OMAHA STEAKS MEAT

JOHN HARRISSON

WITH FREDERICK J. SIMON

PHOTOGRAPHS BY TIM TURNER

CLARKSON POTTER / PUBLISHERS
NEW YORK

Omaha Steaks
11030 O Street
Omaha, NE 68137
To order: (800) 228-9055
Customer Service: (800) 228-9872
www.omahasteaks.com

Published by Clarkson Potter/Publishers, New York, New York
Member of the Crown Publishing Group

Random House, Inc. New York, Toronto, London, Sydney, Auckland
www.randomhouse.com

CLARKSON N. POTTER is a trademark and POTTER and
colophon are registered trademarks of Random House, Inc.

Printed in Singapore

Design and composition by Terrace Publishing

Library of Congress Cataloging-in-Publication Data
Harrisson, John.
Omaha Steaks Meat/ John Harrisson with Frederick J. Simon;
photographs by Tim Turner.—1st ed.
1. Cookery (Meat). I. Simon, Frederick J.   II. Title
Tx749.H235 2001
641.6'6—dc21   2001031335

ISBN 0-609-60777-4

10 9 8 7 6 5 4 3 2 1

First Edition

ACKNOWLEDGMENTS

Terry Finlayson (New York) developed and tested a number of recipes in this book, and her expertise, professionalism, and good taste are much appreciated.

Lynn Gagné (Chicago) not only retested the recipes chosen for photography, but helped with some fine-tuning suggestions too—many thanks. Susan Taves (Chicago) assisted in testing some of the recipes, and her input also proved valuable.

A number of both professional chefs and home cooks provided inspiration, as well as some wonderful recipes, for this book. Special thanks are due to Jean Alberti, Jim Coleman, Kirsten Dixon, Hubert Keller, Waldy Malouf, Mark Miller, Martín Rios, Allen Susser, Roy Yamaguchi, and Jean-Marie Josselin.

Tim Turner, our photographer, is much more than a gifted artist and a consummate professional. He knows his food and is a man of sensible and insightful opinions. All of these qualities contributed enormously to the look of the book. We also thank Tim's extraordinary team: Renée Miller, prop stylist; Cindy Melin, Lynn's assistant; Rod La Fleur and Bart Witowski, Tim's untiring assistants; and Tiffany Butler, studio manager.

Katie Workman, senior editor at Clarkson Potter, made this book possible and believed enthusiastically in the project. We thank her for her guidance and patience.

We would also like to thank Elaina Lin, Katie's assistant; our designers, Martha Hopkins and Randall Lockridge, at Terrace; Marysarah Quinn, art director at Clarkson Potter; and Jan Derevjanik, designer.

Thanks are also due to Trez, Duncan, and Noa Harrisson, and to Eve Simon, for their patience and their help.

We are also indebted to many colleagues and employees at Omaha Steaks. Todd Simon, Fred's son, served as business advisor and marketing partner, as he has for our previous cookbooks. Dave Hershiser, the company's chief financial officer, provided much help with the business details. Bob Bezousek, our director of plant operations, supervised the preparation and shipping of all the Omaha Steaks products for recipe preparation, testing, and photography. Greg Smolen, master butcher, cut some great pieces of meat to exact specifications for these purposes with good grace and at short notice. Jackie Thompson, staff home economist, read the manuscript and offered helpful suggestions. Thanks in advance to Vickie Hagen, director of marketing, and our public relations team, Sharon Bargas and Lynn Kampschneider, for organizing and executing the marketing and promotion of this book. And last, but by no means least, thanks to Deb Righter, Fred's assistant, who made sure everything ran smoothly.

CONTENTS

INTRODUCTION

For as long as our species has been standing upright, we have been opportunistic carnivores. From the earliest hunter-gatherer cultures, meat has undoubtedly played a major role in our diets. With the establishment of the first agrarian societies more than 10,000 years ago came the domestication of wild animals, such as sheep and goats, for meat. The most recent food animal of importance to be domesticated was cattle. History shows that the demand for meat has always directly correlated with wealth, a trend that continues worldwide to this day.

Each of the different meats included in the chapters of this book have, at one time or another, played a major role in local, regional, and national cuisines over the centuries. Just about every culture has enjoyed a diet based on domesticated livestock, and the recipes in this book reflect and celebrate the diversity of ingredients, flavors, and techniques from around the world. America has always been a land where red meat was an important food. Its wide-open range land; its history of buffalo, cattle drives, and cowboys; and Americans' renewed love affair with steakhouses, grilling, and barbecued foods have all shaped and defined our penchant for juicy, satisfying meat.

Although we think of the United States as a land of beef, it has not always been so. One hundred and fifty years ago, pork served as the principal meat, as it still is in so many different countries today. Before

pork, Plains Indians got the protein they needed from wild game like buffalo and deer, and were even able to enjoy preserved sun-dried meat in the winter—the original jerky. Lamb is the meat of choice in many regions of the world, especially the Mediterranean, and even veal is a preferred meat in parts of Europe. As more and more Americans travel to increasingly exotic parts of the world, our appreciation of foreign foods, including different preparations for meat, broadens.

Meats provide an enormous range of flavors, from the delicate mildness of veal to the hearty richness of beef and venison. Then there are the nutritional aspects of meat that are often overlooked. Meat contains important amino acids, nutrients, and minerals, such as iron, as well as vitamins. It is high in protein and nutrient-dense, meaning that meat is high in essential nutrients compared to the calorie content. In support of this point, archaeological research suggests that individuals in meat-eating hunter-gatherer societies were physically healthier and taller than those in non-meat-eating, purely agrarian ones.

As you leaf through this book or prepare one of the recipes, stop for a moment to consider that meat reflects the great continuum that is our history. The types of meat we eat today and the way we prepare it now are not so very different from times long since passed by. Meat provides a connection to our extended ancestry and offers a simpler way of life.

GENERAL NOTES ON MEAT

BUYING, STORING, AND HANDLING MEAT

The chapter introductions provide notes on what to look for when buying each type of meat. In general, you should always use top-quality ingredients; those of only average quality will give you only average results.

All meat should be refrigerated as soon as possible after purchase and kept refrigerated. Cook it as soon as possible after purchasing, or at least within a reasonable amount of time (preferably no more than two or three days). If using meat that has been frozen or shipped with dry ice or a freezer pack, be sure to thaw it in the refrigerator to allow for juicier, more flavorful results. Never thaw meat at room temperature, and avoid microwaving at all costs. To speed the process, thaw vacuum-sealed meat in cold water. You can refreeze cuts of meat that have been thawed in the refrigerator for only a day or two if they still contain some ice crystals or are cold to the touch (at or below 40°F.) Seal the meat tightly in freezer bags with as little air inside as possible, and for best results, use within 3 months.

To be sure of handling meat safely, do not use the same cutting board or platter for raw meats and cooked meats. Thoroughly wash hands, utensils, cutting boards, and countertops that come into contact with raw food. Once cooked, do not let meats stand at room temperature for longer than it takes to serve, and refrigerate leftovers immediately.

COOKING MEAT

It is always preferable to cook meat from a thawed state. There are several common methods for cooking meat: grilling, broiling, sautéing, roasting, and braising. For a successful cooking experience, be sure to preheat the grill, broiler, sauté pan, or oven to the ideal temperature before proceeding.

When grilling with a gas or charcoal grill, using a lid will make it easier to regulate the cooking temperature, help speed up cooking time, and reduce flare-ups. Make sure the charcoals are covered with a thin layer of gray ash and have a red glow before adding the meat. Broiling is a high heat method; the meat should be at least 2 to 3 inches, but no more than 4 or 5 inches, away from the heat source. When broiling with an electric oven, leave the oven door ajar. Use heavy pans or skillets when sautéing meat to distribute the heat evenly across the bottom of the pan. Roast meat either quickly at high temperatures, or slowly at lower temperatures. In either case, the meat should be placed in the center of the oven. Braising works well with tougher cuts of meat that require a long cooking time to become perfectly tender.

In timing meat as it cooks, remember that bone-in cuts take longer than boneless ones. The cooking times given in the recipes are intended as general guidelines rather than hard-and-fast rules, as there are many factors that can affect timing. When grilling, for example, the exact size and heat of the fire tends to vary, and factors, such as weather (especially wind, humidity, and air temperature), the openness of air vents, the height of the grill rack, and the placement of the meat on the grill can all affect exact cooking times. Likewise, gauging "medium-high heat" when sautéing on a gas stove is a rather imprecise and subjective measure, and it generally takes longer to adjust the heat using an electric stove. The exact thickness of meat will also affect recommended cooking times, so be flexible. When grilling, keep the rack clean with a wire brush and wash the rack after each use. In most cases, lightly oiling the rack before grilling meat will prevent it from sticking, especially if it has been coated with a dry rub.

DONENESS

To test doneness, we recommend inserting an instant-read meat thermometer into the center of the meat. The following table shows recommended fully cooked temperatures for each stage of doneness, allowing for a few minutes of standing time to let the meat juices redistribute internally for best results. (Cuts of meat less than 1 inch thick do not need time to reset and can be served immediately.) At the time you remove the meat from the heat, internal temperature should be 5°F. to 10°F. lower than those listed because residual heat will cause the temperature of the meat to continue rising.

PORTION SIZES

Finally, a word about portion sizes: most of the recipes in this book serve main course portions, and assume healthy appetites. While most meat portions fall within the 6- to 8-ounce range, others call for more—the 16-ounce bone-in Porterhouse steaks, for example. By all means choose smaller cuts that fit within your budget and appetite and dietary restrictions. Once again, use your judgment and adjust the recipes accordingly.

INTERNAL TEMPERATURES—READY TO EAT (NUMBERS IN °F.)				
	RARE	MEDIUM-RARE	MEDIUM	MEDIUM-WELL
BEEF	130	140	150	165
VEAL	130	140	150	165
PORK	*	*	160	165–170
LAMB	130	140	150	165
VENISON	130	140	150	165
POULTRY	*	*	*	175
FOWL	*	150	160	170

* Where no figures are given, consumption is not recommended. Note that USDA recommendations are 5°F. to 10°F. higher at each stage of cooking than the temperatures listed here, primarily because of food safety concerns. If you wish to err on the side of caution, bear this in mind. The internal temperature at which all meat bacteria are killed is 160°F., although poultry should be cooked to at least 175°F.

BEEF

Ancient cave paintings and petroglyphs attest to the long and flavorful relationship between man and cattle. All cattle are descended from aurochs, Eurasian wild animals that were worshiped in ancient times and domesticated at least 6,000 years ago. Romans introduced cattle to large parts of Europe, making beef the most common type of meat available in medieval times, and particularly popular in France. Some of the largest herds were found in Spain, and once the early explorers took them to the New World, there was no looking back. English breeds, such as Angus, Hereford, and Shorthorn, were soon introduced to the colonies, and most of today's herds descended from them.

The turning point for beef in the United States was in the mid-1860s. By then, bison had disappeared from the prairies, and semi-wild longhorn cattle (descended from the original Spanish breeds) had taken their place. As the Civil War ended, shortages of other types of meat, especially pork, caused the demand for beef to skyrocket. At the same time, the West was opening with the expansion of the railroads, and crucially, the refrigerated railroad car meant that fresh beef could be shipped far and wide—especially to the large, expanding markets on the East Coast. As a result, the first cattle drives began. Over the next three decades, cowboys rounded up more than 10 million longhorns that roamed the range of the Midwest, Texas, and the Southwest and herded them to railheads and from there to the stockyards of Fort Worth, Kansas City, and Chicago. This legendary era established the great demand for beef and the booming American cattle industry gained its stronghold with it. Today, more beef is consumed per person in the United States than in any other country. From big juicy steaks to tender, slow-cooked barbe-cued brisket and the ubiquitous burger, beef is regarded elsewhere as a distinctly American food.

Most beef consumed in the United States is steer meat. Look for beef graded by the U.S. Department of Agriculture (USDA), the standardized yardstick of quality. These grades have three main criteria: conformation—the proportion of meat to bone; finish—the proportion of fat to lean meat; and overall quality. There are several grades, with the top three being Prime (the best quality), Choice, and Select. Prime (usually sold only to hotels and restaurants) and Choice contain more marbling and therefore tend to be juicier, more tender, and more flavorful than other cuts. Choice, a little less tender and flavorful than Prime, is the most common grade of all. Select (formerly Good) is still a superior grade, falling below the quality of Choice. For best results, choose high-quality beef at the highest grade you can afford. Professionally aging beef—and especially steaks—in refrigerated lockers for at least 7 days, and up to 21, improves the flavor because the natural enzymes in the meat break down the fibers. If you are looking to buy a steak with great flavor, aged beef is the way to go.

When buying beef, look for moist (but not damp) meat with a uniform bright red color. The most important contributor to flavor in beef, as in other meats, is the marbling, or internal fat. Some people assume that the leaner the meat, the more tender it is likely to be, but the opposite is true. As the meat cooks, the fat melts and surrounds the fiber cells, holding in water-soluble proteins that are high in aroma and flavor, as well as in valuable nutrients. Marbling should be white in color, not yellow, and it should run throughout the meat. In response to declining sales due in part to health concerns regarding beef, improved animal husbandry techniques and breeding programs have successfully produced leaner beef over the years, resulting in up to 40 percent less fat and lower cholesterol and calorie levels. Today's lean beef actually has less fat than skinless chicken legs. Consumption is rising once again, and beef is now firmly back on menus and dinner tables as we recognize that its flavor, texture, and nutritional value cannot be beaten.

Beef should be cooked medium-rare to medium, rather than well done, as today's beef looks and tastes best this way. This compares with the old days, when even old-time cowboys were notorious for liking their steaks cooked to a crisp. We particularly enjoy the story of the grizzled cowboy staying at a good Kansas City hotel after a cattle drive. He ordered a steak, but when it arrived, beautifully medium-rare, the cowpoke complained, "I've seen cows git well that was hurt worse 'n' that."

Whatever your personal taste in doneness, these recipes are sure to please. When your guests tell you "well done," they will certainly be referring to your skill and good taste.

BREAKFAST CHIPPED BEEF
OVER BISCUITS WITH FRIED GREEN TOMATOES

Southern food tends to be comforting, filling, and none-too-easy on the waistline. Chipped beef, made from shredded meat, stands as a favorite throughout the region, and the typical serving tends to contain more sauce than beef. This recipe breaks the mold with a hearty proportion of beef to a tasty, low-fat sauce. Buttermilk biscuits and fried green tomatoes are also hallmarks of Southern cooking. Once you have made them, we suspect you'll use them again with all kinds of other dishes. They're just that good! For a change, you can use red tomatoes or green tomatillos instead of the green tomatoes. If using tomatillos, a distant relative of tomatoes, husk and rinse them first.

FOR THE BUTTERMILK BISCUITS:

1 cup all-purpose flour

1 teaspoon baking powder

1/2 teaspoon salt

1/4 teaspoon baking soda

4 tablespoons butter (1/2 stick)

3/4 cup buttermilk

FOR THE FRIED GREEN TOMATOES:

1 cup all-purpose flour

1 teaspoon baking soda

2 teaspoons paprika

1/2 teaspoon freshly ground black pepper

1/4 teaspoon salt

1 cup dark beer

1 egg, beaten

Vegetable oil, for frying

4 large green (unripe) tomatoes or tomatillos, cut into 1/4-inch slices

FOR THE CHIPPED BEEF:

4 tablespoons butter (1/2 stick)

12 ounces corned beef brisket, shredded (about 2 1/2 cups)

1/4 cup all-purpose flour

2 1/2 cups low-fat (1%) milk

Freshly ground white pepper to taste

Pinch of nutmeg

Preheat the oven to 425°F.

To prepare the biscuits, mix the flour, baking powder, salt, and baking soda in a mixing bowl. Add the butter and mix with your hands until crumbly. (Do not overwork.) Add the buttermilk and stir with a wooden spoon until thoroughly combined but sticky.

Using a 1/4 cup measure, scoop 8 evenly sized dollops of the dough onto an ungreased baking sheet. Bake in the oven for 12 to 15 minutes, or until golden brown. Remove and let cool for 5 minutes.

While the biscuits are baking, prepare the tomatoes. Place the flour, baking soda, paprika, pepper, and salt in a mixing bowl. In another bowl, whisk together the beer and egg. Whisk the flour mixture into the beer mixture. Heat 1/2 inch of vegetable oil in a large skillet until just smoking. Dip the tomato slices in the batter and transfer to the hot pan. Sauté for about 1 minute per side, or until golden brown. Remove, drain on paper towels, and keep warm.

To prepare the chipped beef, heat the butter in a saucepan, add the beef, and sauté over medium heat for 3 minutes. Remove the pan from the heat and slowly add the flour while stirring. Add the milk, pepper, and nutmeg; return to medium heat. Cook until the mixture is smooth and thick, 4 or 5 minutes, stirring constantly.

Place 2 biscuits on each serving plate, and split them in half, if you wish. Serve the chipped beef next to, or partly over, the biscuits and serve the fried tomatoes to one side.

SERVES 4

EVE'S OMAHA
OXTAIL SOUP

Fred's wife, Eve, an accomplished cook, says this straightforward recipe is one of her favorites. Oxtail, actually derived from cattle rather than oxen these days, is intensely flavorful but tough, so long, slow cooking is required. Ideally, large oxtail sections should be used for this soup. If you like, add chopped tomatoes and/or diced fennel bulb to the soup before cooking it for 3 hours, and serve it with a good crusty bread.

In a large, heavy saucepan or soup pot, melt 1 tablespoon each of the butter and oil, add the oxtails, and cook over medium heat for 7 or 8 minutes, or until browned on all sides. Using tongs, transfer the oxtails to a large plate and set aside. Add the onion and sliced carrot to the pan, and cook for 7 or 8 minutes, or until softened. Add the flour and stir continuously until it lightly browns. Remove the pan from the heat and let cool slightly.

Gradually whisk in the stock to deglaze the pan. Return the pan to the heat and return to a boil. Reduce the heat to a simmer, continuing to stir until the soup is smooth and begins to thicken, about 5 minutes longer. Tie together the parsley, thyme, celery, and leek with kitchen twine (or tie in cheesecloth). Add to the pan together with the Herbes de Provence, peppercorns, and oxtails. Raise the heat to high and bring to a boil. Skim the surface with a spoon to remove any fat or impurities, and then reduce the heat again to simmer. Partially cover the pan and simmer for 3 hours, skimming often.

Remove the oxtails with a slotted spoon and discard. Strain the soup through a fine strainer into a clean saucepan. Skim again and season with salt and pepper. Heat the remaining tablespoon each of butter and oil in a sauté pan, and add the diced carrot, parsnip, and turnip. Sauté for 3 minutes, stirring often, and add to the soup. Add the pearl barley and bring the soup to a simmer. Cook over low heat for 30 minutes, skimming the surface of the soup occasionally. Stir in the sherry and serve in large soup bowls.

SERVES 6 TO 8

2 tablespoons butter ($\frac{1}{4}$ stick)

2 tablespoons olive oil

3 pounds oxtails, cut at the joints

1 sweet onion, thinly sliced

1 carrot, thinly sliced, plus 1 carrot, finely diced

2 tablespoons all-purpose flour

8 cups Beef Stock (page 225)

3 fresh curly parsley sprigs

3 fresh thyme sprigs

1 stalk celery, cut in half

1 small leek, trimmed

1 teaspoon Herbes de Provence or mixed dried herbs

8 crushed black peppercorns

Salt and freshly ground black pepper to taste

$\frac{1}{2}$ cup finely diced parsnip

$\frac{1}{2}$ cup finely diced turnip or potato

$\frac{1}{3}$ cup pearl barley

$\frac{1}{4}$ cup dry sherry

STEAK CANAPÉS
WITH ROQUEFORT CREAM AND CARAMELIZED PEARS AND ONIONS ON GARLIC TOASTS

Some canapés work simply as bite-size accompaniments to cocktails, but these small, tasty open-faced sandwiches offer something a little more substantial. They are a knockout on an appetizer platter and they taste perfect with soup or salad for a light lunch. The sweetness of the pears deliciously contrasts with the sharp, salty flavor of Roquefort. The recipe is easy (even if doubled or tripled) because all of the components can be prepared in advance. You can even use leftover grilled steak or roast beef. A multi-grain health bread would work just as well as the baguette for the toast.

FOR THE CARAMELIZED PEARS AND ONIONS:

1 tablespoon butter

3 Bartlett or Anjou pears, ripe but still firm, peeled, cored, and sliced lengthwise into eighths

1 tablespoon sugar

1 tablespoon olive oil

2 onions, thinly sliced

FOR THE ROQUEFORT CREAM:

8 ounces Roquefort cheese, softened

1/4 cup heavy cream

2 tablespoons freshly squeezed lemon juice

1 1/2 teaspoons white wine Worcestershire sauce or regular Worcestershire sauce

Freshly ground white pepper to taste

FOR THE GARLIC TOASTS:

1 small French baguette (at least 8 inches long)

3 tablespoons butter, softened

2 cloves garlic, minced

FOR THE STEAK:

1 pound shell steak, bone-in beef strip loin, or New York steak (about 1/2 inch thick), Prime or Choice grade

Salt and freshly ground black pepper to taste

2 teaspoons olive oil

16 small arugula leaves, for garnish (optional)

To prepare the pears and onions, melt the butter in a large sauté pan over medium-low heat. Place the pears in the pan in a single layer and sauté for 5 minutes on each side. Sprinkle the sugar over the pears and continue to sauté for about 5 minutes longer on each side, or until cooked through but not mushy. Remove the pears and let cool. Wipe out the pan with a paper towel. Heat the olive oil in the pan and sauté the onions over medium heat for about 10 minutes, or until golden brown. Set aside.

For the Roquefort cream, combine the Roquefort, heavy cream, lemon juice, Worcestershire sauce, and pepper in a small mixing bowl. Set aside.

Preheat the oven to 400°F. Slice the baguette on the diagonal into 1/2-inch slices. (You will need 16 slices.) Combine the butter and garlic and spread a thin layer on each slice of bread. Place the bread, garlic-side up, on a baking sheet and toast in the oven for 6 to 8 minutes, or until lightly golden. Remove from the oven and set aside to cool.

Season the steaks with salt and pepper. Heat the olive oil in a cast-iron skillet and sear the steaks over medium-high heat for about 3 minutes on each side for medium-rare, 4 minutes for medium, or to the desired doneness. Remove from the pan and let rest for 5 minutes. Slice the steaks against the grain into 1/4-inch strips that are long enough to fit the toast slices.

To assemble the canapés, spread 1 tablespoon of Roquefort cream on each garlic toast. Lay 2 slices of steak on top of the cream. Arrange 1 slice of caramelized pear and some of the onions on top of the steak. Garnish with the arugula. Serve at room temperature.

SERVES 4 TO 8 (16 CANAPÉS)

VIETNAMESE SUMMER ROLLS
WITH BEEF, SHRIMP, AND PEANUT DIPPING SAUCE

Serve these wonderful Asian rolls either as an appetizer or a light lunch. They are a little labor intensive, but well worth the effort. If you're making them for a party, have some friends help you assemble them; you can easily double or triple the recipe. Once you have mastered the simple technique of making these rolls, you'll want to experiment later on with different ingredients. If rice wrappers are not available, wrap the rolls in Boston or Bibb lettuce. And if you prefer, sauté the beef rather than grilling it. The rolls are best if eaten immediately, but they can be covered with a damp cloth and held in the refrigerator for up to 4 hours.

To prepare the sauce, combine the peanut butter, ginger, garlic, scallions, vegetable stock, fish sauce, vinegar, sugar, cilantro, and sambal oelek in a mixing bowl. Thin with additional broth if necessary. Transfer to a smaller serving bowl.

Prepare the grill. Soak the cellophane noodles in lightly salted hot water for 20 to 30 minutes, until just tender. Drain and cut the noodles into pieces 2 or 3 inches long. (This can be easily done in the colander using kitchen shears.) Season the steak with salt and pepper. Grill over direct medium-high heat for about 3 minutes per side for medium-rare, or 4 minutes per side for medium. Let cool, and then slice into at least 24 thin slices. Meanwhile, place the shrimp in a steamer basket or colander set over a large saucepan of boiling water, cover tightly, and steam for 2 or 3 minutes, or until just cooked through. Drain, peel, devein, and slice in half lengthwise. Blanch the bean sprouts in a saucepan of boiling water for 30 seconds. Drain and let cool.

Cover a large platter with lettuce leaves. Tear the remaining leaves into small pieces to use in the rolls. Place the dipping sauce in the center of the platter. To assemble the spring rolls, fill a medium bowl (large enough to hold a rice wrapper) with warm water and lay a kitchen towel in front of it. Dip 1 rice wrapper in the bowl for 20 to 30 seconds and lay it on the kitchen towel. Leaving about 1 inch at each end of the wrapper empty, place the following ingredients in a strip down the middle: 4 shrimp halves, 2 strips of beef, about 2 tablespoons of the cellophane noodles, 4 or 5 bean sprouts, 2 or 3 slices of tomato, some scallions, a few pieces of lettuce, a few mint leaves, and 2 halves of basil leaf. Fold in the top and bottom of the wrapper and roll up the spring roll. Place on the platter of lettuce leaves and repeat the process for the remaining rolls, arranging them around the dipping sauce.

SERVES 4 TO 6

FOR THE DIPPING SAUCE:
6 tablespoons smooth peanut butter

2 teaspoons peeled and finely minced fresh ginger

3 cloves garlic, minced

3 scallions, finely sliced

$1/2$ cup vegetable stock or Chicken Stock (page 225)

$1/4$ cup Asian fish sauce

3 tablespoons rice vinegar

1 tablespoon sugar

$1/4$ cup chopped fresh cilantro leaves

$1/2$ tablespoon sambal oelek or other Asian hot sauce

FOR THE SPRING ROLLS:
1 (2-ounce) package cellophane noodles, or vermicelli

1 pound beef top sirloin ($3/4$ inch thick), Prime or Choice grade

Salt and freshly ground black pepper to taste

24 unpeeled medium shrimp (about 1 pound)

1 cup fresh bean sprouts

3 heads Boston or Bibb lettuce

12 rice wrappers (6 to 8 inches in diameter)

4 plum tomatoes, sliced into very thin wedges

4 scallions, finely sliced

1 cup loosely packed fresh mint leaves or cilantro

12 fresh basil leaves, cut in half lengthwise

BEEF

GRILLED STEAK SANDWICH
WITH HORSERADISH CHEESE SAUCE
AND ONION RINGS

What could be better with steak than the pungent flavor of horseradish and sharp Cheddar cheese? Serve these rich, filling sandwiches on a cool spring day or in the fall and winter (the steak can be sautéed rather than grilled). Offer a crisp green salad to offset the richness of the sandwich. We recommend not using the innermost rings of the onions as they are hard to separate and get gloppy (a technical culinary term, this) with too much flour; save and use them for other recipes. The trick with preparing the onion rings is to maintain the oil at 350°F. during cooking. When the temperature drops below that, the onion rings take longer to cook, absorb too much oil, and do not crisp properly.

FOR THE HORSERADISH CHEESE SAUCE:

1 1/2 cups grated extra-sharp white Cheddar cheese

1/2 cup sour cream

1/4 cup drained prepared horseradish

Salt and freshly ground white pepper to taste

1/4 cup milk

FOR THE ONION RINGS:

1 cup all-purpose flour

1/4 cup cornstarch

1 teaspoon salt

1 tablespoon freshly ground black pepper

Vegetable oil, for deep frying

4 large onions, thinly sliced, rings separated

FOR THE SANDWICHES:

2 tablespoons butter (1/4 stick), softened

2 cloves garlic, minced

4 French bread rolls or hero rolls (large enough to accommodate the steaks)

4 beef strip loin steaks (about 6 ounces each and 1/2 inch thick), Prime or Choice grade

Salt and freshly ground black pepper to taste

2 tomatoes, thinly sliced (8 or 12 slices)

8 cornichons or miniature gherkins, chopped

To prepare the sauce, combine the Cheddar cheese and sour cream in a saucepan and cook over low heat until the cheese is melted; do not let the sauce boil or it will separate. Add the horseradish and season with salt and pepper. Remove from the heat and set aside. When ready to serve, reheat over low heat and thin with the milk as necessary.

Prepare the grill.

To prepare the onion rings, combine the flour, cornstarch, salt, and pepper in a large mixing bowl. Pour enough of the oil into a deep-fryer or large heavy saucepan to come 2 or 3 inches up the sides and heat to 350°F., or until almost smoking. Toss the onion rings in the flour mixture and gently shake off any excess. Fry the onions in 3 or 4 batches, so they do not crowd the pan: use tongs to carefully place some of the coated onions in the hot oil and fry until crispy and golden brown, 2 to 3 minutes. Remove the onions with a slotted spoon and drain on paper towels. Season with additional salt and keep warm.

To prepare the sandwiches, combine the butter and garlic in a small bowl. Split the rolls open lengthwise and spread a small amount of garlic butter on each half. Grill each roll until lightly golden, about 5 minutes. Lightly pound the steaks 2 or 3 times with a meat mallet or rolling pin and season with salt and pepper. Grill the steaks for about 3 minutes on each side for medium-rare, 4 minutes for medium, or to the desired doneness.

To serve, place the steak on the bottom half of the roll, top with 2 or 3 tomato slices and cover with a generous portion of the cheese sauce. Sprinkle some of the chopped cornichons over the sauce. Serve open-faced. Pile the onion rings around the sandwiches.

SERVES 4

STIR-FRIED BEEF TOP SIRLOIN
WITH GINGER, GARLIC, CHILES, AND BOK CHOY WITH RICE

Top sirloin has a pleasantly firm texture and robust beefy flavor, but little marbling—internal fat—which gives it fewer calories than other cuts. Sirloin works very well in this classic stir-fry recipe that features unmistakably Asian flavors, such as soy sauce, sake, and ginger. Another Asian ingredient here is the white-stemmed bok choy (literally, "white vegetable"), also called Chinese white cabbage. In some Asian markets, it may also be labeled "pak choy." There are several closely related species of this vegetable, and strictly speaking, the mild, slightly sweet, and juicy bok choy is not the same thing as Chinese cabbage, although the latter would also work fine here.

Cut the beef into 2 x ¼-inch strips and place in a mixing bowl. Add the soy sauce, sake, fish sauce, and cornstarch, stirring to combine. Marinate the beef in the refrigerator for 30 minutes.

Meanwhile, prepare the rice. Place the rice, 2½ cups water, and the salt in a saucepan with a tight-fitting lid. Bring to a boil, and then reduce the heat to a simmer. Stir once, cover, and cook for 15 to 20 minutes, or until the rice has absorbed all the liquid. Remove from the heat and let sit for 5 minutes. Fluff with a fork and season with salt before serving.

While the rice is cooking, prepare the stir-fry. Cut the bottom (stem end) and the outer leaves off the bok choy and discard. Cut the leaves lengthwise and then crosswise into 1-inch pieces. Heat the peanut oil in a wok or large skillet over high heat. Using a slotted spoon or tongs, remove the beef from the bowl, add it to the wok and stir-fry for 1 minute, until just browned. (To avoid overcrowding the wok, you may wish to do this in two or three batches.) Remove the beef from the wok and set aside. Add the sesame oil to the wok. When the oil is hot, add the ginger, garlic, and jalapeño, and stir-fry over high heat for 2 to 3 minutes. Add the bok choy and scallions, and stir-fry for 1 or 2 minutes, or until the stems begin to soften.

Reduce the heat to medium, pour in any remaining marinade, add the reserved stir-fried beef along with any juices that have been released from the meat, and toss gently to heat through. Make sure the marinade cooks for 2 to 3 minutes. Season with more soy sauce to taste and serve immediately with the rice.

SERVES 4

FOR THE BEEF:
1½ pounds beef top sirloin butt (about ½ inch thick), Prime or Choice grade
¼ cup soy sauce
2 tablespoons sake
1 tablespoon Asian fish sauce
2 teaspoons cornstarch

FOR THE RICE:
1 cup long-grain rice
Pinch of salt

FOR THE STIR-FRY:
1 pound bok choy
3 tablespoons peanut oil
1 tablespoon roasted sesame oil
3 tablespoons peeled and minced fresh ginger
2 tablespoons minced garlic
1 tablespoon minced red jalapeño chile, or red serranos
3 scallions, finely sliced

T-BONE STEAKS
WITH MUSTARD BEURRE BLANC, KASHA, AND MUSTARD GREENS

Kasha (roasted buckwheat groats), though long a staple of Eastern Europe, is a relative newcomer to the American diet. Look for it in natural foods stores and some supermarkets. It has a nutty flavor and can be served plain or with vegetables; here, we have added tomatoes and mushrooms. Kasha is invariably cooked with egg, which not only provides nutrients but also helps keep the grains crisp and separate during the cooking process. Although mustard and garlic are not classic ingredients of the French sauce beurre blanc, they enhance it and pair well with the robust flavor of beef and the mustard seed's mother plant, mustard greens.

FOR THE KASHA:

1 egg, lightly beaten

1 cup coarsely cracked roasted kasha (buckwheat groats)

2 cups boiling Chicken Stock (page 225)

Salt to taste

1 tablespoon olive oil

2 tablespoons diced onion

2 ounces button mushrooms, diced (about ⅔ cup)

2 plum tomatoes, blanched, peeled, seeded, and diced (page 228)

Freshly ground black pepper to taste

Mustard Greens (page 226)

FOR THE MUSTARD BEURRE BLANC:

½ cup dry white wine

¼ cup white wine vinegar

1 teaspoon minced garlic

2 tablespoons heavy cream

2 tablespoons Dijon mustard

1 stick butter (8 tablespoons), diced

Salt and freshly ground white pepper to taste

FOR THE STEAKS:

4 T-bone steaks (about 1 pound each and 1 inch thick), Prime or Choice grade

Salt and freshly ground black pepper to taste

2 tablespoons olive oil

To prepare the kasha, place the egg in a mixing bowl, add the kasha, and stir until well coated. Set a large nonstick saucepan over medium-high heat, add the kasha, and toast for 2 or 3 minutes, stirring constantly, until the grains are separated and the egg is cooked. Reduce the heat to medium-low, add the stock, and season with salt. Cover and slowly simmer for about 8 minutes, or until all the liquid has been absorbed and the kasha is just tender. Let sit, covered, for about 10 more minutes before fluffing with a fork.

While the kasha is cooking, heat the olive oil in a sauté pan and sauté the onion over medium heat for about 5 minutes. Add the mushrooms and sauté for about 5 minutes, or until they are tender and have released most of their juices. Add the tomatoes and a pinch of salt and pepper; cook for another 2 or 3 minutes. Add the mushrooms and tomatoes to the kasha, stir in, and adjust the seasonings. Cover and set aside.

Prepare the mustard greens according to the recipe on page 226.

To prepare the beurre blanc, combine the white wine, white wine vinegar, and garlic in a saucepan and bring to a boil over medium-high heat. Continue cooking until the liquid is reduced to about 3 tablespoons, and then whisk in the cream and mustard. Reduce the heat to low and gradually add the butter, whisking slowly until all is incorporated. Be careful not to let the mixture boil, or it will separate. Season with salt and pepper, and transfer to a double boiler to keep warm if not using immediately.

Preheat the broiler. Season the steaks with salt and pepper, heat the oil in a cast-iron skillet, and sear the steaks over high heat for about 2 minutes on each side. Transfer the steaks to the broiler and cook another 3 to 4 minutes per side for medium-rare, 5 to 6 minutes per side for medium, or to the desired doneness. Transfer the steaks to warm serving plates and spoon with 2 or 3 tablespoons of the sauce. Arrange the kasha and greens next to the steaks.

SERVES 4

PROVENÇAL BEEF STEW
WITH RED WINE, OLIVES, AND POLENTA

This stew combines the hearty red wine of southern France with the tiny cured black olives from that same region. Niçoise olives, named after the coastal resort city of Nice, are small, oval, and brown in color with a firm texture and rich flavor. Serve polenta, the classic northern Italian cornmeal staple, in a cake form, as we have done here, or soft, like grits (in which case, do not cool or sauté). If you prefer, substitute noodles or potatoes for the polenta.

To prepare the stew, season the beef with salt and pepper. Heat the oil in a large Dutch oven or large, heavy saucepan over medium heat. Adding the beef in batches, sauté for 8 to 10 minutes, stirring occasionally, until browned on all sides. Remove with a slotted spoon and set aside. Add the onions and sauté for about 5 minutes, or until light golden, adding a little olive oil to prevent the onions from sticking, if necessary. Add the garlic and cook 2 minutes longer. Add the beef stock and stir to deglaze the pan. Return the beef to the pan and add the red wine, olives, thyme, and bay leaves. Lightly season with salt and pepper. Bring the stew to a simmer, cover, and cook for 1 1/2 hours, skimming the surface occasionally to remove any fat. Add the carrots and continue to simmer for 15 minutes. Add the mushrooms and cook for another 20 to 30 minutes, or until the beef is tender but not falling apart.

While the stew is cooking, prepare the polenta. In a large heavy saucepan, bring the chicken stock to a boil over high heat. Gradually add the polenta in a steady stream, whisking continuously. Reduce the heat to low and continue to whisk for about 30 minutes, or until the polenta thickens. (Thin with a little more stock or water if it thickens too quickly.) Stir in the Parmesan and butter, and season with salt and pepper to taste. Pour into a 9-inch greased baking pan; the polenta will be 1/2 to 3/4 inch thick. Refrigerate for about 30 minutes, or until firm. Cut the polenta into squares, or use cookie cutters to make rounds or other shapes. Just before serving, heat the olive oil in a large nonstick sauté pan and sauté the polenta over medium heat for 2 or 3 minutes on each side, or until golden brown and warmed through.

To serve, remove and discard the thyme sprigs and bay leaves from the stew. Stir in the orange zest and adjust the seasonings. Place a portion of the sautéed polenta into a warm shallow soup plate and spoon the stew all around the polenta. Garnish with a thin sliver of Parmesan sticking up from the center.

SERVES 4

FOR THE BEEF STEW:

2 pounds beef top round, Prime or Choice grade, cut into 1 1/4-inch chunks

Salt and freshly ground black pepper to taste

2 tablespoons olive oil

2 onions, chopped

3 cloves garlic, minced

1 cup Beef Stock (page 225)

2 cups red wine, preferably Provençal or Burgundy

1/2 cup niçoise or Nyons olives (about 3 ounces)

4 sprigs fresh thyme

3 bay leaves

12 ounces precut and trimmed "baby" carrots

6 ounces button mushrooms, stemmed and cut in half

1/2 tablespoon minced orange zest

FOR THE POLENTA:

4 cups Chicken Stock (page 225)

1 cup polenta or coarse yellow cornmeal

1/4 cup freshly grated Parmesan cheese

1 tablespoon butter

Salt and freshly ground black pepper to taste

1 to 2 tablespoons olive oil

4 long, thin slivers of fresh Parmesan cheese, for garnish

BLACKENED RIB-EYE STEAKS
WITH FRIED OKRA AND CREAMY SLAW

Here's a truly Southern-influenced dish. Blackening is a cooking technique popularized by Louisiana's own Paul Prudhomme and emulated by many of America's leading chefs. When the spice-crusted meat is cooked over such high heat, it results in an enormous amount of smoke. So if you do not have adequate ventilation in your kitchen, you can place the pan on a hot grill outside. Do not crowd the steaks in the skillet—cook in two batches, if needed, but wipe out and reheat the skillet between batches. Buy the smallest okra, as they are the most tender.

FOR THE CREAMY SLAW:
1/2 cup sour cream

1/2 cup mayonnaise

2 tablespoons freshly squeezed lemon juice

2 teaspoons whole-grain Dijon mustard

2 tablespoons minced fresh flat-leaf parsley

1 clove garlic, minced

Salt and freshly ground black pepper to taste

1 pound green cabbage (about 1/2 cabbage), thinly sliced or shredded

1 red onion, thinly sliced

1 carrot, grated

FOR THE FRIED OKRA:
1 1/2 pounds okra, stemmed and sliced into 1/2-inch rounds

1 tablespoon plus 1 teaspoon salt

1 cup cornmeal

1 teaspoon freshly ground black pepper

Corn oil, for frying

Salt to taste

FOR THE BLACKENING SPICES AND STEAKS:
2 teaspoons freshly ground black pepper

1 teaspoon salt

1/2 teaspoon garlic powder

1/2 teaspoon onion powder

1/2 teaspoon cayenne

1/2 teaspoon ground cumin

1/2 teaspoon dried oregano

1/2 teaspoon dried thyme

1/4 to 1/2 cup melted butter, as needed

4 beef rib-eye steaks (about 8 ounces each and 1 inch thick), Prime or Choice grade

To prepare the slaw, combine the sour cream, mayonnaise, lemon juice, mustard, 1 tablespoon of the parsley, and the garlic in a mixing bowl. Season with salt and pepper. Refrigerate for at least 1 hour to allow the flavors to blend. Just before serving, add the cabbage, red onion, and carrot, and toss with the dressing. Adjust the seasonings if necessary. Garnish with the remaining parsley.

Place the okra slices in a large mixing bowl, sprinkle 1 tablespoon of the salt over the rounds and cover with ice water. Refrigerate for about 1 hour. Rinse the okra under cold running water and drain well. On a plate, mix together the cornmeal, the remaining teaspoon of salt, and the pepper. Pour enough corn oil into a large skillet or saucepan to come about 3/4 to 1 inch up the sides and heat to 350°F., or until almost smoking. Dredge the okra in the cornmeal and gently shake off any excess. Using a slotted spoon, carefully place some of the okra in the hot oil; fry until crispy and golden brown, 3 to 5 minutes. Fry the okra in batches so as not to crowd the skillet. Remove the okra with a slotted spoon and drain on paper towels. Season with salt to taste and hold in a warm oven.

To prepare the steaks, combine the pepper, salt, garlic powder, onion powder, cayenne, cumin, oregano, and thyme in a small bowl. When you are ready to cook the steaks, brush about 1/2 tablespoon of the melted butter on 1 side of each rib-eye. Sprinkle about 1/2 teaspoon of the blackening spices over the butter on each steak and press gently so the spices adhere. Turn the steaks over and repeat the process on the other side.

Heat a large, dry cast-iron skillet over very high heat until it is very hot—at least 5 minutes. Place the steaks in the pan and cook for about 4 minutes, or until a crust forms. Turn the steaks over and cook on the other sides for 3 or 4 more minutes for medium-rare, 4 or 5 minutes for medium. Drizzle more butter over the steaks if they begin to stick. For the best crust, avoid turning the steaks more than once. Serve immediately with the okra and slaw.

SERVES 4

LEMON-PEPPER
BEEF TOURNEDOS
AND FETTUCCINE WITH ASPARAGUS,
LEMON CREAM SAUCE, AND GREMOLATA

Tournedos are rounded slices of tenderloin about 1 inch thick and weighing 3 to 4 ounces each—simply melt-in-the-mouth morsels. This is the perfect dish for cool spring evenings when asparagus reaches its peak. The flavors are light and fresh, even with the addition of the heavy cream. Try to track down the freshest, thin asparagus you can find for the most tender results; if asparagus is not available, broccoli, green beans, or sautéed spinach all make good substitutes here. Gremolata, a classic Italian garnish traditionally served with Osso Buco (page 81), adds a further spark of flavor. We suggest adding gremolata to other dishes that you might otherwise garnish with chopped parsley.

FOR THE STEAKS:

2 pounds center-cut beef tenderloin, Prime or Choice grade

3 tablespoons freshly squeezed lemon juice

Salt and freshly ground black pepper to taste

12 ounces dried fettuccine

1 tablespoon olive oil

FOR THE ASPARAGUS:

1 1/2 pounds asparagus

1 cup Chicken Stock (page 225)

1 teaspoon salt

1 tablespoon freshly squeezed lemon juice

To prepare the tournedos, slice the tenderloin into 8 equal portions of about 4 ounces each; cut the portions longer from the tapered end of the tenderloin and flatten each steak so that the tournedos are approximately the same size. Place the tournedos on a platter, season each side with 1/2 teaspoon of the lemon juice, and sprinkle with salt and a generous amount of pepper. Let the steaks rest at room temperature for about 30 minutes while preparing the rest of the dish.

Cook the fettuccine al dente according to the package directions. Drain, rinse, and set aside.

Trim the asparagus, removing any large or woody ends. Put the chicken stock, 1 cup of water, and the salt in a large saucepan and bring to a boil. Add the asparagus, reduce the heat to low, cover, and simmer until just tender, 7 or 8 minutes. (Pencil asparagus will take half this time.) Remove the asparagus with tongs or a slotted spoon, reserving the cooking liquid, and drain on paper towels. Cut the asparagus into 3/4-inch lengths (or 1-inch lengths for pencil asparagus) and sprinkle with the lemon juice. Return the cooking liquid to the heat and reduce the liquid over medium-high heat until 1/2 cup remains. Set aside.

To prepare the sauce, melt the butter in a large sauté pan and sauté 1 tablespoon of the garlic over medium heat for about 2 minutes, until softened. Add the reduced cooking liquid from the asparagus and the heavy cream, and reduce until thick enough to coat the back of a spoon, about 5 minutes. Add 2 tablespoons of the parsley and 1 tablespoon of the lemon zest, and season with salt and white pepper. Remove from the heat.

To prepare the gremolata, combine the remaining 1 teaspoon of garlic with the remaining 1 tablespoon each of parsley and lemon zest in a small bowl. Set aside. When ready to serve, add the cooked fettuccine and asparagus to the sauce, stir gently, and cook over low heat until the fettuccine and asparagus are warm. Season with more salt and white pepper, if necessary.

To complete the tournedos, heat the olive oil in a cast-iron skillet and sauté the tournedos over medium-high heat for about 3 to 4 minutes per side for medium-rare, about 5 minutes per side for medium, or to the desired doneness.

Serve 2 tournedos per person with the fettuccine on the side. Garnish the fettuccine with the gremolata and the pine nuts.

SERVES 4

FOR THE LEMON CREAM SAUCE AND GREMOLATA:

1 tablespoon butter

1 tablespoon plus 1 teaspoon minced garlic

$3/4$ cup heavy cream

3 tablespoons minced fresh flat-leaf parsley

2 tablespoons minced lemon zest

Salt and freshly ground white pepper to taste

$1/4$ cup pine nuts, toasted (page 229), for garnish

TAPENADE-
STUFFED TOURNEDOS
WITH RATATOUILLE AND PARSLEY COUSCOUS

This menu incorporates many essential ingredients of Provençale cuisine: garlic, tomatoes, eggplant, anchovies, capers, and olives. Tapenade is a classic Provençale condiment, often served with meat and fish or spread on garlic toast. Ratatouille is best when prepared in advance so that the flavors have a chance to blend. It is perfect picnic fare, a welcome change from the more traditional potato salad or coleslaw. It is nothing if not versatile—it can be served warm, room temperature, or cold, and it tastes wonderful with omelets and pasta. Couscous, a semolina dish from North Africa (across the Mediterranean from Provence), pairs well with the Gallic flavors. For notes on niçoise olives, see page 21.

FOR THE RATATOUILLE:

1/4 cup extra-virgin olive oil, or as needed

2 onions, coarsely diced

3 cloves garlic, minced

4 plum tomatoes, blanched, peeled, seeded, and diced (page 228)

1 teaspoon minced fresh rosemary leaves

1 teaspoon minced fresh thyme leaves

2 bay leaves

Salt and freshly ground black pepper to taste

1 small red bell pepper, seeded and coarsely diced

1 small green bell pepper, seeded and coarsely diced

1 unpeeled zucchini (about 8 ounces), coarsely diced

1 small, unpeeled eggplant (about 8 ounces), coarsely diced

FOR THE TAPENADE:

1/2 cup niçoise or Nyons olives (about 3 ounces), pitted and minced

2 cloves garlic, minced

2 teaspoons drained capers

1 teaspoon freshly squeezed lemon juice

1 canned anchovy, chopped

1 teaspoon oil from canned anchovies

1/2 teaspoon minced fresh thyme leaves

FOR THE PARSLEY COUSCOUS:

1 1/4 cups Chicken Stock (page 225)

1 1/2 cups couscous

1 tablespoon minced fresh flat-leaf parsley

1/2 teaspoon minced lemon zest

Salt and freshly ground black pepper to taste

To prepare the ratatouille, heat 1 tablespoon of the olive oil in a large heavy sauté pan and cook the onions over medium-low heat for 7 or 8 minutes, until soft and translucent. Add the garlic and cook for 2 or 3 minutes longer. Add the tomatoes, rosemary, thyme, bay leaves, and a pinch of salt and pepper. Continue cooking for 6 or 7 minutes, or until fairly dry. Transfer to a large bowl and wipe out the sauté pan. Heat 1 more tablespoon of the olive oil in the sauté pan and cook the bell peppers over medium heat for about 5 minutes, until softened. Season with salt and pepper, add the bell peppers to the onion-tomato mixture, and return the pan to the stove. Heat another tablespoon of olive oil in the pan, and sauté the zucchini over medium heat for 4 or 5 minutes, or until softened and lightly colored. Season the zucchini with salt and pepper, add to the vegetables in the mixing bowl, and return the pan to the stove. Heat the remaining tablespoon of olive oil in the pan, and sauté the eggplant over medium heat for 5 to 7 minutes, or until softened. Season with salt and pepper and return all of the vegetables to the pan. Cook over medium heat for about 5 minutes, or until fairly dry, stirring occasionally. Adjust the seasonings if necessary; remove the bay leaves before serving.

To prepare the tapenade, place the olives, garlic, capers, lemon juice, anchovy, oil from the anchovies, and thyme in a blender and purée. (Alternatively, mash with a mortar and pestle, adding a little olive oil if necessary to achieve a coarse paste.)

To prepare the couscous, bring the chicken stock to a boil in a saucepan. Reduce the heat to low, add the couscous, cover, and cook for 5 minutes. Turn off the heat and let the couscous stand for 10 minutes. Fluff the couscous with a fork, add the parsley and lemon zest, and season with salt and pepper.

To prepare the tournedos, slice the tenderloin into 8 equal portions of about 4 ounces each; cut the portions from the tapered end of the tenderloin longer and flatten each steak so that the tournedos are approximately the same size. Cut a pocket in the side of each steak and fill with a heaping tablespoon of tapenade. Season the tournedos with salt and pepper and set aside. When you are ready to cook the steaks, heat the olive oil in a large cast-iron skillet and sauté the tournedos over medium-high heat for 3 or 4 minutes per side for medium-rare, about 5 minutes per side for medium, or to the desired doneness. Transfer 2 of the tournedos to each serving plate and serve with the ratatouille and couscous.

SERVES 4

FOR THE TOURNEDOS:

2 pounds center-cut beef tenderloin, Prime or Choice grade
Salt and freshly ground black pepper to taste
1 tablespoon olive oil

POLYNESIAN KABOBS:
PINEAPPLE-MARINATED BEEF SKEWERS WITH PEPPERS, TOMATOES, AND PINEAPPLE SERVED WITH CILANTRO RICE

Those of us who grew up in the late '50s and early '60s well remember the South Seas craze that hit America by storm, partly due to the elevation of Hawaii to statehood and the growth in air travel and tourism to the 50th state. Trader Vic's was all the rage. Re-create those days by throwing a luau: string some colorful lanterns in your backyard, or better yet install some bamboo tiki torches; serve exotic punches (mai tais, Blue Hawaiians, and zombies come to mind), and treat your guests to these Polynesian Kabobs. The recipes on pages 48 and 107 would also fit the event well. Suggest a dress code of Hawaiian aloha shirts and full-length flowery muumuu dresses, and for a special touch, have plenty of leis (flower garlands) on hand.

FOR THE MARINADE AND KABOBS:

2 cups pineapple juice

¼ cup soy sauce

2 tablespoons freshly squeezed lemon juice

2 tablespoons minced garlic

2 tablespoons peeled and minced fresh ginger

1 tablespoon dark brown sugar

1 tablespoon roasted sesame oil

2 star anise, broken into pieces

1 serrano chile, with seeds, minced

Salt and freshly ground black pepper to taste

2 pounds boneless strip steak, Prime or Choice grade, cut into 1½-inch chunks

1 pineapple, peeled, cored, and cut into 1-inch chunks

2 green bell peppers, seeded and cut into 1½-inch pieces

2 onions, quartered and then cut in half crosswise

16 cherry tomatoes

FOR THE CILANTRO RICE:

1 cup long-grain rice

Pinch of salt, plus more to taste

1 tablespoon minced fresh cilantro leaves

Freshly ground black pepper to taste

Soak 8 bamboo skewers (preferably 12 inches long) in water for at least 10 minutes so they won't burn up on the grill, and then drain. (Alternatively, use metal skewers.)

In a small mixing bowl, combine the pineapple juice, soy sauce, lemon juice, garlic, ginger, sugar, sesame oil, star anise, serrano, salt, and pepper. Thread the beef, pineapple, peppers, onions, and cherry tomatoes onto each skewer and lay them in a roasting pan. Any extra pineapple and vegetables can be threaded on skewers as well. Pour the marinade over the kabobs and marinate in the refrigerator for about 1 hour, turning occasionally if they are not fully immersed.

About 30 minutes before serving, prepare the rice. Place the rice, 2½ cups of water, and the salt in a saucepan with a tight-fitting lid. Bring to a boil and reduce the heat to a simmer. Stir once, cover, and cook for 15 to 20 minutes, or until the rice has absorbed all the liquid. Remove from the heat and let sit for 5 minutes. Add the cilantro, fluff with a fork, and season with salt and pepper to taste.

Meanwhile, prepare the grill. Remove the kabobs from the marinade. Pour the marinade into a saucepan, bring to a boil, and reduce until about 1 cup remains. Reserve half of the reduced marinade to pass at the table; use the rest while grilling. About 15 minutes before serving, grill the kabobs for about 4 minutes on each side, or until the peppers start to blacken. Brush the kabobs a few times with the reduced marinade as they cook. Discard the marinade used for brushing the meat.

Serve 2 kabobs per person with a heaping mound of cilantro rice on the side. Transfer the reserved marinade to a gravy boat and serve at the table, if you like.

SERVES 4

GRILLED PORTERHOUSE STEAKS
WITH CHIMICHURRI AND YUCA HASH BROWNS

Chimichurri is a parsley-based Argentinean condiment served with grilled meat. For maximum flavor, it should be prepared at least 2 or 3 hours in advance; adjust the seasonings after the flavors have had a chance to blend. Chimichurri should be thick like pesto or mayonnaise, and leftover chimichurri is good with pasta or for seasoning eggs, poultry, and cheese toasts, for example. These Yuca Hash Browns are inspired by the Cuban dish Yuca con Mojo. Yuca, also called cassava, is a root vegetable as common to the Caribbean and Central and South America as potatoes are to North America. It has a sweet, dense flavor and is starchier than potatoes. If you don't plan to make this recipe within a day or two of buying the yuca, boil it and store in the refrigerator, covered with a damp cloth. It holds much better boiled than fresh.

To prepare the chimichurri, place the parsley, oil, vinegar, oregano, garlic, cayenne, salt, and pepper in a blender or food processor and purée until smooth. Refrigerate until ready to use. Before serving, adjust the seasonings if necessary.

About 45 minutes before serving, prepare the hash browns. Cut the yuca into 3-inch sections and peel with a sharp knife. Place in a large saucepan and cover with enough cold salted water to cover the yuca by 2 inches. Bring to a simmer and cook for about 20 minutes, or until just tender. Drain and let cool slightly.

Prepare the grill.

Cut the yuca into $1/2$-inch dice, removing and discarding any thick fibers. Cook the bacon in a large skillet over medium heat until all the fat is rendered, about 3 minutes. Add the onions and sauté for 6 to 7 minutes, or until golden. Toss in the yuca and cook for 3 minutes longer. Add the orange juice, lime juice, and 1 heaping tablespoon of the chimichurri. Cook for about 5 minutes, or until fairly dry. Season with salt and pepper and keep warm.

Season the steaks with salt and pepper and grill for about 5 minutes per side for medium-rare, about 6 minutes per side for medium, or to the desired doneness. Transfer to warm serving plates, place 1 heaping tablespoon of the chimichurri sauce on each steak, and garnish with the parsley. Pile the yuca beside the steak, and pass the remaining chimichurri sauce at the table.

SERVES 4

FOR THE CHIMICHURRI:
$3/4$ cup coarsely chopped fresh flat-leaf parsley

$1/2$ cup extra-virgin olive oil

$1/4$ cup red wine vinegar

2 tablespoons chopped fresh oregano leaves

4 cloves garlic, coarsely chopped

$1/4$ teaspoon cayenne, or to taste

Salt and freshly ground black pepper to taste

FOR THE YUCA HASH BROWNS:
2 pounds yuca

2 slices bacon, diced

2 onions, diced

$1/4$ cup freshly squeezed orange juice

$1/4$ cup freshly squeezed lime juice

Salt and freshly ground black pepper to taste

FOR THE STEAKS:
4 Porterhouse steaks ($1 1/4$ pounds each and about $1 1/8$ inches thick), Prime or Choice grade

Salt and freshly ground black pepper to taste

4 sprigs fresh flat-leaf parsley, for garnish

Spinach and Duxelles–
Stuffed Meat Loaf
with Cremini Mushroom Sauce

Duxelles, a paste made with finely chopped mushrooms, shallots, and herbs, originated in France and was probably first created for the Marquis d'Uxelle, hence the name. It is astonishing to think that only about 20 types of the 50,000 species of fungi are edible—or at least worth eating for their flavor and texture. Cremini mushrooms are a darker and more flavorful variety than regular domestic mushrooms that develop into the popular portobello. If unavailable, substitute the fully matured portobellos or regular button mushrooms. The stuffing and meat loaf have so many similar ingredients that they could be combined, but the stuffing works so well as a filling for poultry, zucchini, or tomatoes, that we've kept them separate.

For the Spinach and Duxelles Stuffing:

2 tablespoons butter (¼ stick)

2 shallots, finely chopped

10 ounces button mushrooms, finely chopped

8 ounces spinach, cleaned, trimmed, and chopped

2 tablespoons minced fresh flat-leaf parsley

Pinch of nutmeg

Salt and freshly ground black pepper to taste

¼ cup prepared plain bread crumbs

¼ cup sour cream

For the Meat Loaf:

1 tablespoon olive oil

1 onion, finely chopped

2 cloves garlic, minced

¼ cup minced fresh flat-leaf parsley leaves

2 eggs

2 teaspoons Worcestershire sauce

2 pounds high-quality lean ground beef

½ cup prepared plain bread crumbs

1 teaspoon salt

½ teaspoon freshly ground black pepper

4 or 5 slices bacon, cut in half

To prepare the stuffing, melt the butter in a sauté pan and sauté the shallots over medium-low heat for 3 to 5 minutes, or until softened. Add the mushrooms and sauté for 6 or 7 minutes, until cooked through and fairly dry. Stir in the spinach, parsley, and nutmeg, and season with salt and pepper. Cook for 1 minute, until the spinach begins to wilt. Transfer to a small mixing bowl and let cool. Stir in the bread crumbs and sour cream, and season with salt and pepper to taste. Set aside.

Preheat the oven to 350°F. To prepare the meat loaf, heat the olive oil in a sauté pan and sauté the onion over medium-low heat for 5 to 7 minutes, until softened. Add the garlic and sauté for 2 to 3 minutes longer. Stir in the parsley, transfer to a mixing bowl, and let cool. In a small bowl, lightly beat the eggs with the Worcestershire sauce. Place the ground beef, bread crumbs, salt, and pepper in the mixing bowl with the onions. Add the Worcestershire sauce mixture, and mix gently to combine; do not overwork the meat or it will become tough. Using a lightly oiled 9 x 6-inch loaf pan, evenly spread out half of the meat loaf mixture. Pile the duxelles stuffing in the center of the meat loaf, running down the length of the rectangle. Place the remaining meat loaf mixture over the stuffing and mold to form a loaf, pressing gently around the edges to seal in the stuffing. Cover the top of the meat loaf with the bacon slices and transfer to the oven. Bake the meat loaf for about 1 hour, or until it is no longer pink on the inside and the internal temperature reaches 160°F.

While the meat loaf is cooking, prepare the sauce. Melt the butter in a large sauté pan, add the onion, and sauté over medium heat for 5 to 7 minutes, until golden. Add the mushrooms and cook for about 5 minutes longer, until softened. Reduce the heat to medium-low, add the stock, and cook the mushrooms and onions for 10 to 15 minutes, or until the liquid is reduced by half. Add the heavy cream and sherry, season with salt and pepper, and cook for about 10 minutes, until the sauce is the consistency of the heavy cream. Do not let the sauce boil once the heavy cream and sherry have been added.

Prepare the egg noodles according to the instructions on the package—typically 10 to 12 minutes in boiling salted water. Drain and transfer to a serving bowl. Toss with the melted butter and season with salt and pepper. Unmold the meat loaf onto a large serving platter and cut into slices. Place on serving plates and spoon the sauce around the meat loaf. Serve with the egg noodles.

SERVES 4

FOR THE CREMINI MUSHROOM SAUCE:
2 tablespoons butter (¼ stick)
1 onion, sliced
8 ounces cremini mushrooms, sliced
1 cup Beef Stock (page 225)
1 cup heavy cream
¼ cup dry sherry
Salt and freshly ground black pepper
1 pound egg noodles
1 tablespoon melted butter

T-BONE STEAKS "ARANJUEZ"
WITH PEANUT SAUCE AND JULIA'S GREEN SUMMER SALAD WITH PAPA'S REAL FRENCH VINAIGRETTE

This Spanish-style recipe is named for not only the famous Iberian composer, but also the city south of Madrid, where such a presentation might be found. Then again, it was the Spanish who took cattle to the New World, to roam the plains of North America and the pampas of South America. Our consumption of large, juicy steaks, such as T-bones, owes much to these early settlers. Julia Wright, a young French friend of ours, impressed us with her salad-making capabilities on a recent visit, and this is her recipe. Her father, Jon, helped her with the vinaigrette, which is the house dressing of choice back home in Vauhallan. Enjoy the rustic sauce with rice or Asian noodles as a great meal on its own. For a colorful side dish, serve cooked rice in a radicchio leaf next to the steaks.

FOR THE PEANUT SAUCE:

2 tablespoons olive oil

1 large onion, chopped

2 cloves garlic, chopped

2 plum tomatoes, blanched, peeled, seeded, and chopped (page 228)

1 red bell pepper, roasted, peeled, seeded, and chopped (page 228)

3 tablespoons peanut butter

1 cup Chicken Stock (page 225)

1 teaspoon hot chile sauce

Salt and freshly ground pepper to taste

FOR JULIA'S GREEN SUMMER SALAD AND REAL FRENCH VINAIGRETTE:

3 tablespoons balsamic vinegar

2 teaspoons Dijon mustard

1 small clove garlic, minced

2 tablespoons minced shallot

Pinch of salt

$1/2$ cup safflower oil

$1/3$ cup extra-virgin olive oil

6 cups mesclun salad mix

FOR THE STEAKS:

4 T-bone steaks (1 pound each and 1 inch thick), Prime or Choice grade

1 tablespoon olive oil

Salt and freshly ground black pepper to taste

Prepare the grill.

To prepare the sauce, heat the olive oil in a heavy skillet, and sauté the onion and garlic over medium-high heat for 2 minutes. Add the tomatoes and bell pepper and sauté for 2 minutes longer. Add the peanut butter, stock, chile sauce, salt, and pepper. Cover the pan and bring to a simmer. Cook for 15 to 20 minutes, stirring occasionally, until thickened slightly.

To prepare the salad, whisk together the vinegar, mustard, garlic, shallot, and salt in a small bowl. Drizzle in the safflower oil and olive oil, whisking continuously. Place the salad greens in a separate mixing bowl and toss together with the vinaigrette just before serving.

To prepare the steaks, brush the T-bones with the oil and season with salt and pepper. Grill over medium-high heat for 5 to 6 minutes for medium-rare, about 7 minutes for medium, or to the desired doneness. Transfer the steaks to serving plates and pour the sauce next to the steaks. Serve with the tossed green salad.

SERVES 4

TEXAS BBQ BEEF RIBS
WITH CORN AND GREEN CHILE FRITTERS

There are as many recipes for barbecue sauce as there are stars in the Texas sky. This one is slightly sweet, slightly tangy, and slightly smoky. You can increase the heat and the smokiness by adding canned chipotle chiles or more adobo sauce, and you can also use soaked wood chips for a smokier flavor. Corn fritters, a wonderful Southern tradition, require some last-minute work, but they are well worth the effort. Ours taste light, fluffy, and full of flavor.

To prepare the sauce, heat the oil in a sauté pan and sauté the onion over medium-low heat for 5 to 7 minutes, or until softened. Add the garlic and sauté for 2 to 3 minutes longer. Add the lemon slices, ketchup, 1/2 cup of water, the Worcestershire sauce, vinegar, brown sugar, chile powder, adobo sauce. Season with salt and pepper, and simmer 20 to 30 minutes, or until slightly thickened. Let cool slightly and whisk in the butter. Adjust the seasonings as necessary. You can serve the sauce immediately, but is best if allowed to chill for several hours.

Place the ribs in a roasting pan, and add enough water to come 1/2 inch up the sides. Add the onion and bay leaves to the water, season with salt and pepper, and tightly cover the pan with aluminum foil. Place the pan in the oven and braise for about 1 hour, or until the ribs are tender, but not falling off the bone. Meanwhile, prepare the grill. Remove the ribs from the pan and drain on paper towels. Discard the cooking liquid. Brush the ribs with the melted butter. Combine the salt, pepper, paprika, and cayenne and rub the mixture onto all sides of the beef ribs. Grill the ribs over medium-high heat, turning often, for about 15 minutes, or until crisp and dark on all sides.

About 30 minutes before serving, prepare the fritters. Cut the corn kernels off the cobs, transfer to a large mixing bowl, and combine the kernels and their milk with the egg yolks and green chiles. Stir in the cornmeal, flour, baking powder, sugar, and salt. Beat the egg whites to medium peaks in a separate bowl and fold them into the fritter batter. Pour enough vegetable oil into a deep-fryer or large heavy saucepan to come 2 or 3 inches up the sides and heat to 375°F. Drop the batter, using heaping tablespoon portions, into the oil. Cook, turning once, for about 4 minutes, or until golden brown. Remove with a slotted spoon and drain on paper towels. Sprinkle with salt and serve immediately. (The fritters may be held briefly in a warm oven.) Serve the ribs with the sauce on the side, and pass the fritters.

FOR THE BARBECUE SAUCE:
1 tablespoon vegetable oil
1 onion, chopped
2 cloves garlic, minced
1/2 lemon, thinly sliced and seeded
1/2 cup ketchup
1/4 cup Worcestershire sauce
1/4 cup apple cider vinegar
1/4 cup packed dark brown sugar
1 tablespoon pure red chile powder
1 tablespoon adobo sauce (from canned chipotle chiles)
Salt and freshly ground black pepper to taste
2 tablespoons butter (1/4 stick)

FOR THE BBQ BEEF RIBS:
4 pounds bone-in beef short ribs
1 onion, coarsely chopped
2 bay leaves, crumbled
Salt and freshly ground black pepper to taste
2 tablespoons melted butter
2 teaspoons salt
2 teaspoons freshly ground black pepper
2 teaspoons paprika
1/2 teaspoon cayenne

FOR THE CORN FRITTERS:
4 ears fresh corn
3 eggs, separated
2 fresh green New Mexico or poblano chiles, roasted, peeled, seeded, and diced (page 228)
1/2 cup cornmeal
3/8 cup all-purpose flour
2 teaspoons baking powder
1 teaspoon sugar
1 teaspoon salt, plus more for seasoning
Vegetable oil, for deep frying

SERVES 4

BEEF

GRILLED BEEF TENDERLOIN
WITH CELERIAC RÉMOULADE AND GARLIC OVEN FRIES

It is our loss that celeriac, also known as celery root, is more common in French cooking than American. It is mostly available from September through May, so we have called for roasting the beef in this recipe, though grilling is still a viable alternative. Celeriac is most often served in rémoulade, a chilled sauce traditionally made with mayonnaise, mustard, capers, cornichons, and herbs, but we prefer the mustard cream sauce prepared here as a base. If the celery root is very hard, it may be grated by hand or in a food processor. Note that the mixed peppercorn blend (also called rainbow peppercorn blend) used for the beef usually consists of black, white, green, and pink peppercorns. Look for it in specialty food stores and gourmet markets.

FOR THE CELERIAC RÉMOULADE:

1 cup heavy cream

2 tablespoons freshly squeezed lemon juice

1 tablespoon Dijon mustard

Salt and freshly ground white pepper to taste

1 1/2 pounds celeriac, peeled and finely julienned (1/6 inch thick)

FOR THE GARLIC OVEN FRIES:

2 pounds small russet potatoes, peeled and cut into 1/2-inch wedges

2 tablespoons olive oil

2 tablespoons butter (1/4 stick)

3 cloves garlic, minced

Salt and freshly ground white pepper to taste

FOR THE BEEF TENDERLOIN:

2 pounds center-cut beef tenderloin, Prime or Choice grade

1 tablespoon olive oil

Salt to taste

1/4 cup mixed peppercorn blend, crushed

To prepare the rémoulade, combine the heavy cream, lemon juice, and mustard in a large mixing bowl, and season with salt and white pepper. Immediately add the julienned celery root to the dressing to prevent the celery from darkening, and toss well. Keep refrigerated and drain slightly before serving, if necessary.

Preheat the oven to 400°F. Toss the potatoes with the olive oil, spread in a roasting pan, and roast for 45 to 50 minutes, tossing occasionally, until cooked through and golden brown. After the potatoes have roasted for about 15 minutes, rub or brush the tenderloin with olive oil and season with salt. Rub on all sides with the crushed peppercorns, pressing gently so they adhere. Place the tenderloin in a roasting pan and roast in the oven for about 30 to 35 minutes for medium-rare, about 5 minutes longer for medium, or to the desired doneness. Remove from the oven, cover loosely with aluminum foil, and let rest for 10 minutes.

Just before the potatoes have finished roasting, melt the butter in a small sauté pan. Add the garlic and sauté over medium-low heat for 2 or 3 minutes, until it begins to soften. Set aside. Transfer the potatoes to a large serving bowl and drizzle the garlic and butter over them. Season generously with salt and pepper, and toss to combine. Keep warm until ready to serve.

Slice the tenderloin and serve with the fries and rémoulade.

SERVES 4

CLASSIC BEEF POT PIES
WITH VEGETABLES IN A PASTRY CRUST

It would seem that as long as there have been pots, there have been pot pies. They are certainly a tradition in Europe, where they have been prepared with all kinds of different meats for centuries. The pot pies here have only a top crust; double the dough recipe if you prefer both a top and bottom crust. Top round, cut from the leg, is also sold as London Broil. It is reasonably priced and gives flavorful, tender results when cooked slowly, as here.

Season the beef with salt and pepper and dredge in the flour so that all pieces are lightly covered; shake off any excess flour. Heat the oil in an ovenproof casserole over medium heat, add the beef, and cook for 6 to 8 minutes, stirring occasionally, until browned on all sides. (To avoid crowding the pan, you may need to do this in 2 or 3 batches.) Remove with a slotted spoon and set aside. Add the onions to the casserole and sauté for 5 or 6 minutes, until light golden brown. Add the garlic and sauté for 2 minutes longer. Add the beef stock and scrape the bottom of the pan with a spatula to incorporate any drippings. Secure the lemon zest, thyme, oregano, and bay leaf in cheesecloth, and add to the pan. Return the beef to the pan, and stir in the red wine vinegar, horseradish, and Worcestershire sauce. Season with salt and pepper. Bring to a low simmer, cover, and cook for $1\frac{1}{2}$ hours. Add the green beans, carrots, potatoes, and mushrooms. Cover and slowly simmer for 30 to 45 minutes longer, or until the beef and vegetables are tender. Remove the cheesecloth packet and adjust the seasonings.

While the stew is cooking, prepare the pastry crust. Place the flour, shortening, butter, and salt in a food processor and pulse until the mixture becomes crumbly. Gradually add $\frac{1}{2}$ cup of water and mix until the dough just comes together in clumps; do not overwork the dough. Divide into 4 balls and chill in the refrigerator for 30 minutes. On a lightly floured work surface, roll out each ball of dough to a thickness of about $\frac{1}{8}$ inch. The dough should be large enough to cover the top of the gratin dishes or pie tins you are using, allowing for $\frac{1}{2}$ inch overhang. Preheat the oven to 425°F. Ladle the stew evenly into 4 gratin dishes or individual 2-cup pie tins. Lay the dough over the stew and crimp the edges around the dish to seal. Lightly brush the top of the pastry with the beaten egg. Cut 3 small slits or holes in the pastry to let the steam escape. Place in the oven and bake for 15 minutes, until the crust is golden. Reduce the heat to 350°F. and bake for 15 minutes longer, until the filling is hot.

SERVES 4

FOR THE BEEF:
$1\frac{1}{2}$ pounds top round, Prime or Choice grade, cut into $\frac{3}{4}$-inch chunks

Salt and freshly ground black pepper to taste

$\frac{1}{2}$ cup all-purpose flour, or as needed

2 tablespoons olive oil

8 ounces pearl onions

2 cloves garlic, minced

1 cup Beef Stock (page 225)

1 strip lemon zest (about 1 x 2 inches)

2 sprigs fresh thyme

1 sprig fresh oregano

1 bay leaf

3 tablespoons red wine vinegar

$\frac{1}{2}$ tablespoon drained prepared horseradish

$\frac{3}{4}$ teaspoon Worcestershire sauce

12 ounces green beans, cut into 1-inch lengths

6 ounces baby carrots, cut in half crosswise

1 pound new potatoes, peeled and quartered

10 ounces button mushrooms, cut in half

FOR THE PASTRY CRUST:
2 cups all-purpose flour

$\frac{1}{3}$ cup chilled vegetable shortening, diced

$5\frac{1}{3}$ tablespoons ($\frac{1}{3}$ cup) chilled butter, diced

$\frac{1}{2}$ teaspoon salt

1 large egg, beaten

BEEF

CHICKEN-FRIED STEAK
WITH MASHED POTATOES AND
PEPPERED CREAM GRAVY

Long a favorite of the Southern and Midwestern states, this dish, as its name implies, is steak cooked in the style of fried chicken. Our good friend Stephan Pyles, the acclaimed Dallas-based chef, tells us the Texas Restaurant Association estimates that more than three-quarters of a million chicken-fried steaks are consumed in Texas alone every day. The recipe we present here is chicken-fried steak in its most simple form, with the only seasoning being plenty of salt and freshly ground black pepper. If it seems bland to you, you probably haven't added enough salt and pepper! If you wish to add more seasonings, try dusting the steaks with cayenne, adding roasted garlic to the mashed potatoes, or using chicken or bacon drippings and onions to prepare the gravy. Serve plenty of sautéed greens on the side—the chard recipe on page 114 works well with it.

FOR THE MASHED POTATOES:

1 1/2 pounds russet potatoes, peeled and quartered

3 tablespoons butter

1/2 cup milk, or as needed

Salt and freshly ground black pepper to taste

FOR THE CHICKEN-FRIED STEAK:

8 top sirloin or top round steaks (about 8 ounces each and 1/2 inch thick), Prime or Choice grade

Salt and freshly ground black pepper to taste

1 cup all-purpose flour, or as needed

2 large eggs, beaten

Vegetable oil, for frying

FOR THE PEPPERED CREAM GRAVY:

3 tablespoons all-purpose flour

Salt and freshly ground black pepper to taste

1 1/2 cups milk, at room temperature

Place the potatoes in a saucepan of cold salted water and bring to a boil. Reduce the heat and simmer for about 20 minutes, or until just tender. Drain the potatoes and return to the saucepan. Place the pan over low heat and let the potatoes dry for 2 or 3 minutes, shaking constantly. Add the butter and mash with a potato masher until fairly smooth. Stir in enough milk to reach a creamy consistency, season with salt and pepper, and continue to cook until heated through.

While the potatoes are boiling, pat the steaks dry and season with salt and pepper. Sift the flour onto a plate and dredge the steaks in the flour. Using the flat side of a meat cleaver or a rolling pin, pound out the steaks until they are about 1/4 to 3/8 inch thick. Dredge again in the flour, shaking off any excess. Dip the steaks into the beaten eggs, and then again in flour, making sure all of the beef is well covered with flour. Pour enough oil into a large skillet to come about 1/4 inch up the sides and set over medium-high heat. When the oil is hot, carefully add the steaks with tongs and cook for 3 or 4 minutes on each side, until golden brown. Remove the steaks and keep warm.

To prepare the gravy, pour off all but 2 tablespoons of the oil and remove any burnt drippings from the skillet. Reduce the heat to medium, and add the flour, salt, and pepper. Cook for 2 or 3 minutes, stirring constantly, until the flour is light golden. Slowly whisk in the milk, about 1/2 cup at a time. Reduce the heat to medium-low, and simmer until the gravy is thick and creamy, stirring constantly, about 7 or 8 minutes. Season again with salt and pepper, if necessary. Serve the gravy over the chicken-fried steaks and mashed potatoes.

SERVES 4

ALLEN SUSSER'S CHARRED BLUE MOUNTAIN
COFFEE BURGERS
WITH POLENTA "FRIES"

Allen Susser, owner of Chef Allen's in North Miami Beach, is one of the pioneers of South Florida's "New World Cuisine"—which is also the title of Allen's cookbook (published by Doubleday), which contains this recipe. This innovative regional style of cooking combines the flavors of the Caribbean and Central and South America with local produce and, in many cases, classic technique. Allen's inspiration for this recipe came from an unexpected quarter: he was challenged by a local magazine to create a meal using ingredients in a couple's refrigerator and cupboards, only to find they were about to move. Their pantry was almost bare, but as Allen aptly puts it, "inspiration was born of necessity." The coffee coating on the burgers is surprisingly mild, yet robust, and a delightful surprise on the palate. Instead of grilling burgers and polenta "fries," you can sauté them both in a cast-iron skillet over high heat.

FOR THE POLENTA:

3 cups Chicken Stock (page 225), vegetable stock, or water

2 cups milk

1 cup polenta

2 tablespoons butter (¼ stick)

⅓ cup freshly grated Parmesan cheese

1 teaspoon salt

½ teaspoon freshly ground black pepper

FOR THE BURGERS:

2 scoops Jamaica Blue Mountain coffee beans (about 1½ tablespoons)

10 black peppercorns

2 pounds high-quality lean ground sirloin

3 tablespoons minced garlic (7 or 8 large cloves)

2 tablespoons coarse salt

¼ cup olive oil

To prepare the polenta, pour the stock and milk into a saucepan and bring to a boil. While stirring with a wooden spoon, gradually pour in the polenta in a steady stream and continue stirring until the mixture is thickened, about 15 minutes. Reduce the heat to low and simmer for 20 minutes, stirring frequently. Stir in the butter, cheese, salt, and pepper.

Lightly butter an 8-inch square pan and pour in the polenta. Let cool and refrigerate until chilled, at least 2 or 3 hours.

Meanwhile, prepare the grill. In a coffee mill, roughly grind the coffee beans and peppercorns together. Transfer to a plate. Season the ground sirloin with half of the garlic and the coarse salt and form into oblong-shaped hamburgers (about 4 x 3 x 1 inch thick). Combine the remaining garlic with half of the olive oil in a small bowl and rub the mixture onto the burgers. Roll the burgers in the coffee-pepper mixture until coated thoroughly.

Drizzle the remaining oil over the burgers and grill over medium-high heat until the internal temperature reaches 160°F., about 7 or 8 minutes. Cut the polenta into "fingers" about 1 x 2½ inches. Grill for 3 to 4 minutes on each side, until crisp and golden brown. Serve the burgers with the polenta "fries."

SERVES 4

Beef Filet
with Roasted Corn–Wild Mushroom Salsa and Ancho Chile Aïoli

Nothing beats filet mignon for richness and tenderness. If it's expensive compared to other cuts, it's not just because of its premium quality, but also because of its required trimming. It takes almost a full pound of meat to yield a 7-ounce filet. In this recipe, the deep flavor of the filet is complemented perfectly by the earthy tones of the mushrooms, the smoky corn, and the spicy aïoli. Ancho chiles—dried poblano chiles—are mild to medium in heat, with a delicious sweetness. If you enjoy mushrooms and want to really amplify the flavor of the salsa, sauté two more cups of wild mushrooms in two tablespoons of olive oil and serve them over the steaks. To complete the meal, serve with a rustic, crusty bread.

To prepare the aïoli, rehydrate the chile in a bowl of warm water for 30 minutes, using a pan or plate to keep the ancho submerged. Strain, reserving about 1/4 cup of the soaking liquid, and place the ancho in a blender. Purée to a paste-like consistency, adding just enough soaking liquid to make puréeing possible. Strain into a clean mixing bowl, and add the mayonnaise, garlic, and paprika. Whisk to combine thoroughly; add up to 1 tablespoon of milk or water if you want a thinner aïoli.

Preheat the oven to 300°F.

To prepare the salsa, heat the olive oil in a sauté pan and sauté the mushrooms over medium-high heat for 5 or 6 minutes, or until tender. Transfer to a mixing bowl, and add the corn, garlic, hazelnut oil, sun-dried tomatoes, chipotles, cilantro, lemon juice, lime juice, and salt. Serve at room temperature.

To prepare the beef, heat the olive oil in a sauté pan until lightly smoking. Add the filets and sear over high heat for 4 to 5 minutes per side for medium-rare, about 6 to 7 minutes for medium, or to the desired doneness. Spoon the aïoli on one side of each serving plate and arrange the steaks so they partly overlap the aïoli. Serve with the salsa and garnish the steaks with the chives.

SERVES 4

FOR THE ANCHO CHILE AÏOLI:
1 dried ancho chile, toasted (page 230)
1/2 cup mayonnaise
1 tablespoon roasted garlic purée (page 229)
1/2 teaspoon paprika
1 tablespoon milk or water (optional)

FOR THE SALSA:
3 tablespoons extra-virgin olive oil
3/4 cup diced cremini, chanterelle, or shiitake mushrooms
2 cups fresh corn kernels (about 3 or 4 ears), roasted (page 229)
1/2 tablespoon roasted garlic purée (page 229)
1 tablespoon hazelnut oil
1/4 cup diced sun-dried tomatoes (packed in oil)
1 tablespoon minced canned chipotle chiles in adobo
2 tablespoons minced fresh cilantro leaves
1 teaspoon freshly squeezed lemon juice
1 teaspoon freshly squeezed lime juice
1/4 teaspoon salt

FOR THE BEEF:
2 tablespoons olive oil
4 filet mignons (about 7 ounces each and 1 1/2 inches thick), Prime or Choice grade
1 tablespoon sliced chives, for garnish

CHINESE MANGO BEEF
WITH RED BELL PEPPERS, GINGER, AND CASHEW NUTS

China is a land of many geographical contrasts. To the north lie the arid plains of Mongolia; to the west, the Himalayan mountains; and to the south, the subtropical regions of Kwangtung (which includes Canton) and Yunnan. Mangoes grow in these latter regions, as well as other fruits, such as banana, pineapple, papaya, and guava. The local cuisines reflect this bounty. A favorite means of preparing these fruits is to preserve them in honey and to eat them as a snack; other times, these and other fruits are stir-fried with meat and vegetables, as in this recipe. Peanut oil provides an excellent choice for stir-frying, as it has a high "smoking point"—the temperature at which it will smoke and begin to burn—and stir-frying is best done at high temperatures.

To prepare the marinade, place the soy sauce, sherry, sesame oil, rice vinegar, ginger, garlic, salt, and pepper in a mixing bowl, and mix together. Add the beef, combine well, and let sit in the refrigerator for 1 hour, turning occasionally.

Prepare the rice according to the recipe on page 227.

Heat the peanut oil in a wok or large sauté pan until lightly smoking. Add the garlic and ginger and sauté over high heat for 1 minute. Lightly drain the beef mixture and add it to the wok. Stir-fry for 4 to 5 minutes, until browned on all sides. Add the chile sauce, red bell pepper, and the cashews and stir-fry for 2 minutes longer. Add the mango and cook for 1 minute longer, stirring gently.

Spoon the rice onto serving plates and top with the beef mixture. Garnish the beef with the cilantro.

SERVES 4

FOR THE MARINADE AND BEEF:

$2\frac{1}{2}$ tablespoons soy sauce

3 tablespoons dry sherry

$1\frac{1}{2}$ tablespoons dark sesame oil

1 tablespoon rice vinegar

$\frac{1}{2}$ tablespoon peeled and minced fresh ginger

1 clove garlic, minced

Salt and freshly ground black pepper to taste

$1\frac{1}{2}$ pounds top sirloin steak, Prime or Choice grade, finely julienned into strips 4 x $\frac{1}{2}$ x $\frac{1}{4}$ inch thick

Jasmine Rice (page 227) or medium-grain rice, such as Calrose

FOR THE STIR-FRY:

$\frac{1}{2}$ tablespoon peanut oil

1 clove garlic, minced

1 teaspoon peeled and minced fresh ginger

1 teaspoon chile sauce with garlic (such as sambal oelek)

1 red bell pepper, seeded and finely julienned

$\frac{1}{3}$ cup chopped cashew nuts

2 large mangoes, peeled, pitted, and diced (about $2\frac{1}{2}$ cups)

3 tablespoons chopped fresh cilantro leaves, for garnish

BEEF

CURRIED BEEF–
STUFFED CABBAGE
WITH GINGERED BEETS AND
SOUR CREAM–HORSERADISH SAUCE

Wrapped food not only involves an element of surprise, but the packages also make for a neat presentation. Cabbage, bell peppers, and tomatoes all make good mediums for stuffing, and in this recipe, the texture of the cabbage contrasts well with the meat curry. Likewise, the colorful beets set off the cabbage leaves and blond sauce to good effect. Leaving 1 inch of beet tops and the bottoms untrimmed will prevent them from bleeding. This dish is best served with crusty French bread, which will also serve the delicious job of mopping up the flavored beet juices.

FOR THE GINGERED BEETS:

3 beets (about 7 or 8 ounces each)

¼ cup packed dark brown sugar

3 tablespoons white wine vinegar

2 cloves garlic, minced

1 teaspoon peeled and finely minced fresh ginger

1 tablespoon butter

FOR THE BEEF-STUFFED CABBAGE:

¼ cup olive oil

1 large onion, diced

1 leek, white part and a little of the green, sliced

2 large cloves garlic, minced

2 teaspoons peeled and minced fresh ginger

1 tablespoon curry powder

1 teaspoon mild paprika

1 pound high-quality lean ground beef

½ cup tomato paste

¼ cup freshly squeezed lemon juice

Salt to taste

1 small savoy or other green cabbage (about 2 pounds)

FOR THE SOUR CREAM–HORSERADISH SAUCE:

1 cup sour cream

2 tablespoons prepared horseradish

1 tablespoon sliced fresh chives or very finely sliced scallions

1½ tablespoons minced fresh dill leaves

To prepare the beets, place them in a steamer basket set inside a saucepan of boiling water. Cover tightly and steam for 35 to 40 minutes, or until tender. Drain, peel, and coarsely dice. (There should be about 3 cups.) Set aside. Place the brown sugar, vinegar, garlic, and ginger in a saucepan, and stir together over medium heat until warm. Add the butter, and when melted, add the cooked beets. Cook for 5 minutes, stirring occasionally. Keep warm or reheat just before serving.

Meanwhile, to prepare the cabbage, heat 2 tablespoons of the olive oil in a saucepan, and add the onion, leek, garlic, and ginger. Sauté over medium-high heat for 5 minutes, until soft. Stir in the curry powder and paprika. Add the beef and sauté, stirring to break up the beef, for 8 to 10 minutes, until the beef is evenly browned. Add the tomato paste, lemon juice, and salt. Cover and cook over low heat for 10 minutes, stirring occasionally.

Fill a stockpot with salted water and bring to a boil. Place the cabbage in a steamer basket, cover tightly, and steam for 15 minutes, or until the leaves are tender. Transfer to a colander and when cool enough to handle, carefully peel off 12 leaves and lay flat on a work surface. Evenly divide the meat mixture among the center of the leaves, fold in the sides of the leaves, and roll up neatly. Keep warm.

To prepare the sauce, place the sour cream and horseradish in a mixing bowl, and stir in the chives and dill.

To serve, place 3 or 4 cabbage rolls on each plate and spoon the beets next to the leaves. Garnish the cabbage with the sour cream sauce.

SERVES 4

MARINATED RIB ROAST DUBARRY
WITH CAULIFLOWER CHEESE

This recipe was a favorite of Madame Dubarry, a prominent courtesan in French King Louis XIV's court. Classic rib roast Dubarry is not marinated, and some would say that marinating a perfectly fine rib roast is a crime. But just taste this and we think you'll disagree. The smooth, rich, velvety texture of the beef makes it well worthwhile. One of the most evocative kitchen aromas, in our unbiased opinion, is that of roasting beef, and this dish certainly delivers here, too. Our cauliflower recipe is no ordinary cauliflower cheese with its delicate, subtle sauce. For gravy lovers, melt a teaspoon of butter in a small saucepan, stir in 1 teaspoon of flour, and add some of the juice and drippings from the roast.

Pour the wine, olive oil, mustard, garlic, pepper, and bay leaf in a small mixing bowl; stir to combine. Add the beef, and marinate in the refrigerator for at least 5 hours or overnight, turning occasionally.

Preheat the oven to 400°F. Remove the roast from the marinade and pat dry. Heat the butter in a heavy sauté pan. Over high heat, sear the beef on all sides, about 5 minutes. Transfer the beef and butter to a roasting pan and cover the roast with the bacon, overlapping the slices if necessary. Roast in the oven for 55 to 60 minutes for medium-rare, 65 to 75 minutes for medium, or to the desired doneness. Remove from the oven, let rest for 10 minutes, and slice before serving.

Meanwhile, to prepare the cauliflower, place the shallot, carrot, celery, bay leaf, peppercorns, and 2 sprigs of the parsley in a heavy saucepan. Add the milk and cream and bring to a boil over medium heat. Remove the pan from the heat, cover, and let sit for 30 minutes to infuse. Strain and reserve the cooking liquid; discard the vegetables. In a clean saucepan, melt the butter over medium heat. Stir in the flour, and continue stirring for 1 minute. Remove the pan from the heat and whisk in the infused milk. Slowly bring to a boil and cook until the mixture thickens, about 5 minutes. Stir in 1/2 cup of the cheese and the mustard. Season with salt and pepper. Keep warm.

Cut the cauliflower into florets and place in a steamer basket set inside a saucepan of boiling water. Cover tightly and steam for 15 minutes, or until just tender. Drain and transfer to an ovenproof baking dish, and sprinkle with the sauce and the remaining 1/2 cup of cheese. Once the beef is removed from the oven to rest, turn on the broiler and broil the cauliflower cheese until the top turns golden brown, 2 to 3 minutes. Remove from the oven, garnish with the remaining parsley, and serve with the sliced beef.

SERVES 4

FOR THE BEEF:
2 cups red wine, such as Cabernet Sauvignon

1/4 cup olive oil

2 tablespoons Dijon mustard or prepared horseradish

3 cloves garlic, minced

1 1/2 tablespoons freshly ground black pepper

1 bay leaf

3 pounds boneless rib-eye roast, Prime or Choice grade, trimmed of fat

3 tablespoons butter

6 slices bacon

FOR THE CAULIFLOWER CHEESE:
1 shallot, sliced

1 small carrot, sliced

1 small stick celery, sliced

1 bay leaf

1 teaspoon black peppercorns

4 large sprigs fresh curly parsley

1 cup milk

1/2 cup heavy cream

2 tablespoons butter (1/4 stick)

1/4 cup all-purpose flour

1 cup grated fresh Gruyère or Parmesan cheese

2 teaspoons Dijon mustard, or to taste

Salt and freshly ground black pepper

1 cauliflower (about 2 1/2 pounds)

BEEF

BEEF CHIMICHANGAS
WITH GUACAMOLE AND SALSA MEXICANA

Chimichangas are deep-fried, stuffed burritos, a specialty of the state of Sonora in northern Mexico and the border region. They have also become popular menu items in Arizona and New Mexico, and in Southwestern and Tex-Mex restaurants everywhere. Stuff "chimis" with seasoned beef, pork, poultry, or even vegetables. Here, they contain picadillo, a traditional Mexican-seasoned ground beef mixture. For a lower-fat version of this recipe, lightly heat (rather than deep-fry) the flour tortillas and fill them to make Beef Picadillo Burritos.

To prepare the salsa, place the tomatoes, cilantro, garlic, onion, lime juice, chiles, salt, and sugar in a mixing bowl and combine thoroughly. Let sit for 30 minutes at room temperature before serving. Serve at room temperature or chilled.

To prepare the guacamole, place the tomatoes, onion, garlic, chiles, 2 tablespoons of the cilantro, lime juice, and salt in a mixing bowl. Add the avocados and gently fold together. Cover with plastic wrap (with the wrap touching the guacamole) and let sit in the refrigerator for at least 10 minutes before serving. Garnish with the remaining tablespoon of cilantro.

To prepare the chimichangas, heat the tablespoon of vegetable oil in a large, heavy skillet and sauté the garlic, onion, and chile over medium-high heat for 2 minutes. Add the beef and cook for 5 or 6 minutes longer, or until evenly browned, using a wooden spoon to break up any lumps. Add the raisins, vinegar, chile powder, cinnamon, cumin, salt, and pepper. Cook for 6 or 7 minutes longer, or until the mixture is almost dry, stirring often. Place the tortillas on a work surface and evenly spread 1 tablespoon of the beans in a strip down the center of each tortilla. Top with about 1 1/2 tablespoons of the beef mixture for each tortilla. Tuck in the ends of the tortilla first, tightly roll up into a narrow burrito, and secure the seams lengthwise with toothpicks.

Pour enough vegetable oil in a large, heavy skillet or large saucepan to come 2 inches up the sides and heat to 350°F., or until just smoking. Using tongs, carefully add the burritos and fry until all sides are crisp and golden brown. Remove the chimichangas, quickly drain on several paper towels, and remove the toothpicks. Transfer to serving plates, sprinkle with the cheese so it melts a little, and serve with the salsa and guacamole.

SERVES 4

FOR THE SALSA MEXICANA:
1 pound plum tomatoes, seeded and finely diced
1 tablespoon chopped fresh cilantro leaves
1 clove garlic, minced
1/4 cup minced onion
1 tablespoon freshly squeezed lime juice
2 serrano chiles, seeded and minced
1/3 teaspoon salt
1/2 teaspoon sugar

FOR THE GUACAMOLE:
2 ripe plum tomatoes, finely diced
1/4 onion, finely diced
2 cloves garlic, minced
2 serrano chiles, seeded and minced
3 tablespoons minced fresh cilantro leaves
1 tablespoon freshly squeezed lime juice
1/2 teaspoon salt
3 ripe avocados, peeled, pitted, and diced

FOR THE BEEF CHIMICHANGAS:
1 tablespoon vegetable oil, plus more for deep frying
2 cloves garlic, minced
1 onion, diced
1 jalapeño chile, seeded and minced
1 pound high-quality lean ground beef
1/4 cup golden raisins
1 tablespoon red wine vinegar
1 teaspoon pure red chile powder
1/2 teaspoon ground cinnamon
1/2 teaspoon ground cumin
1/2 teaspoon salt
1/2 teaspoon freshly ground black pepper
12 flour tortillas (8 inches across)
3/4 cup canned refried beans
1 cup grated Monterey Jack cheese

GRILLED BEEF SANDWICH
WITH CARAMELIZED SWEET ONIONS, HONEY-GINGER MUSTARD, AND WATERCRESS

For those times when only a thick, juicy steak sandwich will satisfy your hunger, look no further than this recipe. These sandwiches are perfect for lunch or brunch, and once you've made them we can almost guarantee you'll come back to use the onion and mustard recipes for other dishes. Though you can halve the recipe, we recommend making the amount of mustard called for here, even though it is more than you will need for the sandwiches; store the extra in an airtight container and keep in the refrigerator for another use. Add tomato slices to the sandwich, if you wish. The square-ish steaks fit the size of regular bread the best, but you can trim them to fit baguette rolls, or leave the steaks overhanging for a rustic look. Serve with a green salad or a salsa.

FOR THE HONEY-GINGER MUSTARD:
1/2 cup Dijon mustard

1/4 cup honey

1 teaspoon white wine vinegar

1 teaspoon dried ginger

1 teaspoon dried red pepper flakes

1/4 teaspoon salt

1/4 teaspoon paprika

FOR THE CARAMELIZED ONIONS:
2 tablespoons olive oil

2 sweet onions, such as Vidalia, sliced

1/2 teaspoon salt

3/4 teaspoon sugar

1/2 tablespoon white wine vinegar

FOR THE STEAKS:
4 Prime rib filets (rib-eye steaks) (7 ounces each and 7/8 inch thick), Prime or Choice grade

Salt and freshly ground black pepper to taste

FOR THE SANDWICHES:
8 slices rustic country-style bread; 4 individual crusty rolls; or 1 French-style baguette, 2 feet long, cut crosswise into 4 pieces each 6 inches long

2 to 3 packed cups watercress tops and leaves (about 1 bunch)

Place the mustard, honey, vinegar, ginger, pepper flakes, salt, and paprika in a small mixing bowl. Stir until well blended and thickened. Set aside.

Prepare the grill. (Alternatively, pan-sear the steaks.)

To prepare the onions, heat the olive oil in a sauté pan and add the onions, salt, and sugar. Sauté over medium-high heat for 10 to 12 minutes, or until lightly browned. Add the vinegar, stir to deglaze the pan, and remove from the heat. Set aside.

To prepare the steaks, season on both sides with salt and pepper. Grill over medium-high heat for about 4 minutes per side for medium-rare or about 5 minutes per side for medium. (If pan-searing, do so over medium-high to high heat for about the same length of time.)

To assemble the sandwiches, lightly toast the bread slices on the grill or under the broiler. (If using French bread or rolls, cut in half first.) Spread 4 slices of bread (or the bottom half of each roll) with 1 to 1 1/2 tablespoons of the mustard. Add the steaks, cover with the caramelized onions, and top with the watercress. Close the sandwiches and serve.

SERVES 4

PLUM SAUCE AND MIRIN-MARINATED BEEF
AND BROCCOLI SALAD

This recipe is typical of the Pacific Rim fusion cuisine so popular these days, which combines ingredients and flavors from different Asian countries and sets them in a distinctly American context. The main influences here are Chinese and Japanese, although a Thai or Vietnamese hot chile sauce will further extend this recipe's reach. Chinese plum sauce (also called duck sauce) is a sweet-and-sour condiment made from plums and apricots that is available in most supermarket Asian food sections; the same is true of mirin, a Japanese sweet cooking wine made from rice. Also consider serving this dish warm, with rice, as a hot main course.

Place the sesame oil, mirin, soy sauce, plum sauce, chile sauce, and garlic in a shallow bowl or dish and add the steaks. Let marinate in the refrigerator for 1 hour, turning once or twice. Prepare the grill. Grill the steaks over medium-high heat for 4 to 5 minutes for medium-rare, 5 to 6 minutes for medium, or to the desired doneness. Set aside, let cool, and slice thinly.

To prepare the vegetables, heat $1/4$ cup of the peanut oil in a wok or large heavy skillet. Cut the broccoli into florets and stems, and chop or slice the stems. When the oil is hot, stir-fry over medium-high heat for 2 minutes. Add the florets and continue to stir-fry for 4 more minutes, or until tender, but still crisp. Using a slotted spoon, transfer to a serving bowl. Heat the remaining $1/4$ cup of peanut oil in the wok and stir-fry the mushroom and garlic for 5 minutes. Add to the broccoli, using a slotted spoon.

In a bowl, mix together the vinegar, soy sauce, and sugar, and pour over the vegetables. Add the beef, bell peppers, and artichoke hearts and thoroughly combine. Transfer to the refrigerator and chill for at least 2 hours. Sprinkle with the sesame seeds just before serving.

SERVES 6

FOR THE MARINADE AND STEAKS:

2 tablespoons roasted sesame oil

3 tablespoons mirin

2 tablespoons soy sauce

3 tablespoons Chinese plum sauce

1 teaspoon Asian hot chile sauce

2 cloves garlic, minced

3 boneless strip steaks (about 9 ounces each and $7/8$ inch thick), Prime or Choice grade

FOR THE VEGETABLES:

$1/2$ cup peanut oil

1 pound broccoli

1 small portobello mushroom (4 or 5 ounces), chopped

2 cloves garlic, minced

$1/4$ cup balsamic vinegar

$1/4$ cup soy sauce

$1/4$ teaspoon sugar

1 red bell pepper, roasted, peeled, seeded, and julienned (page 228)

1 yellow bell pepper, roasted, peeled, seeded, and julienned (page 228)

12 ounces frozen artichoke hearts, defrosted and quartered, or 14 ounces canned

1 tablespoon sesame seeds, toasted

The fresh pineapple and pineapple juice in this recipe gives it a distinctly tropical feel. The Hawaiian island of Maui produces large quantities of pineapple, much of which is canned, but some of which is flown "jet fresh" to markets in the rest of the United States. Buy Hawaiian pineapple when you see it—it is invariably juicy, deliciously sweet and flavorful, and fresher than imported fruit. Hawaiian cuisine borrows ingredients and flavor combinations from many Asian countries, reflecting its diverse population, and you might well expect to find these burgers with "two scoops rice" and a macaroni salad at roadside lunch wagons and local diners.

2 cups "sticky" white rice, such as Calrose

FOR THE SWEET-AND-SOUR SAUCE:

1 tablespoon peanut oil
2 scallions, finely sliced
1 teaspoon peeled and minced fresh ginger
1 cup pineapple juice
¼ cup white wine vinegar
¼ cup sugar
1 tablespoon cornstarch
½ tablespoon soy sauce
1 green bell pepper, roasted, peeled, seeded and finely diced (page 228)
1 red bell pepper, roasted, peeled, seeded and finely diced (page 228)
½ cup finely diced fresh or canned pineapple

FOR THE SPICY MIXED GREEN SALAD:

3 cups mizuna lettuce or arugula
2 cups radicchio or red leaf lettuce, torn or shredded
1 cup baby spinach or torn regular spinach leaves
½ tablespoon balsamic vinegar
1 tablespoon white wine vinegar
3 tablespoons peanut oil
1 teaspoon minced shallot
½ teaspoon minced garlic

FOR THE BURGERS:

4 fresh pineapple rings, cored, or canned pineapple rings
1¼ pounds high-quality lean ground beef
2 teaspoons peeled and grated fresh ginger
1 teaspoon dried red pepper flakes
Salt and freshly ground black pepper to taste
1 tablespoon peanut oil

To prepare the rice, place in a strainer and rinse under cold running water until the water no longer looks milky. Soak the rice in a bowl of water for 1 hour. Drain the rice and place in a saucepan with 2 cups of cold water. Bring to a boil, reduce the heat to low, and cover the pan with a tight-fitting lid. Simmer for about 15 minutes, or until the water has been absorbed and the rice is sticky and soft. Keep warm.

Meanwhile, to prepare the sauce, heat the oil in a saucepan and add the scallions and ginger. Sauté for 1 minute over medium-high heat. Add ¾ cup of the pineapple juice, the vinegar, and sugar, and stir well. Cook over medium-high heat for 2 minutes, or until the sugar is dissolved. Combine the cornstarch with the remaining ¼ cup of pineapple juice in a bowl and stir into the saucepan. Add the soy sauce and bring to a boil. Reduce the heat to a simmer, and stir in the bell peppers and pineapple. Keep warm.

To prepare the salad, place the mizuna, radicchio, and spinach in a salad bowl. In a small bowl, mix together the balsamic and white wine vinegars, peanut oil, shallot, and garlic. Just before serving, toss the dressing with the salad; it is not necessary to use all of the dressing.

Heat a dry cast-iron skillet and add the pineapple slices. Sear over medium heat for 6 or 7 minutes per side, or until caramelized and golden brown. Set aside. In a large mixing bowl, combine the beef, ginger, and pepper flakes, and season with salt and pepper. Divide into 4 portions, shaping them into burgers about ¾ inch thick. Add the peanut oil to the pan and sauté the burgers over medium-high heat for about 5 minutes on each side, or until the internal temperature reaches 160°F. (for medium).

Spoon the rice onto serving plates and place the caramelized pineapple rings next to the rice. Top the rings with the burgers and spoon with the sauce. Serve with the salad.

SERVES 4

SWEDISH MEATBALLS
IN CREAMY DILL SAUCE WITH ROASTED GARLIC MASHED POTATOES

This is a filling, satisfying recipe that's a must for all meatball lovers. While dill is a popular herb for flavoring food in Scandinavia, it is not a traditional ingredient with Swedish meatballs. Instead, they are usually made with parsley, which you can substitute here. These meatballs can also be served with noodles rather than potatoes, although the texture of the potatoes and their garlicky flavor seem ideally matched with the meatballs.

To prepare the potatoes, place them in a saucepan of boiling salted water and boil for 15 to 20 minutes, or until soft. Drain the potatoes and transfer to a mixing bowl. Add the garlic, butter, and half-and-half. With an electric whisk (or by hand), whisk together until smooth. Season with salt and pepper.

While the potatoes are boiling, prepare the meatballs. Place the bread crumbs and half-and-half in a mixing bowl and soak for 5 minutes. Meanwhile, heat the butter in a sauté pan and sauté the onion over medium-high heat for 5 minutes; do not brown. Add the onion, along with the beef, garlic, dill, egg, allspice, salt, and pepper, to the breadcrumb mixture. Combine thoroughly until all the ingredients are incorporated, and then divide the mixture into 4 equal portions. Form each portion into 6 meatballs, making a total of 24 meatballs. Place on a platter, cover with plastic wrap, and chill in the refrigerator for at least 1 hour.

Heat the butter in a large, heavy nonstick skillet and sauté half of the meatballs over medium-high heat for 10 minutes, or until browned on all sides and completely cooked through. Remove with a slotted spoon and drain on paper towels. Sauté the remaining meatballs and drain. Keep warm.

To prepare the sauce, place the dill, vinegar, salt, pepper, and mustard in a saucepan. Stir in the sour cream and milk and heat until warm; do not boil. To serve, spoon the dill sauce on serving plates and place 6 meatballs on the sauce. Serve with the mashed potatoes.

SERVES 4

FOR THE ROASTED GARLIC MASHED POTATOES:

3 russet potatoes (about 8 ounces each), peeled and chopped

1 tablespoon roasted garlic purée (page 229)

1 stick butter (8 tablespoons), at room temperature

1/2 cup half-and-half, warmed

Salt and freshly ground black pepper to taste

FOR THE SWEDISH MEATBALLS:

1/2 cup fresh bread crumbs

1/3 cup half-and-half or milk

1 tablespoon butter

1 sweet onion (about 12 ounces), minced

1 pound high-quality lean ground beef

3 cloves garlic, minced

1/3 cup minced fresh dill leaves or 1 1/2 tablespoons dried

1 egg, beaten

1/2 teaspoon ground allspice

Salt and freshly ground black pepper to taste

2 tablespoons butter (1/4 stick)

FOR THE CREAMY DILL SAUCE:

2 tablespoon minced fresh dill leaves or 2 teaspoons dried

1 tablespoon white wine vinegar or freshly squeezed lemon juice

Salt and freshly ground black pepper to taste

2 teaspoons Dijon mustard

1 cup sour cream

1 1/2 tablespoons milk

BEEF

Pepper-Mustard
FILET STEAKS
WITH QUINOA–SHIITAKE MUSHROOM RAGOUT
AND CLARET SAUCE

50

Each element of this delicious recipe is spectacular, and it makes for an elegant combination that you will want to return to often. Claret, a word dating from medieval England that describes the graceful red wines from the Bordeaux region, provides the foundation for a rich sauce that stands up well to the spicy, tender steaks. The unusual and colorful ragout rounds out the dish. Quinoa is thought of—and cooked—like a grain, but it's actually the high-protein seed of an herb. (It also goes by the nicknames of "super grain" and "mother grain.") Highly nutritious, quinoa was a staple in the diet of the South American Inca civilization. It's important to rinse the quinoa to remove any saponin, a bitter-tasting natural pesticide produced by the plant.

FOR THE CLARET SAUCE:

2 tablespoons olive oil

2 cloves garlic, minced

$1/2$ cup diced onion

$1/2$ cup sliced carrot

$1/2$ cup sliced celery

2 bay leaves

1 teaspoon black peppercorns

Salt to taste

3 cups Claret (red Bordeaux)

3 cups Beef Stock (page 225)

FOR THE PEPPER-MUSTARD FILET STEAKS:

2 teaspoons olive oil

1 tablespoon Dijon mustard

4 teaspoons crushed black peppercorns

Salt to taste

4 filet mignon steaks (about 7 ounces each and $1\,1/2$ inches thick), Prime or Choice grade

FOR THE QUINOA–SHIITAKE MUSHROOM RAGOUT:

3 tablespoons olive oil

8 ounces shiitake mushrooms, sliced

1 cup fresh corn kernels

2 cloves garlic, minced

2 cups quinoa, rinsed and drained

2 cups vegetable stock

Salt and freshly ground black pepper to taste

4 sprigs fresh marjoram, for garnish

To prepare the sauce, heat the olive oil in a saucepan and add the garlic, onion, carrot, celery, bay leaves, peppercorns, and salt. Sauté over medium heat for 6 to 7 minutes, or until the vegetables are tender. Add the wine, bring to a boil, and simmer over medium-low heat until reduced by two-thirds, about 40 minutes. Add the stock and reduce by two-thirds, about 40 minutes longer. Strain into a clean saucepan and continue to reduce until about 1 cup remains and the sauce is thick enough to coat the back of a spoon. Keep warm.

To prepare the steaks, place the olive oil, mustard, peppercorns, and salt in a bowl and spread the mixture onto both sides of the steaks. Let sit at room temperature while preparing the ragout.

To prepare the ragout, heat 2 tablespoons of the olive oil in a sauté pan and add the shiitake mushrooms. Sauté over medium-high heat for 3 minutes, stirring frequently. Stir in the corn and sauté for 2 minutes longer. Remove from the heat. Heat the remaining tablespoon of the olive oil in a saucepan and sauté the garlic over medium heat for 3 minutes. Add the quinoa and stir with a wooden spoon to coat thoroughly. Add the stock and 2 cups of water, and bring to a simmer. Cook for about 10 minutes, or until the liquid is absorbed and the quinoa is almost dry but still moist. Add the mushroom-corn mixture and season with salt and pepper.

Preheat the broiler. When hot, broil the steaks for about 5 minutes for medium-rare, about 6 minutes for medium, or to the desired doneness. Turn the steaks once to ensure even cooking. Transfer to serving plates, spoon the sauce around, and garnish with the marjoram. Serve with the ragout.

SERVES 4

OMAHA STEAKS MEAT

CORNISH PASTIES
WITH BRUSSELS SPROUTS AU GRATIN

Cornwall is a rugged peninsula that forms the southwestern-most county of England. Cornish Pasties (the first syllable rhymes with "gas") are the traditional all-in-one lunch dish made by tin miners' wives. Containing both meat chunks and vegetables and wrapped in short-crust pastry dough, they are an original form of "fast food" that are convenient to eat even down inside mines! Nowadays, commercial Cornish pasties are usually made with minced ground beef, which is not in the authentic style. The vegetables are grated so they all take the same amount of time to cook.

FOR THE PASTRY DOUGH:

1 1/2 pounds all-purpose flour

3/4 teaspoon salt

2 1/2 sticks butter (20 tablespoons), diced

1/2 cup iced water

FOR THE CORNISH PASTY FILLING:

1 pound beef tenderloin tips, Prime or Choice grade, finely diced

3/4 cup grated potato

1 cup grated carrot or sweet potato

1/4 cup grated onion

1/2 cup frozen peas

1 tablespoon cold water

Salt and freshly ground black pepper to taste

1 egg, beaten

2 tablespoons milk

FOR THE BRUSSELS SPROUTS AU GRATIN:

1 1/2 pounds Brussels sprouts, trimmed and stem ends cut with an "X"

1/2 cup diced bacon

1/3 cup grated Monterey Jack cheese

1/3 cup grated mozzarella cheese

1/2 cup fresh bread crumbs

Salt and freshly ground black pepper

To prepare the pastry dough, sift the flour and salt into a mixing bowl and add the butter. Mix with your hands, rubbing the butter into the flour, until the consistency resembles coarse bread crumbs. Add the water gradually until a dough forms (add more water if necessary), and knead gently with your hands until the dough is smooth. Wrap in plastic wrap and refrigerate for 30 minutes.

Preheat the oven to 450°F.

To prepare the filling, place the beef, potato, carrot, onion, peas, and water in a mixing bowl, and season generously with salt and pepper. Unwrap the chilled dough, place on a floured work surface, and roll out to a 1/6-inch thickness. Cut into 6 circles about 8 inches in diameter. Divide the filling between the circles, placing it on one half of each circle. Whisk together the egg and milk and brush the edges of the circles with some of the egg wash. Fold the pastry over to form half-moons and crimp the edges of the pastry with a fork or your fingers to seal. Brush the pasties with the remaining egg wash, and make 2 narrow slits on the top of each so the steam can escape while cooking.

Place the pasties on a lightly greased baking sheet and bake in the oven for 15 minutes, or until the pastry is a pale brown. Reduce the oven temperature to 350°F., and bake for about 30 minutes longer, or until the pastry is a light golden brown.

To prepare the sprouts, place them in a vegetable basket set over a saucepan of boiling water, cover tightly, and steam for 10 minutes, or until just tender. Meanwhile, sauté the bacon in a nonstick pan over medium heat for 5 minutes, until just crispy. Drain the bacon on paper towels and set aside. Place the sprouts in a baking dish, sprinkle with the bacon, and cover with the grated cheese and bread crumbs. After the pasties have baked, turn on the broiler. Transferring the pasties to a middle rack in the oven, broil the sprouts for about 5 minutes, or until the topping is browned. Serve with the pasties.

SERVES 6

MARINATED GRILLED STEAK
WITH RED WINE, BRANDY, AND SHALLOT SAUCE AND A POACHED ASIAN PEAR SALAD

Contrasts in cooking—whether the pairing of ingredients, textures, colors, or flavors—can really "make" a dish, especially if they are unexpected. This is true here, with a classic marinade and sauce, in conjunction with a side salad containing ginger and Asian pears. These crisp, juicy, round fruits, also known as sand pears, are considered the ancestor of other types of common pears that we enjoy today. Note that riper pears will take less time to poach than firmly textured fruit. If you are considering adding a starch to this dish, potatoes make a good accompaniment. For example, serve with wedges of Potato Galette (page 73) or arrange the Pinwheel Potatoes (page 215) beneath the steaks.

To prepare the marinade, place the wine, vinegar, oil, shallot, garlic, pepper, and tarragon in a shallow bowl or dish. Add the steaks and marinate in the refrigerator for 2 hours, turning occasionally.

Prepare the grill.

To prepare the sauce, place 1 tablespoon of the butter in a sauté pan and add the shallots. Sauté over medium-high heat for 3 or 4 minutes, or until a light golden brown. Add the wine and reduce the liquid by half, 2 to 3 minutes. Add the stock and reduce again by half, until about 3/4 cup remains, 7 or 8 minutes. Strain the sauce into a clean saucepan and add the brandy. Bring the sauce to a boil and turn off the heat. Dice the remaining 2 tablespoons of butter and stir into the sauce. Stir in the parsley and tarragon, and keep warm.

To prepare the salad, place the wine, sugar, cinnamon, cloves, allspice, and ginger in a large saucepan; bring to a boil. Add the pear halves in a single layer, cut-side down. (The pears should be almost covered by, or floating in, the liquid.) Cover the pan and poach over low heat for 12 to 15 minutes, or until just tender. Remove the pears and set aside. Strain off most of the poaching liquid, returning 1 cup to the saucepan. Over high heat, reduce the liquid to 1/4 cup, and then transfer to a blender. Add the vinegar, shallot, and garlic and blend until smooth. Add the oil in a steady stream, blending until thoroughly combined. Season with salt. When ready to serve, toss the mesclun salad mix with the dressing.

Grill the steaks over medium-high heat for 4 to 5 minutes for medium-rare, about 6 minutes for medium, or to the desired doneness. Serve the sauce over the steaks and serve the salad on the side. Cut the reserved poached pears into a fan, if desired, and serve on top of the salad.

SERVES 4

FOR THE MARINADE AND STEAKS:
1/2 cup red wine, preferably Merlot
2 tablespoons red wine vinegar
2 tablespoons olive oil
2 tablespoons minced shallot
1 tablespoon minced garlic
2 teaspoons freshly ground black pepper
1 teaspoon minced fresh tarragon leaves
4 top sirloin steaks (about 7 ounces each and 1 inch thick), Prime or Choice grade

FOR THE RED WINE, BRANDY, AND SHALLOT SAUCE:
3 tablespoons butter
1/4 cup minced shallots
3/4 cup red wine, preferably Merlot
1 cup Beef Stock (page 225)
2 tablespoons brandy
1 teaspoon minced fresh flat-leaf parsley
1 teaspoon minced fresh tarragon leaves or 1/2 teaspoon dried

FOR THE POACHED ASIAN PEAR SALAD:
3 cups red wine, preferably Merlot
1/2 cup sugar
1 stick cinnamon
3 cloves
3 allspice berries
2 thin slices peeled fresh ginger
1 large ripe Asian pear, peeled, cut into quarters, and cored, or 2 ripe Anjou pears, peeled, cut in half, and cored
2 tablespoons tarragon vinegar or red wine vinegar
1 teaspoon minced shallot
1/4 teaspoon minced garlic
1/2 cup walnut oil
Salt to taste
4 cups mesclun salad mix

BEEF

HERB-CRUSTED STRIP STEAKS
WITH SAUTÉED ZUCCHINI SQUASH AND RED ONION COMPOTE

New Yorkers call them "Kansas City Strips"; in K.C., they refer to them as "Texas Strips"; while in Texas (and much of the rest of the country), they are described as "New York Strips." Talk about musical steaks! Whatever name used, boneless strips are a favorite of steak connoisseurs. In fact, they are often referred to as "the ultimate cookout steak." Here we broil them, but they can just as well be grilled. Use the flavorful steak crust with other red meats, especially lamb and venison. The compote, which will keep for a few days in the refrigerator, also makes a good accompaniment for other meat dishes.

To prepare the compote, place the onions, honey, vinegar, wine, and rosemary in a saucepan. Cook over low heat for 30 minutes, or until thick and syrupy, stirring occasionally. Remove the rosemary and discard. Season with salt and let cool to room temperature.

Preheat the broiler. To prepare the steaks, combine the butter and mustard in a mixing bowl. Add the bread crumbs, parsley, chives, salt, and pepper, and combine to form a paste. Heat the oil in a sauté pan and season the steaks with salt and pepper. Place the steaks in the pan and sauté over medium-high heat for 2 minutes on each side. Transfer the steaks to a broiling pan and spread the crust on the top of each steak. Place the pan on a rack in the upper part of the oven (but not on the very top rack) and broil for about 10 minutes for medium-rare, 12 minutes for medium, or to the desired doneness; do not turn the steaks over. The crust should be browned.

While the steaks are broiling, prepare the zucchini. Heat the oil in a sauté pan and add the shallots and garlic. Sauté over medium heat for 2 minutes. Add the zucchini and sauté for 2 or 3 minutes on each side, until lightly golden. Season with salt and pepper. Spritz with the lemon juice. Transfer to warm serving plates and place the steaks next to the squash. Spoon the compote next to the steaks and garnish the plate with the parsley.

SERVES 4

FOR THE COMPOTE:
2 red onions, thinly sliced, rinsed in cold water, and drained
$1/4$ cup honey
$1/4$ cup red wine vinegar
$1/4$ cup red wine, preferably Cabernet Sauvignon
1 sprig fresh rosemary leaves
$1/8$ teaspoon salt

FOR THE CRUST AND STEAKS:
3 tablespoons butter, softened
2 teaspoons whole-grain mustard
$1/4$ cup fine bread crumbs
1 tablespoon minced fresh flat-leaf parsley
1 tablespoon finely sliced fresh chives
Salt and freshly ground black pepper to taste
2 tablespoons vegetable oil
4 boneless strip steaks (about 9 ounces each and $7/8$ inch thick), Prime or Choice grade

FOR THE ZUCCHINI:
2 tablespoons olive oil
1 tablespoon minced shallots
2 cloves garlic, minced
1 pound zucchini, thinly sliced on the bias
Salt and freshly ground black pepper to taste
1 tablespoon freshly squeezed lemon juice
4 sprigs fresh flat-leaf parsley, for garnish

VEAL

Veal is considered a great delicacy in Europe where it is widely enjoyed, particularly in Italy, a legacy of the days of the Roman Empire. Some of the most famous classic European dishes showcase veal, such as Osso Buco, Wiener Schnitzel, Blanquette de Veau, and scaloppine recipes like Veal Piccata and Parmigiana. Americans appreciate veal to a lesser extent, mostly because cattle ranchers find it more profitable to raise mature beef animals than to market calves as veal, while Europeans have far less pasture land on which to raise cattle. However, the growing popularity of updated versions of these European and other dishes on American restaurant menus is introducing this mildly flavored meat to a new generation of more sophisticated diners.

Veal meat comes from milk-fed calves less than 6 months old, and usually around 3 to 4 months. This diet ensures lean meat that's creamy white to pale pink and delicately flavored. Historically, veal meat has usually come from young male animals, as the females would be raised for dairy production. Increasingly, with moral concerns regarding the traditional confined quartering of veal calves, free-range and grass-fed animals are appearing on the market. With these animals, the meat has a ruddier color and a meatier flavor. Very young veal meat, marketed as Bob veal, is less expensive, but also less flavorful and with inferior texture.

Many consumers feel qualms about purchasing veal, given the adverse publicity regarding the raising of the calves. However, over recent decades, standards and practices in raising veal have changed considerably, and for the better. In addition, range-raised veal production is on the increase. The argument in defense of veal is probably best summarized by author (and Omaha Steaks consultant) Merle Ellis, in *The Great American Meat Book*:

> Unfortunately, the controversy over veal in the diet will probably last as long as certain vegetarians and animal-rights activists continue with untrue and misleading rhetoric. . . . Fortunately, knowledgeable doctors, nutritionists, consumers, and particularly young creative chefs have ignored the controversy and have greatly increased their acceptance and demand for formula-fed, pen-raised veal.

While veal is graded by the U.S. Department of Agriculture (USDA), it is done so to a lesser extent than with beef, as the system is voluntary. The three top USDA grades are Prime, Choice, and Select. As with beef, most of the Prime grade is sold directly to restaurants and hotels. When buying veal, choose lightly moist, creamy white to pale pink meat (or with some redness in the case of grass-fed veal). Gray or dark red coloration indicates older, lower-quality meat. Look for finely grained texture and soft, white fat.

Like pork and game meat, veal is low in fat (lower even than chicken breast), and because of the absence of marbling, it will dry out and become tough if overcooked. Most cuts of veal are relatively tender because of the age of the calves. The mild flavor of veal suits flavorful, complex, but not overpowering sauces and ingredients, such as cheese, wine, citrus, and tomatoes, particularly well.

ROLLED BREAST OF VEAL
WITH CORN BREAD STUFFING
AND PICANTE TOMATO SAUCE

Your butcher will bone and butterfly the veal breast for you. Many recipes for stuffed veal breasts call for creating a pocket, but this doesn't really give as much room for stuffing or give such attractive results, which is why we roll it here. The stuffing is a little sweet and pairs very well with the sauce, which is a little spicy.

To prepare the stuffing, soak the raisins in the sherry for 15 minutes. Heat the oil in a sauté pan, and sauté the onion over medium heat for 5 to 7 minutes, or until light golden. Add the garlic and sauté for 2 minutes. Add the cumin, cinnamon, and cloves and cook for 2 minutes, or until fragrant. Transfer to a mixing bowl, and stir in the corn bread crumbs, almonds, salt, and pepper. Drain the raisins, reserving the sherry, and add them to the stuffing.

Preheat the oven to 350°F. Lay the veal breast open like a book, and season with salt and pepper. Spread the corn bread stuffing over the veal, to within about 1 inch of the edges. Starting with the shorter side of the rectangle, roll the veal like a jellyroll and tie with butcher's twine. Heat the olive oil in a Dutch oven, stew pot, or flame-proof casserole and sear the veal roll on all sides for about 5 minutes, or until browned. Add 1 cup of water, the stock, carrot, celery, and onion and bring to a simmer on top of the stove. Transfer to the heated oven and braise for about 1¾ hours, or until the veal is tender. Remove the breast from the pan and cover with foil. Strain the pan, reserving the braising liquid and discarding the vegetables. Skim the surface of the braising liquid to remove any impurities.

Meanwhile, prepare the sauce. Heat the olive oil in a sauté pan and sauté the onion over medium heat for 5 to 7 minutes, or until golden. Add the garlic and sauté for 2 to 3 minutes longer. Add the oregano and chile powder and cook for another 2 minutes. Add the tomatoes and adobo sauce and cook until fairly dry, 3 or 4 minutes. When the veal breast has been removed from the oven, add 1 cup of the braising liquid to the sauce. (If necessary, add beef stock or water to make a total of 1 cup.) Bring to a boil, and then reduce the heat to a simmer. Add the reserved sherry, and season with salt and pepper. Simmer over low heat for 10 to 15 minutes, until the tomato sauce has reduced and thickened slightly; do not boil the sauce once the sherry has been added.

Remove the veal from the oven and cut the twine. Carve the veal into ¾-inch slices; place 2 slices of veal on each serving plate, and spoon the tomato sauce around. Serve with the zucchini pancakes.

SERVES 4

FOR THE CORN BREAD STUFFING:
¼ cup raisins
¼ cup dry sherry
1 tablespoon olive oil
1 onion, finely chopped
2 cloves garlic, minced
1 teaspoon ground cumin
¼ teaspoon ground cinnamon
Pinch of cloves
2 cups fresh corn bread crumbs (page 213)
¼ cup slivered almonds
Salt and freshly ground black pepper to taste

FOR THE VEAL:
1 veal breast (3 to 4 pounds), Prime or Choice grade, boned and butterflied
Salt and freshly ground black pepper to taste
2 tablespoons olive oil
1 cup Beef Stock (page 225)
1 carrot, chopped
1 stalk celery, chopped
½ onion, chopped

FOR THE TOMATO SAUCE:
1 tablespoon olive oil
1 onion, chopped
2 cloves garlic, minced
2 teaspoons minced fresh oregano leaves
2 teaspoons mild pure red chile powder
1½ pounds plum tomatoes, peeled, seeded, and coarsely chopped
2 teaspoons adobo sauce (from canned chipotle chiles)
Salt and freshly ground black pepper to taste

Zucchini Pancakes (page 84) (optional)

VEAL

GRILLED VEAL CHOPS
WITH ROASTED CORN SUCCOTASH AND RUSTIC-STYLE ROASTED TOMATO–BALSAMIC SAUCE

There are many olive oils on the market from many countries, made in many different styles. Since this ingredient is an important part of this veal recipe, we recommend a peppery, fruity, Tuscan-style oil rather than a full-bodied one. Any California oil made in the Tuscan style would also be ideal, and any good specialty or gourmet kitchen store should be able to recommend specific brands. Succotash is a popular Southern dish, but the name is derived from a New England Native American word, "msickquatash," meaning corn stew. The tomato sauce contains a little mustard, slightly different from what you might expect with the classic combination of tomatoes, basil, and balsamic vinegar.

FOR THE VEAL:

1/2 cup olive oil

2 cloves garlic, minced

2 tablespoons minced fresh basil leaves

4 veal chops (6 to 7 ounces each and 1 inch thick), Prime or Choice grade

Salt and freshly ground black pepper to taste

Roasted Corn Succotash (page 91)

FOR THE ROASTED
TOMATO–BALSAMIC SAUCE:

2 tablespoons olive oil

1 sweet onion, thinly sliced

2 cloves garlic, minced

1 pound plum tomatoes, roasted, peeled, and coarsely chopped (page 228)

2 tablespoons minced fresh basil leaves

Salt and freshly ground black pepper to taste

1/2 teaspoon sugar

1/2 tablespoon Dijon mustard

1/2 tablespoon balsamic vinegar

1 tablespoon finely sliced fresh chives, for garnish

To prepare the veal, pour the oil into a glass baking dish and add the garlic and basil. Season the chops with salt and pepper, add to the dish, and let marinate in the refrigerator for 1 hour, turning occasionally.

Meanwhile, prepare the succotash according to the recipe on page 91. Prepare the grill.

To prepare the sauce, heat the oil in a saucepan and sauté the onion and garlic over medium heat for 7 or 8 minutes, until translucent and soft. Add the tomatoes and basil, and season with salt and pepper. Add the sugar and cook for 7 or 8 minutes, stirring occasionally. Transfer to a blender or food processor and purée. Return to a clean saucepan, stir in the mustard, and add the vinegar. Keep warm.

Remove the veal chops from the marinade, and grill over medium-high heat for 4 to 5 minutes per side for medium-rare, about 6 minutes per side for medium, or to the desired doneness.

Spoon a mound of succotash on each serving plate. Place a chop next to the succotash, and spoon the sauce on top of and around the veal. Garnish the sauce with the chives.

SERVES 4

GRILLED SOUTHWESTERN VEAL CHOPS
WITH CILANTRO-POTATO SALAD

Both really simple and tasty, this recipe makes the perfect summer evening dinner. The spicy rub makes an excellent all-purpose seasoning for most types of red meat, and lends the veal deep and complex flavor tones. By all means, cut back on the chile powder if you are looking for milder results. Yukon Gold, fingerling, or new potatoes also make good choices for this zippy potato salad.

To prepare the salad, place the potatoes in a saucepan of salted water and bring to a boil. Boil for about 20 minutes, or until just cooked through. Drain, let cool, and cut into $1/2$-inch chunks. While the potatoes are cooking, combine the mayonnaise, the $1/4$ cup of lemon juice, and the $1/4$ cup of cilantro. Transfer the potatoes to a mixing bowl, and add the radishes, cucumber, and hard-boiled egg. Toss enough of the dressing with the potato salad to create a creamy consistency. Season with salt, pepper, and more lemon juice to taste. Garnish with the remaining 2 tablespoons of cilantro. Chill until ready to serve.

Prepare the grill. To prepare the rub, combine the chile powder, cumin, oregano, cinnamon, salt, and pepper in a small bowl. Lightly brush both sides of the chops with the melted butter and sprinkle with the dry rub, pressing it onto both sides of each chop to make sure it adheres. Grill the chops over direct medium-high heat for about 5 minutes on each side for medium-rare, 6 minutes per side for medium, or to the desired doneness. Serve immediately with the potato salad.

SERVES 4

FOR THE CILANTRO-POTATO SALAD:

2 pounds unpeeled Red Bliss potatoes, scrubbed

$3/4$ cup mayonnaise

$1/4$ cup freshly squeezed lemon juice, plus more to taste

$1/4$ cup minced fresh cilantro leaves, plus 2 tablespoons, for garnish

5 radishes, halved and thinly sliced into half-moons

1 cucumber, peeled, seeded, quartered lengthwise, and sliced $1/4$ inch thick

1 hard-boiled egg, chopped

Salt and freshly ground black pepper to taste

FOR THE SOUTHWESTERN RUB AND VEAL CHOPS:

2 tablespoons pure red chile powder

2 tablespoons ground cumin

1 tablespoon dried oregano

$1/2$ tablespoon ground cinnamon

$1/2$ teaspoon salt

$1/2$ teaspoon freshly ground black pepper

4 veal rib chops (about 8 ounces each and $1 1/4$ inches thick), Prime or Choice grade

2 tablespoons melted butter

VEAL

GRILLED VEAL T-BONES
WITH CILANTRO-JALAPEÑO BUTTER AND GREEN BEANS WITH TOMATOES AND PINE NUTS

If veal T-bones are not available at your local grocery, order them from Omaha Steaks (page 4) or your butcher. You might also use veal chops or poultry. In this recipe, you can sauté rather than grill the T-bones: heat 1 tablespoon of olive oil in a heavy nonstick or cast-iron skillet, season the steaks, and sauté over medium-high heat for the same cooking time. The Cilantro-Jalapeño Butter recipe will make more than double the amount you need for this recipe, but it hardly seems worth making less. Freeze the leftover butter to use again with meat, poultry, or grilled vegetables or toss it with pasta. It is important to make the beans with good-quality, flavorful tomatoes; if they are out of season, substitute 3 or 4 plum tomatoes.

To prepare the cilantro-jalapeño butter, place the butter, cilantro, lime juice, chiles, garlic, salt, and pepper in a food processor or blender and purée until smooth. Transfer to a sheet of wax paper or plastic wrap and roll into a cylinder about 1 inch in diameter. Chill for at least 20 minutes, or until firm. (Alternatively, pack the butter into a small bowl, chill slightly, and form into balls using a melon baller.)

Preheat the grill.

Place the beans in a vegetable steamer basket set over a saucepan of water and bring to a boil. Cover tightly and cook for 6 to 8 minutes, until just tender. Transfer to a colander and stop the cooking process by holding the beans under cold running water. Lay out the beans on paper towels to dry. Heat the olive oil in a large sauté pan and sauté the onion over medium heat for about 8 minutes, or until the edges start to darken. Add the oregano, season with salt and pepper, and cook for 1 minute longer. Add the green beans, toss lightly, and cook for 1 or 2 minutes more. Transfer to a mixing bowl and let cool slightly. Add the tomatoes to the green beans, toss together, and garnish with the pine nuts. Serve at room temperature.

Season the T-bones with salt and pepper, brush with the oil, and grill over direct medium-high heat for 4 to 5 minutes per side for medium-rare, 5 to 6 minutes per side for medium, or to the desired doneness.

Place the steaks on warm serving plates, top each steak with a 1 tablespoon slice or ball of the cilantro-jalapeño butter, and arrange the beans around the T-bones.

SERVES 4

FOR THE CILANTRO-JALAPEÑO BUTTER:
1 stick butter (8 tablespoons), softened
1/2 cup chopped fresh cilantro leaves
3 tablespoons freshly squeezed lime juice
1 1/2 jalapeño chiles, seeded and minced
1 clove garlic, minced
Salt and freshly ground white pepper to taste

FOR THE GREEN BEANS WITH TOMATOES AND PINE NUTS:
1 pound green beans, trimmed
1 tablespoon olive oil
1 onion, sliced lengthwise into 1/4-inch strips
1 teaspoon chopped fresh oregano leaves
Salt and freshly ground white pepper to taste
2 large vine-ripened tomatoes, peeled, seeded, and chopped
1/4 cup pine nuts, toasted (page 229)

FOR THE T-BONES:
4 veal T-bones (about 8 ounces each and 1 inch thick), Prime or Choice grade
Salt and freshly ground black pepper to taste
2 tablespoons olive oil

Crusting meat adds not only flavor, but also texture, and the seasoned corn bread crumbs enhance the Southwestern ambience of this recipe. The advantage of making the corn bread recipe on page 213 for the crumbs is that you can serve the rest of the corn bread with the chops, but by all means take the shortcut of buying store-bought corn bread. The ancho chiles become quite fragrant while toasting in the oven, and their volatile oils can make it hard for some to breathe, so it's best done with windows open and the range vent running. The salsa has a kick to it, so for milder palates, use only two or three anchos.

Preheat the oven to 400°F. Cover the bottom of a large roasting pan with aluminum foil. Place the chiles, tomatillos, onions (cut-side down), and garlic in the pan and place in the oven. After 1 or 2 minutes, turn the anchos, and remove 1 or 2 minutes later; do not allow them to blacken. Return the pan to the oven to continue roasting the tomatillos, onions, and garlic. Meanwhile, rehydrate the anchos in a bowl of warm water for 30 minutes, using a pan or plate to keep them submerged. Roast the tomatillos, onions, and garlic for 15 to 20 minutes longer, turning at least once, until they begin to blacken. Remove from the oven, and when cool enough to handle, remove the husks from the tomatillos, core them, and transfer to a blender or food processor. Add the onions. Squeeze the roasted garlic out of its skin and add to the blender together with the 2 tablespoons of lime juice. Purée until smooth, and season with salt and more lime juice to taste. Set aside.

About 30 minutes before you are ready to serve, prepare the veal chops. Preheat the oven to 350°F. Combine the corn bread crumbs, cumin, and cinnamon in a large shallow bowl. Season the veal chops with salt and pepper. Place the flour on a plate and the eggs in a shallow bowl. Dredge the chops in the flour, shaking off any excess. Then dip in the beaten eggs and finally in the corn bread crumb mixture, so that all of the chop is covered. Set on a dry plate and let the breaded chops rest for about 15 minutes. Pour enough oil into a large skillet to come about 1/4 inch up the sides and set over medium-high heat. When the oil is hot, carefully add the chops and cook for 2 minutes on each side. Transfer to a roasting pan and roast in the oven for about 15 minutes, or until golden brown and medium-rare, about 17 to 18 minutes per side for medium, or to the desired doneness. Remove the chops and drain on paper towels. Transfer to serving plates, garnish with the parsley, and serve with the salsa.

SERVES 4

FOR THE TOMATILLO AND ANCHO CHILE SALSA:

4 dried ancho chiles, stems and seeds removed

1 pound tomatillos, with husks

2 onions, cut in half

4 cloves unpeeled garlic

2 tablespoons freshly squeezed lime juice, plus more to taste

Salt to taste

FOR THE CORN BREAD CRUSTED VEAL CHOPS:

3/4 cup fresh corn bread crumbs (see page 213)

1 teaspoon ground cumin

1/4 teaspoon ground cinnamon

4 veal rib chops (about 8 ounces each and 1 1/4 inches thick), Prime or Choice grade

Salt and freshly ground black pepper to taste

1/2 cup all-purpose flour

2 eggs, beaten

Vegetable oil, for frying

1/2 tablespoon minced fresh flat-leaf parsley, for garnish

ROASTED VEAL TENDERLOIN
WITH SPANISH-STYLE TOMATOES AND OLIVES IN A SHERRY SAUCE

Smaller in girth than beef tenderloin, veal tenderloin has a delicate yet rich flavor. Despite some assertive ingredients, such as poblanos and olives, in this Spanish-influenced sauce, the veal stands up well. The saffron rice is optional, but adding it here continues the Spanish theme and makes for a complete and filling meal. It's a side dish we also use for the Blanquette of Veal (page 76). If you have trouble finding poblano chiles, substitute a roasted large green bell pepper and two roasted jalapeños (or more to taste).

FOR THE SPANISH-STYLE TOMATOES AND OLIVES IN A SHERRY SAUCE:

1 tablespoon olive oil

1 onion, cut lengthwise into thin strips

2 cloves garlic, minced

6 plum tomatoes, peeled, seeded, and coarsely chopped

$1/2$ cup tomato purée or tomato juice

1 cup Chicken Stock (page 225)

2 poblano chiles, roasted, peeled, seeded, and cut into thin strips (page 228)

$1/4$ cup pitted green olives stuffed with pimientos

Salt and freshly ground black pepper to taste

1 cup dry sherry

FOR THE SAFFRON RICE:

1 tablespoon olive oil

1 tablespoon butter

1 cup long-grain white rice

$1/4$ teaspoon saffron threads

$1 1/2$ cups Chicken Stock (page 225)

Salt to taste

FOR THE VEAL TENDERLOIN:

2 pounds veal tenderloin, Prime or Choice grade

Salt and freshly ground black pepper to taste

2 tablespoons olive oil

To prepare the vegetables, heat the olive oil in a large sauté pan and sauté the onion over medium heat for 7 or 8 minutes, or until lightly golden. Add the garlic and sauté for 2 to 3 minutes longer. Add the tomatoes and tomato purée; cook for about 5 minutes, stirring occasionally. Add the stock, chiles, olives, salt, and pepper, and simmer for about 10 minutes, or until the sauce has reduced slightly. Add the sherry and slowly simmer for about 15 minutes, until the sauce thickens; do not let the sauce boil once the sherry has been added. Season with additional salt and pepper, as necessary.

Preheat the oven to 400°F.

To prepare the rice, heat the oil and butter in a saucepan on medium. When the butter has melted, stir in the rice until completely coated. Crumble the saffron into the pan and add the stock. Bring to a boil, cover, and reduce the heat to low. Simmer for 15 minutes, or until the rice has absorbed the liquid. Season lightly with salt and fluff with a fork before serving.

Meanwhile, season the tenderloin with salt and pepper. Heat the oil in a cast-iron skillet and sear the tenderloin over high heat on all sides, about 5 minutes. Place the skillet in the oven and roast the tenderloin for 8 to 10 minutes for medium-rare, 12 to 14 minutes for medium, or to the desired doneness. Remove from the oven, cover with foil, and let rest for about 10 minutes. Slice the tenderloin on the diagonal and place it down the center of a large, oval serving platter. Spoon the sauce around the tenderloin and serve with the rice.

SERVES 4

OMAHA STEAKS MEAT

SAUTÉED CALF'S LIVER,
CARAMELIZED ONIONS AND APPLES, WITH
ROASTED GARLIC MASHED POTATOES

Liver—folks either love it or hate it. Of course we're biased in its favor, which is not a difficult position to take considering that high-quality fresh veal liver has a mild taste and has virtually none of the assertive flavor that some associate with beef. And with its high iron content, it also makes for a nutritious meal. When shopping for this recipe, bear in mind that calf's liver should be a pale pink or light brown, while that of beef is a dark reddish-brown. Liver gets tough when overcooked, so watch it carefully. Mashed potatoes and calf's liver were made for each other, as this simple recipe proves. Although no sugar is added to the onions, their natural sugars will help them caramelize, and the sweetness of the apples enhances their flavor.

Prepare the mashed potatoes according to the recipe on page 49.

To prepare the onions and apples, melt 2 tablespoons of the butter in a large sauté pan over medium-low heat. Place the apples in the pan in a single layer and sauté for 5 to 7 minutes on each side, until lightly golden and cooked through but not mushy. Remove from the pan and set aside. Add the remaining tablespoon of butter to the pan and sauté the onions over medium heat for 7 or 8 minutes, or until lightly golden. Return the apples to the pan, drizzle the apple cider vinegar over the onions and apples, and season with salt and pepper. Gently toss to coat evenly, and cook over medium heat for 2 or 3 minutes. Set aside and keep warm.

Season the liver with salt and pepper. Heat the olive oil in the pan and sauté the liver over medium-high heat for 2 to 3 minutes on each side, or until cooked through. Transfer the calf's liver to 4 warmed serving plates. Pile the apples and onions in a mound over the liver and serve with the mashed potatoes on the side.

SERVES 4

Roasted Garlic Mashed Potatoes (page 49)

FOR THE CARAMELIZED ONIONS AND APPLES:

- 3 tablespoons butter
- 2 Granny Smith apples, peeled, cored, and sliced into 1/8-inch strips
- 2 sweet onions, such as Vidalia, sliced lengthwise into 1/4-inch strips
- 3 tablespoons apple cider vinegar
- Salt and freshly ground black pepper to taste

FOR THE SAUTÉED CALF'S LIVER:

- 1 1/2 pounds calf's liver (1/2 inch thick), Prime or Choice grade, cut into 4 portions
- Salt and freshly ground black pepper to taste
- 2 tablespoons olive oil

VEAL

If you are buying liver at the grocery store rather than from a butcher, it will probably be precut about ¹/₂ inch thick. In that case, simply fold it over before wrapping with bacon so that it becomes 1 inch thick. Note that fresh liver is easier to slice and handle if placed in the freezer for about 30 minutes before slicing. The dressing for the spinach can be prepared in advance and reheated, with the spinach added just before serving, when the skewers are almost ready. The spinach can also be plated raw, with the hot dressing poured over, if you prefer.

FOR THE GARLIC TOAST:

8 slices French bread, cut on the diagonal into ³/₄-inch-thick slices

2 cloves garlic, minced

3 tablespoons butter, softened

FOR THE CALF'S LIVER KABOBS:

1¹/₂ pounds calf's liver (1 inch thick), Prime or Choice grade

Salt and freshly ground black pepper to taste

12 slices bacon (about 12 ounces), cut in half crosswise

16 cherry tomatoes, cut in half

2 large onions, quartered then cut in half crosswise

FOR THE WILTED SPINACH SALAD:

1 tablespoon finely chopped shallots

1 teaspoon Dijon mustard, preferably whole-grain

¹/₄ cup balsamic vinegar

2 tablespoons vegetable oil

10 ounces spinach (about 8 tightly packed cups), cleaned, trimmed, and torn into large pieces

Salt and freshly ground black pepper to taste

Prepare the grill. Soak 8 bamboo skewers (preferably 12 inches long) in water for at least 10 minutes so they won't burn up on the grill, and then drain. (Alternatively, use metal skewers.) Preheat the oven to 400°F.

Place the slices of bread on a work surface, mix together the garlic and butter, and spread a thin layer on each slice of bread. Place the bread on a baking sheet, garlic-side up, and toast in the oven for 6 to 8 minutes, or until lightly golden. Remove from the oven and set aside to cool.

Cut the liver into 1 x 1¹/₂-inch cubes to make about 24 pieces of liver; season with salt and pepper. In a sauté pan, cook the bacon over high heat for about 1 minute to release some of the fat (the bacon should still be soft). Drain the bacon strips on paper towels and reserve 2 tablespoons of the bacon drippings. Wrap each piece of liver with a strip of the bacon and thread onto the skewers, alternating the liver with the tomato and onion pieces. Each skewer should have 3 pieces of liver, 2 pieces of onion, and 2 tomato halves. Grill the kabobs for about 5 or 6 minutes on each side, until the liver is cooked and the onions begin to brown.

To prepare the spinach salad, heat the reserved bacon drippings in a large saucepan, add the shallots, and cook over medium-high heat for about 2 minutes. Reduce the heat to medium-low, and whisk in the mustard, balsamic vinegar, and oil. Add the spinach and toss with the dressing over the heat for 1 or 2 minutes, just until the spinach begins to wilt. Season with salt and pepper, and arrange the spinach on warm serving plates. Top each salad with 2 grilled skewers, crossed to make an "X," with a piece of garlic toast leaning against the skewers on each side.

SERVES 4

VEAL MARENGO:
VEAL BRAISED WITH TOMATOES, MUSHROOMS, AND ONIONS, GARNISHED WITH TOAST POINTS

Napoleon's chef, Durand, is said to have prepared this classic French stew following Napoleon's victory over Austria in 1800 at the battle of Marengo in northern Italy. According to food expert Michael Field, a version of this dish was actually known as Chicken à la Provençal prior to that battle—and is simply a Provençal stew. While the great Escoffier recommended serving heart-shaped croutons fried in butter, toast points are easier, although you can use cookie cutters to make more interesting shapes, if you wish. Toast is the classic accompaniment, but we have found that egg noodles make a great alternative.

2¹/₂ pounds veal breast, Prime or Choice grade, cut into 1¹/₂-inch cubes

Salt and freshly ground black pepper to taste

3 tablespoons olive oil

¹/₂ onion, chopped

2 cloves garlic, minced

2 tablespoons tomato paste

¹/₂ cup white wine

2 cups Beef Stock (page 225)

2 cups canned crushed tomatoes

3 sprigs fresh thyme

1 bay leaf

20 pearl onions (6 to 8 ounces)

5 ounces mushrooms

1 tablespoon chopped fresh flat-leaf parsley

4 slices good-quality, densely textured white bread

2 tablespoons melted butter

Season the veal with salt and pepper. Heat 2 tablespoons of the oil in a large Dutch oven or flame-proof casserole over medium-high heat. Add the veal and sauté for about 7 minutes, stirring occasionally, until browned on all sides. (To avoid overcrowding the pan, you may wish to do this in 2 or 3 batches.) Remove the veal with a slotted spoon and set aside. Reduce the heat to medium, add the chopped onion, and sauté for about 5 minutes, until light golden in color, adding a little olive oil to prevent the onion from sticking, if necessary. Add the garlic and cook for 2 minutes longer. Stir in the tomato paste and cook for another minute. Add the white wine and stir to deglaze the pan; cook for 2 or 3 minutes, until the liquid is reduced by half. Add the stock, tomatoes, thyme, and bay leaf. Return the veal to the pan and lightly season with salt and pepper. Bring the stew to a simmer, cover, and cook for 1¹/₂ hours, skimming the surface occasionally to remove any impurities.

Preheat the oven to 350°F.

While the stew is cooking, heat the remaining tablespoon of olive oil in a sauté pan, and add the pearl onions. Cook over medium heat for 7 to 10 minutes, until dark golden brown and caramelized. Transfer to the stew, add the mushrooms and parsley, and continue cooking for 15 more minutes, or until the veal is tender and the mushrooms are cooked through. Remove the thyme and bay leaf, and season with salt and pepper to taste.

While the stew is cooking, prepare the bread. Cut off the crusts and lightly brush each side with the melted butter. Place the bread on a baking sheet, and toast in the oven for about 5 minutes, or until lightly golden. Cut each slice diagonally into 4 triangles. Serve the stew in warmed soup plates and garnish each serving with 4 toast points.

SERVES 4

Veal Marsala
with Rice and Lentil Pilaf

The pairing of rice and lentils is common in the Eastern Mediterranean, and the pilaf makes a tasty change from the traditional pasta accompaniment for Veal Marsala. Serve pasta—such as vermicelli—if you prefer, but we think you will enjoy the pilaf. Marsala, a fortified wine from Sicily, pairs with veal in this classic Italian dish that's simple to prepare. Marsala is available dry or sweet; be sure to use the dry variety for this recipe. If unavailable, combine three parts dry white wine with one part brandy.

To prepare the pilaf, rinse the lentils under cold running water and pick through them to remove any foreign objects. Transfer to a saucepan and cover with about 1 inch of water. Bring to a boil, reduce the heat to a simmer, and cook for about 20 minutes, or until just tender; drain. While the lentils are cooking, melt the butter in a saucepan over medium heat and sauté the onions for about 7 minutes, until golden brown. Add the rice and stir for 1 or 2 minutes, until all the grains are coated. Add 2$\frac{1}{2}$ cups of water and a pinch of salt, cover the pan, and cook for 15 minutes. With a fork, gently stir in the lentils, cover again, and cook for 5 minutes longer. Remove the pan from the heat and let it rest for about 5 minutes. Fluff with a fork and season with salt and pepper.

For the veal marsala, place the flour on a plate, season the veal with salt and pepper, and dredge in the flour. Lightly pound the veal with the flat side of a meat cleaver or a rolling pin (ideally, the slices should be $\frac{1}{8}$ inch to $\frac{1}{4}$ inch thick). Heat the olive oil and 1 tablespoon of the butter in a sauté pan over high heat and quickly sauté the veal for about 30 seconds per side. (You may wish to do this in 2 batches to avoid overcrowding the pan.) Remove the veal and set aside. Add the Marsala, chicken stock, and lemon slices, and stir to deglaze the pan. Reduce the heat to medium and cook for 3 or 4 minutes, until the liquid is reduced to about $\frac{1}{2}$ cup. Remove the lemon slices, whisk in the remaining 2 tablespoons of butter, and season with salt and pepper. Return the veal to the pan just long enough to reheat, about 1 minute (do not overheat or the veal will become tough.)

Transfer the veal to warm serving plates, spoon the sauce over the veal, and garnish with the chopped parsley. Serve with the rice and lentils.

SERVES 4

FOR THE RICE AND LENTIL PILAF:
1 cup brown lentils
1 tablespoon butter
1 onion, chopped
1 cup long-grain white rice
Salt and freshly ground black pepper to taste

FOR THE VEAL MARSALA:
$\frac{1}{2}$ cup all-purpose flour
1 pound veal top round, Prime or Choice grade, thinly sliced into 8 or 12 scaloppine
Salt and freshly ground black pepper to taste
1 tablespoon olive oil
3 tablespoons butter
$\frac{1}{2}$ cup dry Marsala
$\frac{1}{4}$ cup Chicken Stock (page 225)
$\frac{1}{2}$ lemon, thinly sliced
2 teaspoons chopped fresh flat-leaf parsley, for garnish

ROLLED BREAST OF VEAL
STUFFED WITH SPINACH AND SUN-DRIED TOMATOES WITH MUSHROOM-LEEK SAUCE

Veal breast, an underrated and economical cut, is best stuffed and cooked relatively slowly for an extended time. This veal breast recipe features a much more substantial stuffing than that on page 57, and it really isn't necessary to serve it with a side; however, if you like, serve extra rice or baby carrots. You'll love the rich and flavorful sauce.

To prepare the stuffing, place the spinach in a vegetable basket set over a pan of boiling water, cover tightly, and steam for 2 or 3 minutes. Set aside. When cool enough to handle, finely chop. Heat the olive oil in a sauté pan and sauté the leek over medium heat for about 5 minutes, until softened. Add the parsley and thyme and cook for 2 minutes longer. Transfer to a mixing bowl, and stir in the spinach, rice, sun-dried tomatoes, salt, and pepper. Gently stir in the beaten egg and keep refrigerated if not using immediately.

Preheat the oven to 350°F. To prepare the veal, lay the breast open like a book, and season with salt and pepper. Spread the rice and spinach stuffing over the veal, to within about 1 inch of the edges. Starting with the shorter side of the rectangle, roll the veal like a jellyroll and tie with butcher's twine. Season the roll with salt and pepper. Heat the olive oil in a Dutch oven or ovenproof casserole and sear the veal roll on all sides for about 5 minutes, or until browned. Add 1 cup of water, the stock, carrot, and leek, and bring to a simmer on top of the stove. Transfer to the heated oven and braise for about 1³/₄ hours, or until the veal is tender. Remove the breast from the pan and cover with foil. Strain the pan, reserving the braising liquid and discarding the vegetables. Skim the surface of the braising liquid to remove any impurities and return it to the pan. (You will need about 1 cup of braising liquid; if necessary, add more beef stock or water.)

To prepare the sauce, heat the butter in a sauté pan and sauté the leek over medium heat for about 5 minutes, until softened. Add the mushrooms and cook for 5 minutes longer, until golden. Stir in the tomato paste and thyme and cook for 3 minutes. Add the braising liquid and cook over medium heat for 5 to 7 minutes more, until the broth is reduced by half. Reduce the heat to medium-low, whisk in the cream, and heat until slightly thickened. Season with salt and pepper and remove the thyme sprig.

Remove the veal from the oven and cut away the twine. Carve the veal into ³/₄- to 1-inch slices, and place 2 slices of veal breast on each serving plate. Spoon the sauce around the veal.

SERVES 4 TO 6

FOR THE SPINACH AND SUN-DRIED TOMATO STUFFING:

10 ounces spinach leaves (about 8 tightly packed cups), cleaned and stemmed

1 tablespoon olive oil

1 cup chopped leek (about 1 leek), white part only

2 tablespoons chopped fresh flat-leaf parsley

1/2 teaspoon chopped fresh thyme leaves

2 cups cooked long-grain white rice (page 227)

1/4 cup sun-dried tomatoes (packed in oil), minced

Salt and freshly ground black pepper to taste

1 egg, beaten

FOR THE VEAL:

1 veal breast (3 to 4 pounds), Prime or Choice grade, boned and butterflied

Salt and freshly ground black pepper to taste

2 tablespoons olive oil

1 cup Beef Stock, plus more if necessary (page 225)

1 carrot, chopped

1 cup chopped leek (about 1 leek), white part only

FOR THE MUSHROOM-LEEK SAUCE:

2 tablespoons butter (1/4 stick)

1 cup chopped leek (about 1 leek), white part only

8 ounces mushrooms, sliced

1 tablespoon tomato paste

1 fresh thyme sprig

2 tablespoons heavy cream

Salt and freshly ground black pepper to taste

VEAL

VEAL IN MUSTARD SAUCE
WITH MUSHROOMS AND PEARL ONIONS, SERVED WITH LEEK AND POTATO GRATIN

This delicious rustic recipe of French origin just begs to be made on one of those chilly fall or winter evenings when you feel like something homey and comforting. For a more elegant presentation and flavor, use wild mushrooms, such as chanterelles or morels. If these threaten to exceed your budget, compromise by substituting shiitake mushrooms. If you'd like to double the recipe for extra company, or if you'd like to serve this dish buffet style, you might wish to cut the scaloppine into $1/2$-inch strips and sauté them for about 1 minute before preparing the sauce.

FOR THE GRATIN:

1 pound Yukon Gold potatoes, peeled and cut into $1/4$-inch slices

1 pound parsnips, peeled and cut into $1/4$-inch slices

4 tablespoons butter ($1/2$ stick)

3 leeks, white and light green parts only, cut in half lengthwise and sliced $1/4$ inch thick (about $2 1/2$ cups)

1 large onion, cut in half and sliced $1/4$ inch thick

1 teaspoon minced garlic

Salt and freshly ground black pepper to taste

1 cup grated Jarlsberg or Swiss cheese

1 cup sour cream

$1/2$ cup milk

1 egg, beaten

$1/2$ tablespoon minced fresh marjoram leaves

FOR THE VEAL AND SAUCE:

2 tablespoons olive oil

1 tablespoon butter

$1 1/2$ pounds veal top round, Prime or Choice grade, sliced into 8 scaloppine of 3 ounces each

Salt and freshly ground black pepper to taste

5 ounces pearl onions (about 1 cup)

8 ounces mushrooms, sliced

$1/4$ cup dry sherry

1 cup heavy cream

2 tablespoons Dijon mustard

Preheat the oven to 325°F. To prepare the gratin, place the potatoes and parsnips in a saucepan of boiling salted water and parboil for 5 minutes. Drain and let cool. Heat 2 tablespoons of the butter in a skillet and sauté the leeks, onion, and garlic over medium heat for 5 or 6 minutes, until softened, stirring occasionally. Season with salt and pepper. Transfer half of the mixture to a large buttered baking dish or ovenproof casserole about 9 inches in diameter and 2 inches deep, and cover with a layer of half of the potatoes and parsnips. Cut the remaining butter into thin slices and spread half of it over the potatoes. Sprinkle half of the cheese over the butter. Spread the remaining leek mixture over the cheese, and top with the remaining potatoes, parsnips, and butter. In a mixing bowl, combine the sour cream, milk, egg, and marjoram; season with salt and pepper. Pour over the potatoes and sprinkle with the remaining cheese. Transfer to the oven and bake for about 45 minutes, or until golden and bubbly.

To prepare the veal, heat 1 tablespoon of the olive oil and the butter in a heavy skillet. Season the veal with salt and pepper, and sauté in the skillet over medium-high heat for about 2 minutes per side. Remove the veal from the skillet and set aside on a warm plate. Add the remaining tablespoon of olive oil, and when hot, add the pearl onions. Sauté for about 5 minutes, or until lightly golden. Add the mushrooms and cook for 5 minutes longer, or until tender and fairly dry. Add the sherry and stir to deglaze the pan. Reduce the heat to medium, add the cream, and stir in the mustard, combining thoroughly. Bring just to a boil, and then return the veal to the skillet. Cook over medium-low heat for 2 to 3 more minutes, and then transfer the veal to warm serving plates. Spoon the mushrooms, onions, and sauce over and next to the veal, and serve immediately.

SERVES 4

SAUTÉED VEAL CHOPS,
APPLES AND CALVADOS, WITH POTATO GALETTE

The combination of veal, apples, and Calvados—a dry, smooth apple brandy from Normandy—presents a classic from northern France. Calvados, like French wine, is regulated under its appellation contrôlée; the best comes from the Pays d'Auge region. Calvados is aged for at least one year in oak barrels. You can substitute applejack brandy, although the flavor will be less complex and refined. Galettes are round flat cakes or tartlets in the French tradition, and in this case, they are simply layered potato cakes. The potatoes are best cut with a mandoline, but even thin hand-cut slices will yield a crispy outer crust and a delicious, creamy interior.

To prepare the potatoes, melt the butter in a small saucepan and keep warm. Brush 1 tablespoon of the butter over the bottom and sides of a large, ovenproof skillet or sauté pan and arrange a third of the potato slices in the skillet in a spiral pattern. Start in the center and work out, overlapping the slices slightly. The bottom of the skillet should be covered with potato slices. Brush the potatoes with 1 tablespoon more of the butter, season with salt and pepper, and sprinkle with 1/2 teaspoon each of the rosemary and thyme. Arrange another layer of potatoes the same way and brush with another tablespoon of the butter. Season with salt, pepper, and 1/2 teaspoon each of the rosemary and thyme. Repeat a final layer of the potatoes, and brush the top with the remaining tablespoon of butter.

Preheat the broiler. Sauté the potatoes over medium heat for 7 or 8 minutes, until the bottom begins to brown and turn crisp. Transfer the skillet to the middle rack of the broiler and cook for 7 or 8 minutes longer, or until the tops of the potatoes are golden brown and crisp. Cut into 8 wedges before serving.

While the potatoes are cooking, prepare the veal. Melt the butter in a large sauté pan over medium heat and add the apple wedges. Sauté for 3 or 4 minutes per side, or until softened and slightly browned. Remove from the pan and reserve. Heat the olive oil in the same pan, and season the veal with salt and pepper. Sauté the veal for about 5 minutes per side for medium-rare, about 6 minutes per side for medium, or to the desired doneness. Remove the veal from the pan and set aside. Add the Calvados to the pan, carefully ignite, and when the flames have died down, stir to deglaze the pan. Return the apples and veal to the pan. When warmed through, transfer the veal and apples to serving plates and spoon with the pan juices. Season with freshly ground black pepper and garnish with the parsley. Serve each portion with 2 wedges of the galette.

SERVES 4

FOR THE POTATO GALETTE:

4 tablespoons butter (1/2 stick), softened

4 russet potatoes (about 8 ounces each), peeled and finely sliced

Salt and freshly ground black pepper to taste

1 1/2 teaspoons minced fresh rosemary leaves

1 1/2 teaspoons minced fresh thyme leaves

FOR THE VEAL, APPLES, AND CALVADOS:

2 tablespoons butter (1/4 stick)

2 Granny Smith apples, peeled, cored, and cut into 8 wedges each

2 tablespoons olive oil

4 veal rib chops (about 8 ounces each and 1 1/4 inches thick), Prime or Choice grade

Salt and freshly ground black pepper to taste

1/3 cup Calvados

2 tablespoons minced fresh flat-leaf parsley, for garnish

VEAL

VEAL SALTIMBOCCA:
VEAL, PROSCIUTTO, AND SAGE SERVED WITH ASPARAGUS LINGUINE

In Italian, "saltimbocca" literally means "jump in the mouth," and these little rolls of stuffed veal will jump into your guests' mouths with great ease. If the ready-cut scaloppine called for in this recipe are unavailable, use 4 veal cutlets about 6 ounces each, pounded between sheets of wax paper to a thickness of $^{1}/_{8}$ inch and then cut in half. You can also use $1^{1}/_{2}$ pounds veal loin, leg meat, or top round cut into 4 slices, each about $^{1}/_{3}$ inch thick, and again pound down and cut in half. There are many regional variations of this classic dish. In Rome, for example, this dish is served without cheese. Other recipes call for dredging the veal scaloppine in flour before filling and rolling up.

Preheat the oven to 300°F.

To prepare the linguine, cut off the tough or thick ends of the asparagus spears and discard. Cut the asparagus into 1-inch lengths and transfer to a vegetable basket set over a saucepan of boiling salted water. Cover tightly and steam for 5 minutes, or until al dente. Cook the linguine in a saucepan of boiling water according to the directions on the package. Drain and rinse with cool water. Just before serving, heat the olive oil in a saucepan over medium heat. Add the garlic and pepper flakes, and sauté for 2 minutes. Add the cooked asparagus and the drained linguine and toss gently to ensure that the asparagus is evenly distributed in the pasta. Season with salt and keep warm.

Meanwhile, season the veal with salt and pepper. Lay the scaloppine on a work surface and place 1 or 2 slices of prosciutto, a slice of cheese, and some of the sage on top. Roll up and secure with a toothpick. Heat the olive oil and butter in a large nonstick sauté pan. Sauté the veal over medium-high heat for 2 minutes on each side, or until browned. Transfer to an ovenproof dish and keep warm in the oven. Add the wine and stir to deglaze the pan. Stir in the mustard and lemon juice. Bring the sauce to a simmer, return the veal rolls to the pan, and cook for 2 minutes, turning occasionally. Remove the veal with tongs and place on warm serving plates. Spoon the liquid in the pan over the veal, garnish with the minced sage, and serve with the linguine.

SERVES 4

FOR THE LINGUINE:

1 pound asparagus

1 pound dry linguine

2 tablespoons olive oil

2 teaspoons minced garlic

1 teaspoon dried red pepper flakes

Salt to taste

FOR THE VEAL SALTIMBOCCA:

8 veal scaloppine (about 3 ounces each and $^{1}/_{8}$ inch thick), Prime or Choice grade

Salt and freshly ground black pepper to taste

6 ounces prosciutto ham, cut into 8 or 16 slices

6 ounces Fontina or Swiss cheese, cut into 8 slices (optional)

8 fresh sage leaves, julienned

2 tablespoons olive oil

1 tablespoon butter

6 tablespoons dry white wine or dry Marsala

$^{1}/_{2}$ teaspoon Dijon mustard

2 tablespoons freshly squeezed lemon juice

1 teaspoon minced fresh sage leaves, for garnish

BLANQUETTE OF VEAL
BRAISED WITH VEGETABLES, CREAM SAUCE, AND SAFFRON RICE

The word "blanquette" is derived from "blanc," the French word for "white," and refers to a creamy, thick sauce usually served with veal or lamb. For a lighter version of this dish, use half-and-half or omit the cream altogether, and whisk the eggs with 1 tablespoon more of lemon juice. (Add this off the heat and do not return to a boil or the eggs may curdle.) Veal neck is our cut of choice here; it is underused and often overlooked, but is contains less fat and fewer bones than shoulder or breast, while still maintaining a wonderful flavor. As an alternative to the saffron rice, serve the veal with orzo (page 97) or toast points (page 68).

4 tablespoons butter (1/2 stick)

1 1/2 pounds boneless neck, shoulder, or breast of veal, Prime or Choice grade, cut into 1 1/2-inch cubes

Salt and freshly ground black pepper to taste

2 tablespoons all-purpose flour

2 cups Chicken Stock (page 225) or Veal Stock (page 225)

2 cups dry white wine

2 whole cloves

1 onion

2 sprigs fresh thyme

2 sprigs fresh parsley or oregano

2 cloves garlic, cut in half

8 black peppercorns

1 bay leaf

3 ounces pearl onions (about 2/3 cup)

1/4 cup chopped shallots

4 ounces mushrooms, cut in half

1 tablespoon freshly squeezed lemon juice

1/2 cup heavy cream

2 egg yolks

2 teaspoons minced fresh flat-leaf parsley, for garnish

Saffron Rice (page 64)

Melt 2 tablespoons of the butter in a large heavy saucepan or Dutch oven. Season the veal with salt and pepper, and cook on all sides (without browning) in the butter over medium heat, about 5 minutes. Sprinkle in the flour, and continue cooking for 3 more minutes, stirring continuously. Add the stock and wine, and stir to deglaze the pan. Stick the whole cloves into the onion and add to the pan. Bundle together the thyme, parsley, garlic, peppercorns, and bay leaf. Tie in cheesecloth, and add to the pan. Reduce the heat to a simmer, cover, and cook for about 1 1/2 hours, or until the meat is tender, stirring occasionally.

While the veal is cooking, heat the remaining 2 tablespoons of butter in a large sauté pan, and sauté the onions and shallots over medium heat for 6 or 7 minutes, until tender and lightly golden. Add the mushrooms and cook for about 5 minutes longer, until tender. Stir in the lemon juice and set aside. When the veal is tender, remove the meat, onion, and herbs from the broth, reserving the meat separately. Scoop off any grease from the surface of the broth. In a bowl, whisk together the cream and egg yolks, and whisk in 1/2 cup of the broth to temper the eggs. Return this mixture to the remaining broth, stirring constantly, and bring just to a simmer. Return the veal to the broth, add the reserved pearl onion–mushroom mixture, and adjust the seasonings. Warm through, but do not boil.

While the veal is cooking, prepare the rice. Spoon the rice onto warm serving plates and ladle the veal and broth next to or over the rice. Garnish the veal with the minced parsley.

SERVES 4

SPICE-CRUSTED GRILLED VEAL
WITH CHEF MARTÍN'S ROASTED CORN AND FINGERLING POTATO SALAD

Here is an alternative version of the veal recipe on page 59. It has similar elements, but the results have little in common. The wonderful, all-purpose crust is spicier, and the flavors of the potato salad taste altogether different. The salad recipe comes from a rising Southwestern chef, Martín Rios. Martín is the Executive Chef at The Old House, located in Santa Fe's prestigious Eldorado Hotel. Martín grew up in Mexico and moved to Santa Fe with his family when he was 13 years old. After an earlier stint as Executive Chef at The Old House, Martín trained at the Culinary Institute of America, gained experience in some of the best kitchens in France, and returned to the Southwest. He has been attracting rave reviews and awards ever since. If you would like another side dish, try the fried okra on page 22.

To prepare the spice crust, place the pepper, coriander, cumin, paprika, garlic salt, chile powder, allspice, cloves, sugar, and oregano in a bowl and combine thoroughly. With a sharp knife, lightly score the veal on both sides and dredge in the spice crust, making sure the T-bones are well covered. Cover and let sit for 2 hours in the refrigerator.

Meanwhile, prepare the potato salad. Place the potatoes in a saucepan of boiling salted water, and cook until just tender, 15 to 20 minutes. Drain, let cool, and chop or slice. While the potatoes are cooking, sauté the bacon in a dry skillet over medium heat until crispy, 4 or 5 minutes. Remove and drain on paper towels. When cool enough to handle, crumble the bacon into a mixing bowl. Add the corn, tomato, and yellow pepper, and combine. Add the potato slices and gently mix together.

Prepare the grill. Grill the T-bones over direct medium-high heat for about 5 minutes on each side for medium-rare, 6 minutes per side for medium, or to the desired doneness. Serve immediately with the potato salad.

SERVES 4

FOR THE SPICE CRUST AND VEAL:
1 tablespoon freshly ground black pepper

1 tablespoon freshly ground coriander

1 tablespoon freshly ground cumin

1 tablespoon paprika

1/2 tablespoon garlic salt

1/2 tablespoon pure red chile powder

1/2 tablespoon ground allspice

1/2 teaspoon ground cloves

1/2 tablespoon light brown sugar

1 teaspoon dried oregano

4 veal T-bones (about 12 ounces each and 1 1/8 inches thick), Prime or Choice grade

FOR THE POTATO SALAD:
1 pound fingerling potatoes

3 slices bacon

1 cup roasted corn kernels (page 229)

1 tomato, seeded and finely diced

1/2 small yellow bell pepper, seeded and finely diced

VEAL

KIRSTEN'S RIVERSONG LODGE
BRAISED VEAL
WITH CIDER, ORANGES, AND SPAETZLE

Next time you're roaming the Alaskan wilderness—oh, some 70 miles or so north of Anchorage—make sure the Riversong Lodge is on your itinerary. The salmon fishing on the Yentna River, which rushes by the fishing lodge, is legendary, and the country food served by Kirsten Dixon is worth the visit alone. Kirsten, who has studied with Jacques Pépin and at the Cordon Bleu cooking school in Paris, explains that the inspiration for this veal dish was a luncheon she enjoyed on a visit to the Veuve Cliquot champagne house in France. The spaetzle recipe comes from a German friend of Kirsten's, the late Robert Litti, who stayed at the Lodge every year. This recipe is included in Kirsten's Riversong Lodge Cookbook *(Alaska Northwest Books).*

FOR THE VEAL:

1 cup all-purpose flour

4 slices bone-in veal shanks (about 12 ounces each and 2 inches thick), Prime or Choice grade

Salt and freshly ground black pepper to taste

3 tablespoons olive oil

2 tablespoons butter ($\frac{1}{4}$ stick)

2 tablespoons minced shallot

1 head garlic, separated into cloves and peeled

1 large onion, thinly sliced

$\frac{1}{2}$ cup tomato purée

1 cup Beef Stock (page 225)

1 cup apple cider

1 tablespoon cider vinegar

2 unpeeled, sweet oranges, washed well and cut in half

FOR THE SPAETZLE:

2 cups all-purpose flour

$\frac{1}{4}$ cup milk

$\frac{1}{2}$ cup club soda

2 eggs

$\frac{1}{2}$ teaspoon salt, plus more for seasoning

4 tablespoons butter ($\frac{1}{2}$ stick)

Preheat the oven to 375°F.

Place the flour on a large plate and season the veal with salt and pepper. Dredge the veal in the flour, shaking off any excess. Heat the oil and butter in a large, heavy casserole. Brown the veal over medium-high heat, about 10 minutes. Remove the veal and set aside. Add the shallot and garlic to the casserole, and sauté for 2 to 3 minutes, until softened. Add the onion and sauté for 5 minutes. Add the tomato purée, stock, cider, and cider vinegar. Bring to a simmer and return the veal shanks to the casserole. Arrange the orange halves, cut-side down, around the veal shanks. Transfer to the oven and braise for $1\frac{1}{2}$ hours, or until the shanks are very tender. Before serving, remove the oranges, skim off any grease, and season with salt and pepper, if necessary.

While the veal is braising, prepare the spaetzle. Sift the flour into a mixing bowl, add the milk and club soda, and mix well with a wooden spoon. Stir in the eggs and salt, beating until small bubbles form. Cover the dough and let rest for 30 minutes. In a large saucepan, bring 1 gallon of salted water to a boil. If you have a spaetzle maker, press the dough through it into the boiling water. If you have a colander, grease it well and push the dough through the holes. Alternatively, spread the dough on a small cutting board to a thickness of about $\frac{1}{4}$ inch, and cut the dough into 1-inch pieces. Drop into the water in batches, bring back to a boil, and cook for 7 or 8 minutes. Remove with a slotted spoon, drain in a colander or sieve, and chill under cold running water.

Transfer the spaetzle to a sauté pan set over medium heat and steam off any excess moisture. (This may need to be done in 2 or 3 batches to avoid crowding the pan.) Add the butter, season with salt if necessary, and sauté until the butter has melted and the spaetzle are warm. Serve with the veal and braising liquid.

SERVES 4

SPICY VEAL MEATBALLS
WITH RED BELL PEPPER SAUCE AND PENNE PASTA

These meatballs are a delicious medium for some complex flavors, without losing their own meaty personality. For non-spicy palates, simply omit the pepper flakes—the meatballs will still taste wonderful. You may be surprised to find both fresh and dried bread crumbs in this recipe. The fresh are used inside the meatballs for texture, and the dried give the exterior a golden coating. Spaghetti can be used instead of the penne, but we prefer serving a substantial pasta with meatballs: you'll find penne is a little easier to put on the fork with the meat.

To prepare the sauce, heat the olive oil in a saucepan and sauté the onion and garlic over medium-high heat for 2 minutes. Add the bell peppers, tomatoes, oregano, and honey, and stir to combine. Cover the pan, reduce the heat to low, and simmer for 15 minutes, stirring occasionally. Transfer to a blender and purée. Return to a clean saucepan and season with lemon zest, salt, and pepper. Reheat just before serving.

To prepare the meatballs, heat half of the olive oil in a saucepan, and sauté the onion and garlic over medium heat for 5 or 6 minutes, or until softened and golden. Transfer to a mixing bowl and let cool. Add the veal, sun-dried tomatoes, Worcestershire sauce, red pepper flakes, sage, lemon zest, 1/2 cup of the cheese, the egg, and fresh bread crumbs. Season with salt and pepper and mix thoroughly. Set aside in the refrigerator for 30 minutes.

Place the dried bread crumbs on a plate. Form the veal mixture into 20 round meatballs and roll in the bread crumbs. Heat the remaining 1 1/2 tablespoons of oil in a large saucepan and add the meatballs. (Cook in batches if necessary to avoid crowding the pan.) Sauté over medium-high heat for 4 or 5 minutes, or until browned on all sides. Remove the meatballs with a slotted spoon and set aside. Add the wine and stock, and stir to deglaze the pan. Bring to a simmer and carefully return the meatballs to the pan. Reduce the heat, cover, and cook at a simmer for about 15 minutes, or until the meatballs are no longer pink in the center.

Bring a large saucepan of water to a boil, and cook the penne al dente, according to the directions on the package. Drain and transfer the pasta to warm serving plates. Pour the bell pepper sauce over the pasta and top with 5 meatballs per plate. Sprinkle the remaining 1/4 cup of cheese over the meatballs, and garnish with the oregano.

SERVES 4

FOR THE RED BELL PEPPER SAUCE:
2 tablespoons olive oil
1 onion, diced
1 clove garlic, chopped
3 red bell peppers, roasted, peeled, seeded, and diced (page 228)
3 plum tomatoes, blanched, peeled, seeded, and diced (page 228)
1 teaspoon minced fresh oregano leaves
1 teaspoon honey
1/4 teaspoon minced lemon zest
Salt and freshly ground black pepper to taste

FOR THE MEATBALLS:
3 tablespoons olive oil
3/4 cup finely diced onion
2 cloves garlic, minced
1 1/2 pounds high-quality lean ground veal
2 tablespoons minced sun-dried tomatoes (packed in oil)
1 tablespoon Worcestershire sauce
1/2 tablespoon dried red pepper flakes
1 teaspoon minced fresh sage leaves
1/4 teaspoon finely minced lemon zest
3/4 cup freshly grated Parmesan or Romano cheese
1 egg, beaten
1/2 cup fresh bread crumbs
Salt and freshly ground black pepper to taste
1/2 cup dried bread crumbs
1 cup dry white wine, preferably Sauvignon Blanc or Fume Blanc
1 cup Chicken Stock (page 225) or water

FOR THE PASTA:
1 pound penne pasta
8 sprigs fresh oregano, for garnish

VEAL

OSSO BUCO
WITH A WILD MUSHROOM RISOTTO AND GREMOLATA

Osso Buco means "hollow bones" in Italian, but veal shank (also sold as shin of veal) contains flavorful marrow, which is highly nutritious. In Italy, the marrow is removed with a special thin fork or the tip of a knife, and spread generously on bread. This cut of veal is often labeled "osso buco" in the meat section. If purchasing from a butcher, we recommend that you ask for hind shanks, which have more meat and marrow than the fore shanks, and get him to cut the slices for you. Gremolata is a traditional accompaniment to osso buco.

Prepare the gremolata according to the recipe on page 25.

To prepare the veal, place the flour on a large plate and season the veal with salt and pepper. Dredge the veal in the flour, shaking off any excess. Heat the oil and butter in a large, heavy, ovenproof casserole. When hot, brown the veal over medium-high heat, about 10 minutes. Remove and set aside. Add the garlic, onion, carrots, and celery to the casserole and sauté for 5 or 6 minutes. Add the wine and stir to deglaze the pan. Reduce the liquid by half; this will take 7 or 8 minutes. Add the tomatoes, stock, marjoram, and bay leaves. Bring to a simmer and return the veal to the casserole. Cover and continue to simmer for about 1 hour, or until the meat is tender. Remove the veal with a slotted spoon and keep warm. Strain the sauce into a clean pan and add the lemon zest and parsley. Season with salt and pepper and simmer for 5 minutes.

While the veal is cooking, prepare the risotto. Place the mushrooms in a bowl, add the hot water, and let soak for 20 minutes. Drain and chop the mushrooms, reserving the liquid. Transfer the liquid to a saucepan, bring to a boil, and reduce to 1 cup, about 10 minutes. Add the stock and return to a boil. Reduce the heat to a low simmer. Heat the oil in a heavy saucepan and sauté the onion over medium-high heat for 3 or 4 minutes, until translucent. Add the rice and stir until coated. Add the wine and $1/2$ cup of the stock-mushroom liquid mixture; stir until just absorbed. Add another cup of the liquid mixture, and stir again until it is absorbed by the rice. Continue adding the liquid, $1/2$ cup at a time, until each increment is absorbed. When adding the last $1/2$ cup, add the mushrooms and thyme, and continue stirring until the liquid is absorbed. The rice should be creamy but al dente. Season with salt and pepper and stir in the butter.

Place the veal on warm serving plates and garnish with the gremolata and thyme sprigs. Serve with the risotto and pour some of the sauce next to the veal; serve the rest at the table.

SERVES 4

Gremolata (page 25)

FOR THE OSSO BUCO:

1 cup all-purpose flour

4 slices bone-in veal shanks (about 12 ounces each and 2 inches thick), Prime or Choice grade

Salt and freshly ground black pepper to taste

3 tablespoons olive oil

3 tablespoons butter

2 cloves garlic, crushed

1 onion, diced

2 carrots, finely sliced

1 stalk celery, finely sliced

1 cup dry white wine

1 pound tomatoes, blanched, peeled, and chopped (page 228) or 2 cups canned chopped tomatoes with juice

1 cup Chicken Stock (page 225)

$1/2$ tablespoon chopped fresh marjoram leaves

2 bay leaves

$1/2$ tablespoon grated lemon zest

2 tablespoons minced fresh flat-leaf parsley

FOR THE RISOTTO:

$1/2$ cup dried shiitake mushrooms (about $1/2$ ounce)

2 cups hot water

3 cups Chicken Stock (page 225)

2 tablespoons olive oil

1 onion, finely diced

$1 1/2$ cups Arborio rice

$1/2$ cup dry white wine

2 teaspoons minced fresh thyme leaves

Salt and freshly ground black pepper to taste

2 tablespoons butter ($1/4$ stick)

4 sprigs fresh thyme, for garnish

VEAL

VEAL, PECAN, AND
BOURBON MEAT LOAF
WITH WATERCRESS SALAD AND BOURBON SAUCE

Maybe meat loaf needs some spin doctors to help brush up on its image! Say "terrine" to a connoisseur and you'll gain their attention and interest; say "meat loaf," and they will probably roll their eyes. Although their format is similar, terrines are considered sophisticated, while the humble meat loaf is treated as the plain and dowdy cousin. We think this is unfair because meat loaf can carry some wonderfully elaborate and interesting flavors, as here. You will particularly enjoy the combination of bourbon, pecans, and orange, which go well together, and while the sauce is a little sweet, it provides the perfect counterpoint to the peppery salad.

FOR THE MEAT LOAF:

2 tablespoons olive oil

1 onion, diced

2 cloves garlic, minced

1 cup fresh bread crumbs

1/4 cup milk

1 1/2 pounds high-quality lean ground veal

8 ounces ground pork butt

1 red bell pepper, roasted, peeled, seeded, and minced (page 228)

3/4 cup coarsely ground pecans

1/4 cup bourbon

1 egg, beaten

2 teaspoons minced orange zest

1/2 teaspoon minced lemon zest

1 teaspoon minced fresh chives

1 teaspoon salt

1 teaspoon freshly ground black pepper

4 or 5 strips of bacon

FOR THE BOURBON SAUCE:

3 cups Beef Stock (page 225)

2 tablespoons butter (1/4 stick)

2 tablespoons minced shallots

1 tablespoon freshly squeezed lemon juice

1/4 cup bourbon

FOR THE WATERCRESS SALAD:

1/4 cup peanut oil

3 tablespoons red wine vinegar

1/2 tablespoon Dijon mustard

1/2 teaspoon salt

1/2 teaspoon freshly ground black pepper

6 cups washed and stemmed fresh watercress

Preheat the oven to 350°F. To prepare the meat loaf, heat the olive oil in a sauté pan and add the onion and garlic. Sauté over medium-high heat for 4 or 5 minutes, until softened. Transfer to a large mixing bowl. In another bowl, combine the bread crumbs and milk and let soak for a few minutes. Gently squeeze out the liquid from the bread crumbs, and add the bread crumbs to the mixing bowl. Add the veal, pork, bell pepper, pecans, bourbon, egg, citrus zests, chives, salt, and pepper. Mix thoroughly but gently, and do not over-mix or the meat will toughen. Transfer to a small loaf pan or a low-sided baking dish, smoothing out into a loaf shape. Cover the top of the meat loaf with the bacon strips and transfer to the oven. Bake for about 1 hour, or until the meat loaf is no longer pink inside and the internal temperature reaches 160°F.

To prepare the sauce, bring the stock to a boil in a saucepan. Reduce over medium heat until 1 cup remains, about 15 minutes. Meanwhile, melt the butter in another saucepan and add the shallots. Sauté over medium heat for 3 minutes, making sure the butter does not brown. Add the reduced stock and the lemon juice. Bring to a boil and add the bourbon. Return to a low boil and cook for 5 minutes; keep warm.

To prepare the salad, whisk together the oil, vinegar, mustard, salt, and pepper in a mixing bowl. Place the watercress in a salad bowl, add the dressing, and toss together to coat thoroughly.

Stir the sauce and spoon some of it onto warm serving plates. Slice the meat loaf and arrange over the sauce. Serve with the salad.

SERVES 4

CHEESE AND HAM–
STUFFED VEAL CHOPS
WITH FENNEL-TOMATO CHARLOTTE

This veal recipe is an adaptation of the classic Veal Steak Cordon Bleu, in which thin scaloppines sandwich slices of ham and cheese. The stack is then breaded and sautéed. Here, we stuff thick chops with the same combination of ingredients. The cheese melting deliciously around the ham slices makes these chops extraordinarily appetizing. Traditionally, charlottes are desserts baked in dishes or molds with layers of fruit and buttered bread or sponge cake. This savory version combines the classic flavors of tomatoes, basil, and the anise-like, aromatic fennel to make an immensely satisfying combination.

Preheat the oven to 350°F. To prepare the charlotte, heat the oil in a saucepan and add the onion. Sauté over medium-high heat for 2 minutes and then add the garlic. Sauté for 2 minutes longer and add the fennel. Cook for 2 minutes and then add the wine. Cover and cook for 5 minutes. Remove from the heat. Place half of the tomatoes in a layer on the bottom of a buttered 8 x 6-inch baking dish. Cover with half of the fennel mixture, and sprinkle with 1 tablespoon of the basil. Season with salt and pepper, cover with 1 cup of the bread crumbs, and dot with half of the butter. Add the rest of the tomatoes in an even layer, then the remaining fennel mixture, and the rest of the basil. Season with salt and pepper, cover with the remaining bread crumbs, and dot with the rest of the butter. Bake in the oven for 40 to 45 minutes, or until the breadcrumb topping is golden and crisp.

Prepare the grill. (Alternatively, broil the veal when the charlotte is almost done.)

To prepare the veal, make a horizontal incision with a sharp knife on one side of each veal chop, forming a deep pocket. Line each pocket with 2 slices of cheese, pressing them in as necessary. Mix together the ham and basil, and press into each pocket. Secure with toothpicks. Season the chops with salt and pepper, and brush with the oil on both sides. Place over a medium-hot grill (or under the broiler) for about 6 minutes on each side.

Transfer the stuffed veal chops to warm serving plates and serve with the charlotte.

SERVES 4

FOR THE FENNEL-TOMATO CHARLOTTE:

2 tablespoons olive oil

1 onion, finely sliced

2 cloves garlic, minced

2 fennel bulbs, trimmed, cored, cut lengthwise, and sliced (about 2$\frac{1}{2}$ cups)

$\frac{1}{2}$ cup dry white wine

2 pounds plum tomatoes, blanched, peeled, and diced (page 228)

2 tablespoons chopped fresh basil

Salt and freshly ground black pepper to taste

2 cups coarse fresh bread crumbs

2 tablespoons ($\frac{1}{4}$ stick) chilled butter, thinly sliced

FOR THE VEAL:

4 veal rib chops (about 8 ounces each and 1$\frac{1}{4}$ inches thick), Prime or Choice grade

4 ounces Swiss or Fontina cheese, cut into 8 slices

4 thin slices Parma ham or pancetta (about 2 ounces), chopped

2 tablespoons julienned fresh basil leaves

Salt and freshly ground black pepper

2 tablespoons olive oil

VEAL

VEAL MEDALLIONS
WITH ZUCCHINI PANCAKES AND TOMATO-MUSHROOM SAUCE

Veal medallions, cut from the filet or tenderloin, look almost like toy versions of their beef counterparts, weighing in at about half the size. Like beef medallions, they are rich and dense, and make an elegant meal. Veal medallions have little or no fat, so it's important to keep a close eye on them as they sauté, since they can overcook and toughen very quickly. Keep the zucchini unpeeled; the bright green color makes an attractive presentation. The zucchini pancakes are best served immediately; they may be held in the oven for a short time but will lose some of their crispness.

FOR THE TOMATO-MUSHROOM SAUCE:

2 tablespoons butter (¼ stick)

¼ cup minced shallots

4 ounces mushrooms, sliced

⅔ cup dry white wine

⅔ cup Veal Stock (page 225)

3 plum tomatoes, blanched, peeled, seeded, and diced (page 228)

½ tablespoon minced fresh flat-leaf parsley

1 tablespoon diced butter (optional)

1 teaspoon minced fresh tarragon leaves, for garnish (optional)

FOR THE ZUCCHINI PANCAKES:

1½ pounds zucchini, grated

2 tablespoons kosher salt

¼ cup minced onion

⅔ cup all-purpose flour

1 egg, beaten

1 teaspoon minced fresh oregano leaves

Pinch of cayenne (optional)

4 tablespoons butter (½ stick)

FOR THE VEAL:

12 veal tenderloin medallions (about 2 ounces each and 1 inch thick), Prime or Choice grade

Salt and freshly ground black pepper to taste

2 tablespoons olive oil

To prepare the sauce, heat the butter in a saucepan and add the shallots. Sauté over medium-high heat for 4 or 5 minutes, until lightly golden. Add the mushrooms, stir well, and sauté for 3 minutes longer. Add the wine, bring to a simmer, and cook until the liquid is almost evaporated, 5 to 7 minutes. Add the stock, bring to a boil, reduce the heat to medium-low, and simmer for 5 minutes. Remove from the heat and set aside. Just before serving, warm through and add the tomatoes, parsley, and butter, if desired. Garnish with the tarragon.

To prepare the pancakes, sprinkle the zucchini with the kosher salt. Spread out in a colander and let sit on a large plate or in the sink for about 15 minutes. (Some liquid will be released.) Rinse under cold water, drain, and gently squeeze out any excess liquid. Transfer to a mixing bowl, add the onion and flour, and combine. Stir in the egg, oregano, and cayenne. Shortly before serving and while the veal is cooking, heat 2 tablespoons of the butter in a sauté pan. Using about ¼ cup of the mixture for each pancake (this should make at least 8 pancakes), pour into the pan and form into flat rounds. Cook the pancakes in batches over medium heat for 2 to 3 minutes per side, until cooked through and lightly golden, adding the remaining butter as needed.

To prepare the veal, season the medallions with salt and pepper. Heat the oil in a large sauté pan and when hot, add the veal. Sauté over medium-high heat for 3 to 4 minutes per side for medium, or to the desired doneness. Transfer to warm serving plates and pour the sauce over and around the medallions. Arrange 2 pancakes on each plate.

SERVES 4

Pigs were first domesticated from a species of wild boar at least 8,000 years ago in Asia and have remained a very important source of meat ever since—probably the most popular in the world today. In many countries, from China and Mexico to Indonesia and the southern United States, pork is king. Pigs are able to thrive on grass and leaves, stalks, husks, acorns, root vegetables—just about anything that comes their way. This versatility has ensured their popularity over time with livestock farmers. Some cultures, such as Jewish and Muslim, regard the pig as taboo (in part because the animal is seen as so indiscriminating); colonists from Europe, on the other hand, had no qualms about introducing pigs across the globe.

In the United States, wild boar predated Western contact, probably the result of land migrations across the Bering Strait. It is believed that most of the domesticated pigs in the United States are descended from a small herd brought to Florida from Spain in the 16th century, as well as from a handful of animals brought from England to Virginia in the 17th century. These pigs bred so prolifically (as pigs do) that within a couple of decades, Virginia was supplying a large amount of pork and ham back to England. Pork, and especially preserved salt pork, was the principal meat consumed in the early days of the nation. Until the middle of the 20th century, pigs were also prized for providing the principal cooking fat: lard. As Waverley Root writes in his definitive book, *Food*, "America was built by pioneers and pigs."

These days, pork is bred lean—most cuts are low in fat and cholesterol, comparing favorably with chicken. In fact, pork has about one-third less fat than it did 20 years ago. The calories and fat of lean pork tenderloin, for example, come close to matching skinless chicken breast meat. While the marketing slogan—"the other white meat"—is catchy, and no doubt successful in attracting consumers, let there be no mistake that pork is indeed a red meat. Older pork meat is darker than younger, but with the exception of bacon, much of the pork sold now is from animals less than a year old.

When buying chops or cutlets, look for firm, pale pink meat (not white) without marbling, blotches, or any yellow color, that feels firm to the touch. Like poultry, pork should be cooked through, until the finished internal temperature reaches around 155°F. to 160°F., or medium. At this point, the savory juices will run clear and there will be no pink meat near the bone. However, because of its leanness, overcooked pork will be dry and tough. The trichinosis parasite, which is now believed to have been virtually eradicated in pigs raised commercially in the United States, is killed when the internal temperature reaches around 140°F., well below the recommended 160°F. required for doneness.

Many of the recipes that follow match pork with fruit, as the meat is a natural partner with sweet and tart flavors. Pork is a superb meat for carrying other flavors, too. Brines, marinades, and herbed or spicy rubs also show off pork to its best advantage.

BATON ROUGE
PORK JAMBALAYA

The saying goes that there are as many recipes for jambalaya as there are Cajuns. And considering how good it tastes, it's no wonder why so many Louisianans love it. All versions include rice, but otherwise, it's usually a case of adding whatever meat or seafood is available. This means, for example, that if you feel so inclined, you can add 1 pound of peeled shrimp or diced cooked chicken about 15 minutes before the end. Traditionally, bacon fat is the cooking medium of choice for jambalaya, but you can substitute olive oil or vegetable oil. It is believed that the word "jambalaya" is derived from the French "jambon" ("ham") and "à la" ("in the style of"), and the African word for rice, "yaya," reflecting the mixed antecedents of the Louisiana bayou country.

6 slices bacon

12 ounces pork, such as shoulder or Boston butt, coarsely diced

6 ounces spicy Italian pork sausage, sliced

6 ounces andouille or other smoked sausage, sliced

1 cup diced onion

1 cup sliced celery

1 cup diced green bell pepper

1 tablespoon minced garlic

3 large plum tomatoes, chopped (about 1 1/2 cups)

2 bay leaves

1 1/2 tablespoons chopped fresh oregano leaves

1 tablespoon chopped fresh thyme leaves

1 1/2 cups long-grain white rice

4 cups Chicken Stock (page 225)

2 teaspoons salt

2 teaspoons cayenne, or to taste

1/2 cup sliced scallions (white and green parts)

2 tablespoons chopped fresh curly parsley, for garnish

In a large sauté pan or skillet, cook the bacon in 2 batches over medium heat for 6 or 7 minutes, or until all the fat is rendered. Reserve the cooked bacon for another use. Transfer the bacon fat to a large saucepan, and add the pork and Italian sausage. Sauté over medium heat for 15 to 20 minutes, stirring often, or until browned on all sides and cooked through. Add the andouille and sauté for 5 minutes longer. Add the onion, celery, bell pepper, and garlic, and sauté for 5 minutes. Add the tomatoes, bay leaves, oregano, thyme, and rice, and stir for 2 minutes. Add the stock, salt, and cayenne, and bring to a boil. Reduce the heat to low, cover, and simmer until the rice is tender, 20 to 25 minutes. Stir in the scallions, remove from the heat, and let sit for 5 minutes. Discard the bay leaves before serving and garnish with the parsley.

SERVES 4 TO 6

SCOTCH EGG
HORS D'OEUVRES WITH DUNCAN'S SWEET ONION JAM

Scotch eggs are made by encasing hard-boiled eggs in seasoned ground pork, rolling in bread crumbs, and deep-frying. They are snacks that have long been popular in British pubs, and sure enough, a glass of ale supplies the perfect liquid accompaniment. Alas, this onion jam is unlikely to be found in such mundane surroundings! These appetizers also make an excellent item for parties or buffets—and the recipe can be increased proportionately for large crowds. Add a mixed green salad, double the egg recipe, and you have a lunch dish. You can substitute the fresh herbs in the pork mixture with 1/2 tablespoon of mixed dried herbs. The jam can be prepared in advance; it will keep refrigerated for at least two or three days.

To prepare the onion jam, heat the butter and oil in a saucepan and add the onions. Sauté over medium heat for about 15 to 20 minutes, until golden brown. Add the stock, sugar, sherry, and rice vinegar; cook for 10 minutes. Add the salt, pepper, ginger, and allspice, and reduce the heat to low. Simmer for about 5 minutes longer, or until the mixture is thick and syrupy. Let cool.

To prepare the Scotch eggs, bring a large saucepan of salted water to a boil. Place an egg in a large spoon and gently lower onto the bottom of the pan. Repeat for the remaining eggs and reduce the heat to low or medium-low. Simmer for 10 minutes, or until hard-cooked. Remove with a slotted spoon and transfer to a bowl of ice water. When cool enough to handle, peel the eggs. Place the pork, shallot, parsley, chives, marjoram, thyme, salt, pepper, and orange zest in a mixing bowl. Combine thoroughly. Divide the mixture into 8 portions and flatten each portion to a 1/4- to 3/8-inch thickness on a lightly floured work surface. Place an egg in the center of each rolled out portion of pork and shape the pork around each egg to enclose. Smooth with your fingers so that the pork exterior is seamless.

Place the beaten egg in a saucer or bowl. Spread the bread crumbs on a plate. Pour enough oil to cover the eggs in a deep-fryer or large saucepan and heat to 350°F. Dip the pork balls into the beaten egg, and then dredge in the bread crumbs, pressing them in to make sure the outsides are completely covered. Using tongs or a large spoon, transfer 3 of the eggs (1 at a time) to the deep-fryer. Fry for 4 or 5 minutes, or until deep golden brown, turning once. Remove and drain on paper towels; repeat for the remaining eggs. Spoon some of the jam in the center of each serving plate. Cut the Scotch eggs into halves or quarters, and arrange around the jam.

SERVES 4

FOR THE ONION JAM:
2 tablespoons butter (1/4 stick)
2 tablespoons olive oil
2 sweet onions (about 1 1/2 pounds), thinly sliced
1/4 cup Chicken Stock (page 225)
2 tablespoons dark brown sugar
2 tablespoons dry sherry
2 tablespoons rice vinegar
1/2 teaspoon salt
1/2 teaspoon freshly ground black pepper
1/2 teaspoon ground dried ginger
1/2 teaspoon ground allspice

FOR THE SCOTCH EGGS:
8 eggs
1 1/2 pounds high-quality ground pork
1 shallot, minced
2 teaspoons minced fresh curly parsley
1/2 tablespoon finely sliced fresh chives
3/4 teaspoon minced fresh marjoram
3/4 teaspoon minced fresh thyme
Salt and freshly ground black pepper to taste
3/4 teaspoon minced orange zest
1 egg, beaten
1 cup fine plain bread crumbs
Safflower or vegetable oil, for deep-frying

PORK

Regional variations of barbecue sauce abound. Folks in North Carolina, for example, generally prefer it tangier and hotter than do Texans. In addition, pork is favored in Carolina, while Texans consume more beef (see the typical barbecue recipe in Chapter 1). Both grits and lima beans are common in the South, making them the ideal accompaniments to these barbecued ribs. Prepare the large, buttery beans, as well as the sauce and ribs, a day in advance for maximum flavor and easier assembly.

FOR THE BAKED LIMA BEANS:

1 pound dried small lima beans, soaked overnight and drained

2 tablespoons olive oil

1 onion, chopped

8 ounces salt pork or bacon, roughly chopped

1/3 cup ketchup

1/3 cup dark molasses

2 tablespoons apple cider vinegar

1 tablespoon pure red chile powder

1 teaspoon dry mustard powder

Salt and freshly ground black pepper to taste

FOR THE NORTH CAROLINA–STYLE BARBECUE SAUCE:

1 1/2 cups cider vinegar

2 onions, minced, plus 1 onion, chopped

2 cloves garlic, minced

1/2 cup ketchup

6 tablespoons light brown sugar

1/4 cup dark molasses

1/4 cup Worcestershire sauce

1 tablespoon freshly ground black pepper

2 teaspoons dry mustard powder

2 teaspoons Tabasco sauce

2 teaspoons dried red pepper flakes

Zest of 1/2 orange

2 tablespoons butter (1/4 stick), diced

Put the beans in a large saucepan and add enough water to cover by 2 inches. Bring to a boil, reduce the heat to a simmer, and cook the beans for 25 to 30 minutes, or until almost tender. Drain the beans, reserving 2 cups of the cooking liquid.

Preheat the oven to 350°F. Heat the oil in a sauté pan and cook the onion over medium-low heat for 3 minutes. Add the salt pork and sauté for 3 more minutes, or until the onion is softened. Transfer to a large, heavy, ovenproof casserole. Add the beans and reserved cooking liquid, 1 cup of water, the ketchup, molasses, vinegar, chile powder, dry mustard, salt, and pepper. Cover and bake for 2 to 2 1/2 hours, until the beans are tender and the broth is thick.

To prepare the barbecue sauce, combine 2 cups of water with the vinegar, minced onion, garlic, ketchup, sugar, molasses, Worcestershire sauce, black pepper, dry mustard, Tabasco, red pepper flakes, and orange zest in a saucepan. Bring to a boil, reduce the heat to low, and simmer gently for about 30 minutes. Let cool slightly and whisk in the butter, a piece at a time, until incorporated.

(CONTINUED ON PAGE 90)

FOR THE RIBS:

3 racks baby back ribs (about 1 1/2 pounds each), trimmed of fat and membrane

1 small onion, sliced

1 bay leaf, crumbled

Salt and freshly ground black pepper

FOR THE SOUFFLÉED CHEDDAR GRITS:

1/2 teaspoon salt

1/2 cup stone-ground grits

2 tablespoons butter (1/4 stick)

1/2 cup grated sharp Cheddar cheese (about 3 ounces)

2 eggs, separated, plus 2 egg whites

Salt and freshly ground black pepper to taste

Place the ribs in a large roasting pan and add enough water to come about 1/4 inch up the sides. Add the onion and bay leaf to the water, season with salt and pepper, and tightly cover the pan with foil. Place the pan in the oven and braise for about 1 hour, or until the ribs are tender, but not falling off the bone. Remove the ribs from the pan, drain on paper towels, and cut into smaller 3- or 4-rib mini-slabs. Discard the cooking liquid.

While the ribs are braising, about 1 hour before serving, begin the soufflé. Preheat the oven to 375°F. Bring 2 1/2 cups of water and the salt to a boil in a large saucepan. Pour in the grits, reduce the heat to a simmer, and cook for about 20 minutes, or until thickened, stirring frequently. Stir in the butter and cheese, remove from the heat, and stir in the egg yolks. Season with salt and pepper, set aside, and keep warm. Butter a 1-quart soufflé dish or deep ovenproof casserole. Beat the egg whites just to stiff peaks; do not let them get too dry. Fold the whites into the grits and pour the mixture into the soufflé dish. Bake in the oven for 35 to 40 minutes, until the soufflé has risen and the top is golden brown. Serve immediately.

While the soufflé is baking, prepare the grill. Brush the ribs with the barbecue sauce and grill over medium-high heat for about 7 minutes on each side, or until crisp and dark, basting frequently with the barbecue sauce. Serve the remaining barbecue sauce at the table. Serve the ribs with the barbecue sauce, beans, and soufflé on the side.

SERVES 4

ROAST PORK LOIN
WITH ROASTED CORN SUCCOTASH AND CLASSIC APPLE SAUCE

This simple recipe can be prepared in the time it takes to roast the pork. The leftovers make excellent sandwiches. Traditionally, succotash is made with boiled fresh corn, but we prefer the nuttiness of the roasted corn, especially with the sweetness of the apple sauce. The amount of sugar and cinnamon will depend on the sweetness of the apples (and your preferences). For a tarter apple sauce, add a little freshly squeezed lemon juice.

Preheat the oven to 450°F. Rub the loin all over with the cut garlic cloves and season with salt and pepper. Place in a roasting pan, fat-side down, and roast in the oven for about 15 minutes. Reduce the heat to 350°F., and continue to roast for about 1 hour for medium, or until the internal temperature reaches about 150°F. About 30 minutes before the roast is ready, place the whole garlic head in the roasting pan. When the roast is ready, remove from the oven, cover with foil, and let rest for about 10 minutes before slicing. (The internal temperature will rise to about 160°F.) Reserve the whole roasted head of garlic. Pour the juices released from the roast into a small saucepan. With a spoon, skim off any fat from the surface and discard. Keep the remaining juices warm.

While the pork loin is cooking at 350°F., roast the corn. Lightly dampen the ears of corn and place them on a rack in the middle of the oven. Roast for 15 to 20 minutes, or until they begin to turn light golden; do not let them dry out. (While the corn is roasting, begin preparing the apple sauce.) Remove the corn from the oven, and when cool enough to handle, cut the corn from the cob. Melt the butter in large sauté pan, and add the stock, corn, and lima beans. Simmer for about 5 minutes, until thick and creamy. Stir in the parsley and season with salt and white pepper.

To prepare the apple sauce, place the apples and cider in a large saucepan. Bring to a simmer, cover, and cook for about 20 minutes, until the apples are just tender. Drain, reserving the liquid. Press the warm apple pulp through a ricer or colander, and discard the skins. Return the pulp to the saucepan; stir in the sugar and cinnamon, and cook over low heat until the sugar is dissolved. Meanwhile, reduce the cooking liquid by two-thirds over high heat, and then add it to the sauce. Serve warm or at room temperature.

Place the roast loin on a warm serving platter and spoon with the pan juices. Separate the roasted garlic head into cloves and sprinkle them around the roast—guests can squeeze out the pulp to eat with the roast. Serve the succotash and apple sauce on the side.

SERVES 4

FOR THE ROAST PORK:
3 pounds boneless pork loin

3 cloves garlic, cut in half, plus 1 whole head garlic

Salt and freshly ground black pepper to taste

FOR THE ROASTED CORN SUCCOTASH:
4 ears fresh corn, husked

3 tablespoons butter

¼ cup vegetable stock or water

1 cup fresh (or frozen) lima beans, cooked (page 88)

1 tablespoon chopped fresh flat-leaf parsley

Salt and freshly ground white pepper to taste

FOR THE APPLE SAUCE:
3 pounds unpeeled apples, quartered and cored

1 cup apple cider or apple juice

2 tablespoons sugar (optional)

¼ to ½ teaspoon ground cinnamon (optional)

PORK

FRUITED PORK:
BRAISED SHOULDER WITH APRICOTS AND PRUNES, AND NUTTY BULGHUR PILAF

Here we present another simple dish that demonstrates how well pork and fruit go together. Use fresh pitted apricots if they are in season (and flavorful). You can also add 2 peeled, pitted, and quartered fresh peaches during the last 40 minutes of cooking. However, bear in mind that dried apricots and prunes will hold up better than fresh fruit. Bulghur wheat, a Middle Eastern staple, has a nutty flavor and texture that is enhanced by the addition of walnuts in this recipe. Bulghur, also sold as burghul in some Middle Eastern markets, is the main ingredient in tabbouleh salad. It is parboiled wheat with the bran removed, then dried and coarsely ground.

FOR THE PORK, PRUNES, AND APRICOTS:

4 pounds bone-in pork shoulder

Salt and freshly ground black pepper to taste

2 tablespoons olive oil

1 cup freshly squeezed orange juice

2 tablespoons freshly squeezed lemon juice

2 teaspoons light brown sugar

2 teaspoons balsamic vinegar

2 teaspoons peeled and minced fresh ginger

1/2 teaspoon ground cardamom

1/2 teaspoon cayenne

1/8 teaspoon ground nutmeg

12 dried apricots

12 pitted prunes

FOR THE BULGHUR PILAF:

1 cup bulghur

2 tablespoons butter (1/4 stick)

1/2 onion, finely diced

1 clove garlic, minced

2 cups chicken stock

Salt and freshly ground black pepper to taste

3 tablespoons minced fresh chives

1/4 cup chopped walnuts, toasted (page 229)

Preheat the oven to 350°F. Season the pork shoulder with salt and pepper. Heat the oil in a large flameproof casserole or Dutch oven on medium-high. Add the pork shoulder, and sear on all sides until browned, about 10 minutes. Remove and set aside. Reduce the heat to medium, and add the orange juice, lemon juice, sugar, vinegar, ginger, cardamom, cayenne, and nutmeg. Stir to deglaze the pan, and cook for 2 minutes, or until the brown sugar dissolves. Return the pork shoulder to the pan, cover, and slowly simmer for 2 hours. Turn the meat occasionally. Arrange the apricots and prunes around the shoulder and continue to simmer, covered, for an additional 30 minutes, or until the pork is fork tender.

Transfer the pork shoulder to a large serving platter, cover, and keep warm. Scoop any fat from the pan with a spoon and season the sauce with salt and pepper. Ladle the sauce over and around the shoulder. If the sauce is not as thick as you would like, return the casserole to the stovetop and reduce the broth over medium heat until it thickens.

About 30 minutes before serving, prepare the pilaf. Place the bulghur in a fine-mesh sieve, rinse under cold running water, and drain. Heat the butter in a saucepan, and sauté the onion and garlic over medium heat for about 4 minutes. Add the bulghur and cook for 3 or 4 minutes, until the grains are coated, stirring constantly. Add the stock and season with salt and pepper. Cover the pan and simmer for 20 to 25 minutes, or until the bulghur has absorbed all the liquid. Let sit for 5 minutes. Using a fork, fluff the bulghur and stir in the chives and walnuts. Adjust the seasonings just before serving.

SERVES 4

YUCATÁN PORK
AND BLACK BEAN TORTILLA WRAPS WITH
CILANTRO MAYONNAISE AND APPLE-ANCHO RELISH

Pork, black beans, and ancho chiles are all flavors you'd expect to find together in Mexico's subtropical Yucatán region. Across the Gulf of Mexico in nearby Cuba, similar ingredients are sandwiched between crusty bread or rolls to make a classic, filling meal. In this recipe, we have arranged these components inside flour tortillas, embellished with a flavored mayonnaise, cheese, and an apple relish. You will not need all of the mayonnaise, but it's well worth making for other uses. Store in an airtight container in the refrigerator; it will keep for at least a week or two. For a shortcut, add the cilantro to 2 cups of store-bought mayo, but don't expect the flavor to be quite the same!

To prepare the relish, place the ancho chiles in a bowl and cover with hot water. Let rehydrate for 20 minutes, or until the chiles soften. Meanwhile, place the cider in a saucepan and bring to a boil. Add the apples, reduce the heat to low, and simmer for 5 or 6 minutes, until just tender. Transfer to a mixing bowl. Heat the oil in a sauté pan, add the onion, and sauté over medium-high heat for 5 minutes. Add the sautéed onions, the lemon juice, and vinegar to the mixing bowl. Julienne the ancho chiles and add to the bowl. Add the orange and oregano, and gently combine. Season with salt and pepper and keep refrigerated.

To prepare the mayonnaise, place the egg yolks, lemon juice, cilantro, garlic, salt, and pepper in a food processor or blender and purée until smooth. With the machine running, pour in the oil in a slow and steady stream until thick and completely incorporated. Thin with a little water if necessary; keep refrigerated.

Warm the tortillas in a large dry skillet or sauté pan. Spread each tortilla with 1 tablespoon of the cilantro mayonnaise, leaving a 1-inch border around the edge of each tortilla. Spread 2 tablespoons of the beans over the mayonnaise on each tortilla. Top with a slice of pork loin, cover with a slice of ham, a slice of cheese, and another slice of pork. Roll up the wraps like burritos, folding in the ends, and cut in half on the bias. On each serving plate, arrange one half of the wrap lying down, with the other half leaning against it. Fill a 3- or 4-inch mold or cookie cutter with the relish, and gently release the mold next to the wraps to form a nice presentation. Garnish the relish with the cilantro.

SERVES 4

FOR THE RELISH:
2 dried ancho chiles, stemmed and seeded
1/2 cup apple cider
2 green apples, peeled, cored, and diced
1 tablespoon olive oil
1/4 cup diced onion
1/2 tablespoon freshly squeezed lemon juice
1 teaspoon balsamic vinegar
1 cup diced orange segments, seeded
1 teaspoon minced fresh oregano leaves
Salt and freshly ground black pepper to taste

FOR THE CILANTRO MAYONNAISE:
2 egg yolks
1 1/2 tablespoons fresh lemon juice
1/4 cup chopped fresh cilantro leaves
2 cloves roasted garlic, chopped (page 229)
1/2 teaspoon salt
Freshly ground black pepper to taste
1 cup olive oil

FOR THE TORTILLA WRAPS:
4 large flour tortillas
1/2 cup mashed cooked black beans (page 226) or canned
1 pound roasted pork loin, cut into 8 slices (page 91)
4 slices baked ham, preferably Virginia ham
4 slices Swiss cheese
4 sprigs fresh cilantro, for garnish

MARDI GRAS SPECIAL:
BRAZILIAN FEIJOADA
WITH PORK AND BLACK BEANS SERVED WITH COLLARD GREENS

This traditional Brazilian national dish originated in the ignominious days of the slave trade. Feijoada is a stew containing black beans cooked with smoked, cured, and fresh meats, and no celebration in the country is complete without it. There are many regional variations, but a typical feijoada has at least 5 different cuts of pork, including blood sausage, as well as pig's snout, ears, and tail. This recipe has been adapted for American tastes—we have omitted the snout, ears, and tail! But feel free to substitute or add any pork cuts you wish. The chorizo used here is a hard, Spanish sausage, not the fresh, soft chorizo found in Mexico. You'll find these beans are about as delicious as beans get! In Brazil, feijoada is served in courses; the cooking liquid is served as soup, and then the main ingredients are served separately at the table.

FOR THE BLACK BEANS:

2 smoked ham hocks (about 1 1/4 pounds)

1 pound smoked pork neck bones (optional)

1 pound dried black beans, soaked overnight

2 strips bacon

2 onions, chopped

2 cloves garlic, chopped

3 small dried red chiles, such as de arbol, seeded

2 ounces chorizo (hard Spanish sausage), peeled and cut into 1/4-inch-thick slices

2 ounces high-quality beef jerky, chopped

Salt and freshly ground black pepper to taste

1/2 cup freshly squeezed orange juice

1/4 cup chopped fresh cilantro leaves

2 tablespoons chopped fresh flat-leaf parsley

FOR THE ROAST PORK:

1 center-cut, bone-in, pork loin (about 5 pounds)

Salt and freshly ground black pepper to taste

1 tablespoon olive oil

1 teaspoon Tabasco sauce

3 cloves garlic, slivered

Place the ham hocks and neck bones in a large saucepan and add enough water to cover by 2 to 3 inches. Bring to a boil, reduce the heat to a simmer, and cook for about 2 hours, skimming the surface occasionally to remove any fat or impurities. Remove the ham hocks and neck bones from the broth. Remove the meat from the bones and set aside. Return the bones to the simmering broth and cook for 30 minutes longer. You will need about 3 cups of broth, so add more water if necessary.

While the meat is cooking, place the beans in a large saucepan and add enough water to cover by 2 to 3 inches. Bring to a boil, reduce the heat, and simmer the beans about 1 1/2 hours, until just tender, skimming occasionally. Drain the beans, reserving the beans and the cooking liquid separately. Place the bacon in a large saucepan, and sauté over medium heat for about 3 minutes, or until all the fat is released. Remove the bacon, chop, and set aside. Add the onions to the pan and sauté for 7 or 8 minutes, until golden. Add the garlic, red chiles, and chorizo, and sauté for 5 minutes longer. Return the beans to the pan, and add 2 cups of the reserved pork broth, 1 cup of the reserved bean liquid, the beef jerky, and the reserved pork meat. Season with salt and pepper and simmer for 30 minutes. Add the orange juice, cilantro, parsley, and bacon. Adjust the seasonings and simmer for 15 minutes more. The beans should be somewhat soupy; add more bean broth, if necessary.

While the beans are cooking, prepare the pork. Preheat the oven to 450°F. Season the pork loin with salt and pepper. Combine the olive oil and Tabasco in a bowl, and rub the meat with the mixture. Cut small slits in the pork and insert the garlic slivers. Transfer to a large roasting pan and roast in the oven for 15 minutes. Reduce the heat to 300°F. and roast for 1 1/2 hours more. Remove from the oven, cover with foil, and let rest for 15 minutes.

Prepare the rice according to the recipe on page 227. While the rice is cooking, prepare the collard greens. Heat the olive oil in a large sauté pan, and sauté the garlic and onion over medium heat for 3 or 4 minutes. Add 1 cup of the reserved pork broth and bring to a simmer. Pile the greens into the pan and simmer for about 15 minutes, or until the greens are wilted, tossing frequently. Season with salt and pepper and raise the heat to high. Simmer the greens, uncovered, and continue tossing the greens in the broth until the cooking liquid is reduced.

Slice the pork loin and arrange on a warm serving platter. Serve the beans and the collards on the side, and garnish with the orange slices.

SERVES 4 TO 6

White Rice (page 227) (optional)

FOR THE COLLARD GREENS:

1 tablespoon olive oil

1 teaspoon minced garlic

1/2 onion, diced

1 pound collard greens or kale, stemmed and chopped into large pieces

Salt and freshly ground black pepper to taste

2 navel oranges, peeled, halved lengthwise, sliced, and seeded

PORK CHOP "ENVELOPES"
WITH TOMATOES, OLIVES, FETA CHEESE, AND ORZO

This Mediterranean dish has been attributed to travelers and vagabonds who preferred to cook their meals over an open fire. It uses the technique called "en papillote" by the French, where the food actually steams in the packages. Although we cook the packages in the oven here, you can still hold true to the traditional origins of this dish and make it an elegant picnic or camping dish if prepared ahead of time. Cook the parchment envelopes in foil, place in a cooler, and take them with you. Wrap them in more foil and place over the barbecue coals or in the campfire to reheat while you relax. You can substitute chicken or veal for the pork. Orzo is a small rice-shaped pasta, but you can use small pasta shells or long-grained rice, if you prefer.

Preheat the oven to 350°F. Heat the oil in a large sauté pan and season the pork chops with salt and pepper. Sear the chops over medium-high heat for 1 to 2 minutes on each side, until browned. Remove from the pan and set aside. Reduce the heat to medium and sauté the onion for 5 to 7 minutes, or until golden. Add the garlic and rosemary and sauté for 2 minutes longer. Add the tomatoes, olives, and any juices released from the resting pork chops. Season with salt and pepper, and cook for 2 or 3 minutes.

Cut 4 sheets of parchment paper about 16 x 13 inches. Place a pork chop in the center of each piece of paper and spoon the tomato-olive mixture over the chops, using all of the sauce. Slice or crumble the feta over the tomatoes. Carefully fold the paper over the pork chops, making sure the paper is not punctured, and seal the edges tightly. Place the packages on a baking sheet and bake in the oven for 20 to 25 minutes, or until the pork is tender.

While the pork chops are cooking, prepare the orzo according to the directions on the package. (Typically, it should be simmered in water for 8 to 10 minutes, until al dente.) Drain, rinse, and stir in the oil and parsley. Season with salt and pepper.

Divide the orzo among warm serving plates. Open the packages carefully, as they will contain hot steam. Use 2 forks or spoons to gently lift out the pork chops and place them on the orzo. Pour the vegetables and juices from each package over the pork chops. Garnish with the rosemary.

SERVES 4

FOR THE PORK CHOPS:
2 tablespoons olive oil

4 bone-in pork rib chops (about 6 ounces each and about 3/4 inch thick)

Salt and freshly ground black pepper to taste

1 large onion, cut lengthwise into thin strips

1 clove garlic, minced

1 teaspoon chopped fresh rosemary

6 plum tomatoes, blanched, peeled, seeded, and cut lengthwise into eighths (page 228), or canned tomatoes

1/4 cup Greek black olives, such as kalamata, pitted and sliced

6 ounces feta cheese

FOR THE ORZO:
1 1/2 cups dried orzo

1 tablespoon olive oil

1 tablespoon chopped fresh flat-leaf parsley

Salt and freshly ground black pepper to taste

4 sprigs fresh rosemary, for garnish

PORK CARNITAS QUESADILLAS
WITH MANCHMANTEL SAUCE AND CALABACITAS

Carnitas are morsels of pork often enclosed in tamales or tortillas and usually sold in Mexico as snack food. For large celebrations, we suggest doubling (or tripling) this recipe. Manchmantel (the Spanish translation is "tablecloth stainer," which it certainly can be, so beware!) is a mole sauce sweetened by the addition of fruit. It is often used in Mexico to braise pork ribs or chicken. In this recipe, we have made the sauce with apple, pineapple, and ripe plantain, but bananas, apricots, and prunes are all appropriate substitutions. The flavors in the sauce seem to get better with time, so consider making it a day ahead.

FOR THE CARNITAS:
1 teaspoon cumin seeds

1 teaspoon dried oregano

½ teaspoon anise seeds

1 stick canela (about 1 inch long) or ½-inch stick cinnamon

1½ pounds pork butt, cut into 1-inch cubes

Salt and freshly ground black pepper to taste

2 tablespoons vegetable oil

1 onion, chopped

3 cloves garlic, minced

2 tablespoons dried red pepper flakes

FOR THE MANCHMANTEL SAUCE:
4 dried ancho chiles, stemmed and seeded

2 dried guajillo chiles, stemmed and seeded

4 plum tomatoes

4 cloves garlic

1 onion, cut in half

1 teaspoon cumin seeds

½ teaspoon dried oregano

5 whole cloves

2 bay leaves

1 stick canela (about 1 inch long) or ½-inch stick cinnamon

2 tablespoons vegetable oil

1 cup Chicken Stock (page 225)

1 cup chopped fresh pineapple

1 Granny Smith apple, peeled, cored, and chopped

1 tablespoon cider vinegar

To prepare the carnitas, place the cumin, oregano, and anise in a dry cast-iron skillet. Toast over low heat for about 1 minute, tossing or stirring continuously, until fragrant. (Do not scorch or the mixture will taste bitter.) Transfer to a spice mill or coffee grinder, add the canela, and grind together. Set aside. Season the pork with salt and pepper. Heat the oil in a large, heavy skillet over medium heat. Add the pork and sauté for 4 or 5 minutes, stirring occasionally, until browned on all sides. (To avoid overcrowding the skillet, you may wish to do this in 2 or 3 batches.) Remove with a slotted spoon and set aside.

Add the onion to the skillet and sauté for about 5 minutes, until light golden. (If necessary, add a little more oil to prevent the onion from sticking.) Add the garlic and cook for 2 more minutes. Add the reserved ground spices and the pepper flakes, and cook for 1 minute. Add 2 cups of water, scraping the bottom of the pan to release any drippings. Return the pork to the skillet and bring to a simmer. Reduce the heat to low, cover tightly, and braise for about 1½ hours, or until the pork is tender, adding more water if necessary. When the pork is tender, remove the cover and continue to cook until the pork is almost dry. Let cool slightly and shred the pork into thin strips. Set aside in the refrigerator.

While the carnitas are cooking, prepare the sauce. Preheat the oven to 400°F. Clean the ancho and guajillo chiles with a damp towel. Cover a baking sheet with foil and place the chiles, tomatoes, garlic, and onion (cut-side down) on the foil. Toast in the oven; watch the chiles closely, turn them once, and remove after 3 or 4 minutes. (They should puff up slightly, but do not allow them to blacken.) Return the baking sheet to the oven to continue roasting the tomatoes, garlic, and onion. Place the chiles in a nonreactive bowl, cover with hot water, and let soak for about 20 minutes. Roast the tomatoes, garlic, and onion for a total of 20 to 25 minutes, turning at least once, until they begin to blacken.

Remove from the oven, core the tomatoes, and place them in a blender or food processor. Add the onion and rehydrated chiles. Squeeze the roasted garlic pulp out of its skin, add to the blender, and purée until smooth.

Heat a dry cast-iron skillet over medium-high heat and toast the cumin, oregano, and cloves for 1 minute, or until fragrant. Transfer to a spice mill or coffee grinder, add the bay leaves and canela, and grind together. Set the vegetable oil in a large sauté pan over medium heat. Add the puréed chile mixture and the ground spices, and cook for 5 minutes, stirring constantly, until the sauce begins to darken. Add the stock, pineapple, apple, vinegar, salt, and pepper, and simmer for 10 minutes. While the sauce is cooking, peel and cut the plantain into $1/2$-inch dice. Heat the butter in a large sauté pan on medium, add the plantain, and cook for about 4 minutes, until golden brown. Add the plantain to the sauce and simmer for 10 more minutes, until thickened. Adjust the seasonings and stir about $1/2$ cup of the sauce into the prepared carnitas (shredded pork). Reserve the remaining sauce to pass at the table.

About 15 minutes before serving, prepare the calabacitas. Heat the vegetable oil in a large skillet or sauté pan and add the onion, zucchini, and yellow squash. Sauté over medium-high heat for about 5 minutes, stirring occasionally, until golden brown. Reduce the heat to low, and season with salt and pepper. Cover and cook for about 5 minutes, until the squash is tender, but not falling apart.

Warm the carnitas in a saucepan. Warm the tortillas is a large dry skillet or sauté pan. Place 4 of the tortillas on a work surface and spread the carnitas evenly over the tortillas. Sprinkle with the cheese, cover with the remaining tortillas, and return to the skillet. Cook over medium heat for 1 or 2 minutes on each side, until the cheese begins to melt and the carnitas are warmed through.

Cut each quesadilla into 8 wedges. Serve 8 wedges per plate, arranged in a fan shape. Ladle the sauce onto the plates and serve with the calabacitas.

SERVES 4

$1/2$ teaspoon salt
$1/2$ teaspoon freshly ground black pepper
1 ripe plantain
2 tablespoons butter ($1/4$ stick)

FOR THE CALABACITAS:
3 tablespoons vegetable oil
1 onion, cut in half lengthwise and thinly sliced crosswise
2 unpeeled zucchini, cut into $1/4$-inch slices
2 unpeeled yellow squash, cut into $1/4$-inch slices
Salt and freshly ground black pepper
8 large flour tortillas
$1/2$ cup grated Monterey Jack cheese

ROAST PORK LOIN
WITH GARLIC, GINGER, AND SOY, SERVED WITH SWEET POTATOES AND SESAME SPINACH

The pairing of sweet potatoes and Chinese-style pork loin in this recipe may seem unusual, but the potatoes mix wonderfully well with the spiced marinade baste. If you prefer a more traditionally Asian accompaniment, however, rather than the potatoes (native to the South American rainforests), you can use rice instead. Chinese five-spice powder is a blend of equal parts ground cinnamon, cloves, star anise, fennel seed, and Szechwan peppercorns. It is available in most specialty markets and some grocery stores, or you can prepare your own.

FOR THE MARINADE AND PORK:

1/4 cup soy sauce

2 tablespoons minced garlic

2 tablespoons peeled and minced fresh ginger

2 tablespoons honey

2 tablespoons rice vinegar

2 dried Szechwan peppers, de arbol chiles, or other small dried red chiles, crushed, or 1 teaspoon dried red pepper flakes

1 teaspoon Chinese five-spice powder

3 pounds boneless pork loin

FOR THE SWEET POTATOES:

4 sweet potatoes, peeled and quartered

4 onions, cut in half crosswise

FOR THE SESAME SPINACH:

2 teaspoons vegetable oil

2 cloves garlic, minced

10 ounces spinach, cleaned and stemmed

2 tablespoons white sesame seeds, toasted (page 229)

1 tablespoon soy sauce

1 teaspoon roasted sesame oil

Salt and freshly ground pepper to taste

Combine the soy sauce, garlic, ginger, honey, vinegar, peppers, and five-spice powder in a small bowl. Place the pork in a nonreactive baking dish and pour the marinade over the pork loin. Marinate the pork in the refrigerator for 1 hour, turning once. Drain off the marinade, reserving the liquid.

Preheat the oven to 450°F. Place the pork fat-side down in a large roasting pan, and roast in the oven for 15 minutes. Add the sweet potatoes and onions to the roasting pan and baste the meat, potatoes, and onions with the marinade. Reduce the heat to 350°F. Continue to roast for about 1 hour for medium, or until the internal temperature reaches 150°F., brushing the pork and vegetables with the marinade about every 15 minutes. Remove from the oven, cover with foil, and let rest for about 10 minutes before slicing. (The internal temperature will rise to about 160°F.)

About 10 minutes before serving, prepare the spinach. Heat the oil in a large sauté pan, add the garlic, and sauté over medium heat for 2 minutes. Add the spinach, cover, and cook for 2 or 3 minutes longer, until the spinach just begins to wilt. Add 1 tablespoon of the sesame seeds, the soy sauce, and sesame oil to the spinach, tossing to combine. Cook over medium heat for about 1 minute, and season with salt and pepper.

Place the sliced roast pork, sweet potatoes, and onions on warmed serving plates. Serve the sesame spinach on the side and garnish it with the remaining sesame seeds.

SERVES 4

CHINESE-STYLE
HOISIN PORK RIBS
WITH VEGETABLE CHOW MEIN

Hoisin sauce, also called Peking sauce, is based on puréed soy beans. The addition of sweet and spicy seasonings makes it a wonderful condiment and a versatile flavoring for many meat dishes. It goes particularly well with pork, especially combined with the other sweet and savory ingredients in the marinade. The chow mein in this recipe is almost like a Chinese pasta primavera, and you can substitute broccoli florets, mushrooms, or onions, if you like. When cooking the egg noodles, separate them with chopsticks or a fork to prevent them from sticking together.

FOR THE HOISIN-SOY MARINADE AND RIBS:

3/4 cup hoisin sauce
3/4 cup soy sauce
1/2 cup packed dark brown sugar
1/4 cup ketchup
1/4 cup dry sherry
3 tablespoons rice vinegar
3 tablespoons minced fresh cilantro leaves
2 tablespoons peeled and minced fresh ginger
1 tablespoon minced garlic
2 tablespoons chile sauce
1/2 teaspoon Chinese five-spice powder
4 pounds pork spare ribs, trimmed of fat and membrane

FOR THE CHOW MEIN:

1 pound thin dried egg noodles
1 cup sliced green beans
1 cup asparagus tips
1 tablespoon peanut or vegetable oil
1 tablespoon roasted sesame oil
1/2 tablespoon peeled and minced fresh ginger
1/2 tablespoon minced garlic
1 teaspoon dried red pepper flakes
1 cup sliced snow peas
1 cup bean sprouts
1 cup seeded and diced red bell pepper
3/4 cup sliced bamboo shoots
3 scallions, sliced
1/4 cup Chicken Stock (page 225)
3 tablespoons soy sauce
2 tablespoons dry sherry
1 teaspoon honey
Salt and freshly ground black pepper to taste
8 sprigs fresh cilantro, for garnish

Combine the hoisin sauce, soy sauce, and sugar in a medium mixing bowl, stirring until the sugar is dissolved. Add the ketchup, sherry, vinegar, cilantro, ginger, garlic, chile sauce, and five-spice powder, and stir until thoroughly incorporated. Transfer to 1 or 2 baking dishes, and add the ribs, meat-side down. (Cut the racks to fit the dishes if necessary.) Cover with foil and marinate in the refrigerator for at least 4 hours, and preferably overnight, basting occasionally with the marinade.

Prepare the grill. Remove the ribs from the marinade and reserve the marinade. Place the ribs, meat-side up, on the grill over indirect medium heat. Cover and slightly vent the grill, and cook for 1 1/4 to 1 1/2 hours, turning occasionally. Meanwhile, place the marinade in a saucepan and bring to a boil. Reduce the heat to low and simmer for 15 minutes, stirring occasionally. Remove the sauce from the heat and let cool. When the ribs are 30 minutes from being cooked, brush with the sauce every 10 minutes or so. The ribs are done when no pink meat shows when the ribs are pierced with a sharp knife. Heat the remaining sauce through just before serving.

While the ribs are grilling, prepare the chow mein. Cook the noodles in a saucepan of boiling water until al dente, according to the directions on the package. Drain and set aside. Blanch the beans and asparagus in a saucepan of boiling water for 2 minutes and drain. Heat the oils together in a wok or large sauté pan. When hot, add the ginger, garlic, and red pepper flakes, and stir-fry over high heat for 30 seconds. Add the blanched beans and asparagus, the snow peas, bean sprouts, bell pepper, bamboo shoots, and scallions, and stir-fry for 2 minutes, or until just tender. Add the stock, soy sauce, sherry, honey, and cooked noodles, and season with salt and pepper. Stir-fry briefly, until thoroughly combined and the noodles are heated through. Transfer the chow mein to warm serving plates and garnish with the cilantro. Serve with the ribs and pass the sauce at the table.

SERVES 4

HONEY-MUSTARD
GLAZED ROASTED HAM
WITH GARBANZO SALAD AND SUN-DRIED TOMATO SAUCE

Cooked (cured and smoked) hams are usually cut from the hind quarters. In this recipe, we call for a "half" ham, a cut your butcher will be able to provide, but for large parties, consider buying a whole ham and doubling the honey glaze. Because some boneless hams consist of pressed meat or are reshaped, we prefer the real thing—bone-in ham. Besides, the leg bone itself makes a wonderful addition to soups, stocks, or bean dishes. This recipe serves four, but you will also have plenty of leftovers of the ham; use for delicious sandwiches, soups, omelets, and poultry stuffing—and for the recipes on page 106 and 113.

Preheat the oven to 325°F. Score the ham with a sharp knife in a crisscross pattern on all sides, to a depth of about 1/4 inch. Spacing evenly, press the cloves into the ham where the score lines intersect. Place the ham fat-side up on a rack set inside a foil-lined roasting pan. Cover loosely with aluminum foil and roast in the oven for about 1 1/2 hours, or until the internal temperature reaches 120°F. Remove the ham from the oven and raise the oven temperature to 375°F.

Meanwhile, place the orange juice in a saucepan and bring to a boil over high heat. Reduce the heat to medium and cook until reduced to 1 tablespoon. Transfer to a mixing bowl, and add the orange zest, honey, and mustard. Stir until thoroughly combined. Brush the glaze generously over the ham and return to the oven. After 15 minutes, brush again with the glaze. Cook for 15 minutes longer, or until the internal temperature reaches 145°F. Remove from the oven and let rest for 15 minutes before carving. (The internal temperature will rise to at least 150°F.)

Meanwhile, prepare the sauce. Heat the oil in a saucepan and add the garlic and onion. Sauté over medium heat for 2 minutes. Add the plum tomatoes, sun-dried tomatoes, bell pepper, stock, basil, thyme, honey, salt, and pepper. Reduce the heat to low, cover, and simmer for 10 minutes, stirring occasionally. Transfer to a blender or food processor and purée until smooth. Keep warm.

To prepare the salad, place the garbanzos, tomatoes, corn, garlic, oil, lime juice, cilantro, and pepper in a mixing bowl and toss to combine thoroughly.

Ladle the sauce onto warm serving plates. Carve the ham and arrange on top of the sauce. Serve with the garbanzo salad.

SERVES 4

FOR THE HAM AND GLAZE:

1 cooked bone-in half ham (about 7 pounds), skin removed and fat trimmed to 1/4 inch

1 tablespoon whole cloves

1/4 cup freshly squeezed orange juice

1 tablespoon minced orange zest

1 cup honey

1/2 cup Dijon mustard

FOR THE SUN-DRIED TOMATO SAUCE:

2 tablespoons olive oil

1 teaspoon chopped garlic

1/2 cup sliced onion

4 plum tomatoes, blanched, peeled, seeded, and chopped (page 228)

6 tablespoons chopped sun-dried tomatoes (packed in oil)

1 red bell pepper, roasted, seeded, peeled, and chopped (page 228)

3/4 cup Chicken Stock (page 225)

1/4 cup minced fresh basil leaves

1/2 teaspoon minced fresh thyme leaves

1 tablespoon honey

Salt and freshly ground black pepper to taste

FOR THE GARBANZO SALAD:

3 cups canned garbanzos (chickpeas), rinsed

2 plum tomatoes, seeded and diced

1/2 cup roasted corn kernels (page 229)

1/2 teaspoon minced garlic

1 tablespoon extra-virgin olive oil

2 tablespoons freshly squeezed lime juice

2 tablespoons chopped fresh cilantro leaves

Freshly ground black pepper to taste

PORK

WILD RICE AND PUMPKIN–STUFFED
PORK TENDERLOIN
WITH MANGO-CHIPOTLE SAUCE

Pork tenderloin is not only lean, but also very flavorful, and this dish contains some great flavor combinations. The sweet and hot sauce provides a tropical contrast that brightens the other ingredients; canned chipotle chiles in adobo (dried, smoked jalapeño chiles packed in a vinegar-based stew) are sold at Mexican and Southwestern markets and specialty stores. Bottled or canned mango purée (available in health food stores and Asian grocery stores) is the easiest option, but you can also purée fresh or thawed frozen mango.

FOR THE WILD RICE AND PUMPKIN STUFFING:

6 ounces pumpkin, finely diced (about 1 cup)

1 tablespoon butter

1/2 cup minced red onion

3/4 cup wild rice

1/2 tablespoon dried Mexican oregano or dried regular oregano

Salt and freshly ground black pepper to taste

1 tablespoon butter

FOR THE PORK:

2 pork tenderloins (about 12 ounces each)

Salt and freshly ground black pepper to taste

2 tablespoons olive oil

FOR THE MANGO-CHIPOTLE SAUCE:

1 cup mango purée

2 tablespoons apple cider vinegar

1/2 canned chipotle chile in adobo, minced

1 teaspoon adobo sauce (from the canned chipotles)

Salt and freshly ground black pepper to taste

To prepare the stuffing, pour enough water in a saucepan to come 1/2 inch up the sides; bring to a boil. Add the pumpkin, reduce the heat to low, cover, and simmer for 5 minutes. Drain, reserving the cooking liquid, and let cool. Heat the butter in a saucepan, and sauté the onion over medium heat for 2 minutes. Add the wild rice and oregano, and cook for 3 or 4 minutes, stirring constantly. Pour the pumpkin cooking liquid into a measuring cup and add enough water to make 2 1/4 cups liquid. Add to the saucepan and season the mixture with salt and pepper. Cover and simmer for 45 to 55 minutes, or until the rice is tender and has absorbed all the liquid. Set aside and let cool. Gently fold the cooked pumpkin into the wild rice, adjust the seasonings, and set aside.

Preheat the oven to 350°F. Cut the tenderloins in half crosswise and then butterfly them by cutting them lengthwise, almost through to the other side. Open the tenderloin like a book and spread the stuffing down the middle. (Reserve the extra stuffing.) Close the meat, tie with butcher's twine, and season with salt and pepper. Heat the oil in a large sauté pan, add the tenderloins, and sear over medium-high heat for 3 minutes on each side, or until browned. Transfer to a roasting pan and cook in the oven for 12 to 15 minutes for medium, or until the internal temperature reaches 155°F. Remove and let rest for 5 minutes. (The internal temperature will rise to about 160°F.) Meanwhile, heat a sauté pan and melt the butter. Add the reserved stuffing, and sauté over medium heat for about 5 minutes, until cooked through.

To prepare the sauce, combine the mango, vinegar, chipotle, and adobo sauce in a saucepan. Warm through over medium-low heat. Season with salt and pepper and additional adobo sauce, if desired.

Remove the twine from the tenderloins and carefully cut each half into 3 slices. Spoon the sauce in a pool on warm serving plates. Place 3 tenderloin slices in the center of the sauce on each plate, and serve the sautéed wild rice mixture next to the pork.

SERVES 4

OMAHA STEAKS MEAT

FETTUCCINE WITH HAM,
BELL PEPPERS, OLIVES, PEAS, AND HERBS

This simple and flavorful dish makes a great lunch or a main course for dinner. It's just the recipe if you have any leftover ham (for example, from the glazed ham recipe on page 103). You can also buy ham steaks and dice them if you prefer. Other additions you might want to consider are cooked bacon and slices of roasted eggplant. The long, tubular ziti pasta makes an interesting alternative to the fettuccine called for in this recipe.

2 tablespoons olive oil

1 teaspoon minced garlic

1 sweet onion, such as Vidalia, sliced

12 ounces cooked ham (page 103), cut into thin strips about 2 inches long

1 red bell pepper, roasted, peeled, seeded, and sliced (page 228)

1 yellow bell pepper, roasted, peeled, seeded, and sliced (page 228)

1 (14-ounce) can crushed tomatoes

1/2 cup red wine

1/3 cup sliced ripe black olives

2 tablespoons chopped fresh flat-leaf parsley

1 tablespoon chopped fresh basil leaves

Salt and freshly ground black pepper to taste

2/3 cup frozen peas

1 pound dried fettuccine

1/2 cup freshly grated Parmesan cheese

Heat the olive oil in a saucepan and add the garlic and onion. Sauté for 2 minutes over medium-high heat. Add the ham and sauté for 3 minutes longer, stirring often. Add the bell peppers, tomatoes, wine, olives, parsley, basil, salt, and pepper, and bring to a boil. Reduce the heat to a simmer and cook for 15 minutes. Add the peas and cook for 5 minutes longer.

Meanwhile, bring a saucepan of salted water to a boil and add the pasta. Cook according to the directions on the package until al dente (typically, 8 to 10 minutes), and drain. Return the pasta to the pan, add the vegetables, and toss to combine thoroughly. Transfer to warm serving plates and sprinkle with the cheese.

SERVES 4

PACIFIC RIM
GUAVA-GLAZED HAM
WITH EGG RICE AND BLACK BEAN–PAPAYA SALSA

This is ham 'n' eggs with a difference! Flavors here come from different cuisines that border the Pacific—from Mexico to Hawaii and on to China. If you are cooking a whole 12- to 14-pound ham before glazing it, allow about 2$^1/_2$ hours up to that point. A tasty option is to boil the leftover glaze for 3 or 4 minutes and serve it on the side as a sauce. For a nice effect, arrange the egg rice in a mold or cookie cutter (3 or 4 inches across); carefully lift the mold to leave the rice in an attractive circle.

To prepare the salsa, gently combine the papaya, beans, bell pepper, scallions, chile sauce, cilantro, and lime juice in a mixing bowl. Chill in the refrigerator.

Preheat the oven to 325°F. Score the ham with a sharp knife in a crisscross pattern on all sides, to a depth of about $^1/_4$ inch. Place the ham fat-side up on a rack set inside a foil-lined roasting pan. Cover loosely with aluminum foil and roast in the oven for about 1$^1/_2$ hours, or until the internal temperature reaches 120°F. Remove the ham from the oven and raise the oven temperature to 375°F.

Meanwhile, place the guava jelly, plums, hoisin sauce, vinegar, chile paste, plum sauce, ginger, and five-spice powder in a saucepan and set over medium-high heat. Cook for 5 minutes, stirring until thoroughly combined. Transfer to a food processor or blender and purée until smooth. Brush the glaze generously over the ham and return to the oven. After 15 minutes, brush again with the glaze. Cook for 15 minutes longer, or until the temperature reaches 145°F. Remove from the oven and let rest for 15 minutes before carving. (The internal temperature will rise at least to 150°F.)

To prepare the rice, melt 1 tablespoon of the butter in a large saucepan set over medium-high heat. Add the rice and stir until thoroughly coated. Add the stock, stir once, and bring to a boil. Reduce the heat to low, cover, and simmer for 15 to 20 minutes, or until the liquid has been absorbed. Stir in the peas and the remaining tablespoon of butter to the rice. In a small bowl, beat the eggs with the soy sauce and five-spice powder, and add to the pan. Keep stirring until the eggs have set.

Carve the ham and arrange on serving plates. Serve with the rice and the salsa.

SERVES 4

FOR THE SALSA:
1 ripe papaya, seeded, peeled, and diced (about 1$^1/_2$ cups)
1$^1/_2$ cups cooked black beans (page 226) or canned
$^1/_2$ cup finely diced red bell pepper
2 scallions, finely sliced
$^1/_2$ tablespoon hot chile sauce
2 tablespoons chopped fresh cilantro leaves
Juice of $^1/_2$ lime

FOR THE HAM AND GLAZE:
1 cooked bone-in half ham (about 7 pounds), skin removed and fat trimmed to $^1/_4$ inch
1 cup guava jelly or red currant jelly
5 ripe plums, pitted, peeled, and chopped
$^1/_4$ cup hoisin sauce
$^1/_4$ cup rice vinegar
1 tablespoon chile paste
2 tablespoons Chinese plum sauce (optional)
1 teaspoon peeled and minced fresh ginger
$^1/_2$ teaspoon Chinese five-spice powder

FOR THE RICE AND EGGS:
2 tablespoons butter ($^1/_4$ stick)
1 cup long-grain white rice
2 cups Chicken Stock (page 225)
$^1/_2$ cup frozen peas
3 large eggs
1 teaspoon soy sauce
$^1/_8$ teaspoon Chinese five-spice powder

PORK

ASIAN PORK CHOPS
WITH SHERRIED SWEET POTATOES AND PINEAPPLE-GINGER APPLE SAUCE

With the grilled pork, roughly mashed potatoes, and apple-based sauce, this looks like a comfort dish and tastes like one—until the surprising tropical flavors of the pineapple and ginger in the apple sauce hit the palate. Pork is bred much leaner than in the old days, which means it has fewer calories, but it also means that it tends to dry out more quickly during the cooking process. For that reason, marinating lean cuts of pork makes sense as it helps preserve moisture and juiciness, and it also contributes flavor.

FOR THE MARINADE AND PORK CHOPS:

1/4 cup soy sauce

2 tablespoons olive oil

2 tablespoons roasted sesame oil

2 tablespoons sherry vinegar

2 tablespoons dark brown sugar

3 scallions, finely sliced

3 cloves garlic, minced

Juice and zest of 1 orange

1 shallot, minced

1 tablespoon Asian chile paste

1 tablespoon maple syrup or honey

1 teaspoon peeled and minced fresh ginger

4 boneless pork loin chops (6 ounces each and about 1 inch thick)

1/2 tablespoon butter

1 teaspoon all-purpose flour

FOR THE PINEAPPLE-GINGER APPLE SAUCE:

3 apples, such as Fuji or Granny Smith, peeled, cored, and diced (about 1 cup)

1 cup diced fresh pineapple

1/2 cup pineapple juice

2 tablespoons sugar

2 teaspoons peeled and finely grated fresh ginger

1/2 teaspoon ground cinnamon

FOR THE SHERRIED SWEET POTATOES:

2 pounds sweet potatoes, peeled and chopped

4 tablespoons butter (1/2 stick), softened

1/4 cup sweet or medium sherry

3 tablespoons light brown sugar

Salt and freshly ground black pepper to taste

Place the soy sauce, both oils, vinegar, sugar, scallions, garlic, orange juice and zest, shallot, chile paste, maple syrup, and ginger in a baking dish. Whisk to thoroughly combine. Add the pork chops and let marinate in the refrigerator for at least 4 hours, and preferably overnight.

To prepare the apple sauce, place the apples, pineapple, pineapple juice, sugar, ginger, and cinnamon in a saucepan and bring to a simmer over medium heat. Reduce the heat to low, and continue to simmer for 15 minutes, or until the apples are tender. Transfer half of the sauce to a blender and purée until smooth. Pour into a bowl. Transfer the remaining sauce to the blender and pulse just briefly to a chunky consistency. Add to the bowl and mix together. Keep refrigerated.

Prepare the grill.

Place the sweet potatoes in a saucepan of boiling salted water, and cook for 20 minutes, or until tender. Drain, transfer to a mixing bowl, and mash roughly with a fork or ricer. Add the butter, sherry, and sugar, and mash until almost smooth, but still slightly chunky. Season with salt and pepper, and keep warm.

While the potatoes are boiling, prepare the chops. Remove from the marinade, reserving 1 cup of the marinade, and wipe off the chops. Grill over direct medium-high heat for about 5 minutes per side for medium. Meanwhile, strain the reserved marinade into a saucepan and bring to a simmer. Roll the butter in the flour, add to the marinade, and whisk until melted. Cook for 3 or 4 minutes, until the sauce is thick enough to coat the back of a spoon. Spoon the sauce onto warm serving plates, top with the pork, and garnish each chop with 1 tablespoon of the apple sauce. Serve with the sweet potatoes and pass the remaining apple sauce at the table.

SERVES 4

JAMAICAN JERKED
PORK TENDERLOIN
WITH REDDENED SWEET RICE AND SUSAN'S PINEAPPLE SALSA

The centuries-old Jamaican tradition of jerk seasoning—a fiery, spicy marinating paste—results in meat dishes (usually pork or chicken) that will set your taste buds tingling. This recipe is not for the faint of heart. The culprit is the habanero chile, the hottest of all capsicums. (You can substitute the closely related Scotch bonnet chile.) In Jamaica, the "jerk men" have become an institution with their roadside and market food stalls, where they barbecue whole animals over allspice wood. Susan Taves, a Chicago-based recipe tester and caterer, developed the salsa.

To prepare the jerk seasoning, place the chiles, lime juice, Worcestershire sauce, and oil in a food processor or blender, and purée until smooth. Add the onion, scallions, ginger, sugar, garlic, thyme, allspice, celery salt, cinnamon, pepper, and nutmeg in the food processor and pulse. (Do not purée.) Cut the pork in half crosswise and place in a zipper-lock bag. Cover with the jerk paste and fold the bag over so the pork is completely smothered. Refrigerate for at least 4 hours, turning occasionally. (Alternatively, marinate in a baking dish.)

Meanwhile, to prepare the salsa, place the pineapple, scallions, bell pepper, poblano, almonds, vinegar, mint, and cumin in a mixing bowl, and combine thoroughly. Let chill in the refrigerator.

Prepare the grill. To prepare the rice, heat 2 tablespoons of the butter in a saucepan, and add the onion and carrot. Sauté over medium heat for 4 or 5 minutes, stirring often. Meanwhile, rinse the rice in a strainer under cold running water until the water no longer looks milky. Drain and add to the pan, stirring until the rice is thoroughly mixed. Add 1 cup of water, the apple juice, salt, paprika, and cinnamon. Raise the heat to high and bring to a boil. When the water has reduced to the level of the rice, reduce the heat to low, cover, and simmer for about 15 minutes, or until the water is absorbed. Remove from the heat and let sit for 5 minutes. Add the remaining tablespoon of butter and the pecans, and fluff the rice with a fork.

While the rice is cooking, remove the pork tenderloins from the marinade. Grill over direct medium-high heat for about 10 minutes on each side for medium, or until the internal temperature reaches 160 degrees. Cut each loin half into 4 medallions and transfer to warm serving plates. Spoon the rice next to the pork and serve with the salsa.

SERVES 4

FOR THE JERK AND PORK:
2 fresh habanero chiles, seeded and chopped
1 tablespoon freshly squeezed lime juice
1 tablespoon Worcestershire sauce
1 tablespoon olive oil
3/4 cup chopped red onion
1/4 cup sliced scallions
2 tablespoons peeled and chopped fresh ginger
1 tablespoon light brown sugar
1 tablespoon chopped garlic
1/2 tablespoon minced fresh thyme leaves
1 teaspoon ground allspice
1 teaspoon celery salt
1/2 teaspoon ground cinnamon
1 teaspoon freshly ground black pepper
1/2 teaspoon ground nutmeg
2 pork tenderloins (about 12 ounces each)

FOR THE SALSA:
2/3 cup diced fresh pineapple
1/3 cup scallions finely sliced on the bias
1/3 cup diced red bell pepper
1/3 cup diced poblano chile, roasted, peeled, and seeded (page 228)
1/3 cup chopped almonds, toasted (page 229)
2 tablespoons rice vinegar
1 teaspoon minced fresh mint leaves
Pinch of ground cumin

FOR THE REDDENED SWEET RICE:
3 tablespoons butter
1/2 cup finely diced white onion
1 carrot, finely diced
1 1/2 cups long-grain rice
2 cups apple juice or apple cider
1/2 teaspoon salt
2 tablespoons paprika
2 teaspoons ground cinnamon
1/4 cup chopped pecans, toasted (page 229)

PORK MEDALLIONS
WITH HERBED ROASTED POTATO CHIPS
AND RHUBARB SAUCE

Rhubarb, a relative of sorrel and buckwheat, is an overlooked vegetable—partly because it's usually eaten in baked pies, cobblers, and desserts and thought of (erroneously) as a fruit. Only the stalks of the plant can be used, as the leaves contain oxalic acid and are poisonous. Rhubarb makes a wonderful savory ingredient, as this recipes proves. If you use a large zipper-lock bag to marinate the pork, you can cut the marinade recipe in half. The potatoes make an elegant side dish for any meal. They are best cut with a mandoline, but if you do cut them by hand, use a sharp knife and try to slice them as thinly as possible.

Place the oil, herbs, salt, and pepper in a baking dish, and whisk to combine thoroughly. Add the pork tenderloins and marinate in the refrigerator for 2 hours.

Meanwhile, to prepare the sauce, heat the butter in a saucepan and add the onion and garlic. Sauté over medium-high heat for 2 minutes. Add the rhubarb, vinegar, sugar, and ginger, and bring to a boil. Reduce the heat to low, cover, and simmer for 10 to 12 minutes, until the rhubarb is tender. Transfer to a blender and purée until smooth. Season with salt and pepper and warm through just before serving.

Preheat the oven to 375°F. To prepare the potatoes, pour 1 tablespoon of the oil in a large warmed roasting pan and spread to make sure the bottom of the pan is covered. (Use 2 pans if necessary, and double the amount of oil.) Place the potato slices in the pan in a single layer and sprinkle with the herbs, garlic, salt, and pepper. Drizzle with the remaining oil and roast in the oven for 15 to 20 minutes, or until browned and crisp.

While the potatoes are roasting, heat a dry, heavy skillet over medium-high heat. Remove the pork from the marinade and place in the skillet, adding 1 tablespoon or so of the marinade. Sear for about 12 minutes per side for medium, or until the internal temperature reaches 160 degrees. Cut each loin half into 4 medallions. Spoon the warm sauce onto warm serving plates, and arrange the medallions so they are overlapping on top of the sauce. Garnish with the tomatoes and oregano, and serve with the roasted potato chips.

SERVES 4

FOR THE PORK:
1 cup extra-virgin olive oil
1 tablespoon dried mixed herbs
1/2 teaspoon salt
1/2 teaspoon freshly ground black pepper
2 pork tenderloins (about 12 ounces each), cut in half crosswise

FOR THE RHUBARB SAUCE:
1 tablespoon butter or olive oil
1/4 cup finely diced onion
1 clove garlic, minced
12 ounces rhubarb stalks, chopped
1/4 cup cider vinegar
4 tablespoons sugar
1 teaspoon peeled and minced fresh ginger
Salt and freshly ground black pepper to taste

FOR THE HERBED ROASTED POTATO CHIPS:
3 tablespoons olive oil
1 pound small white potatoes, very finely sliced
1/2 tablespoon dried rosemary or 1 tablespoon minced fresh oregano
1 teaspoon minced garlic
Salt and freshly ground black pepper to taste
4 cherry tomatoes, cut in half, for garnish
4 fresh oregano sprigs, for garnish

PORK, CHILE, AND PEAR
BREAKFAST SAUSAGE
WITH POACHED EGGS AND CORN PANCAKES

Do not be intimidated by thinking that all sausage has to be neatly stuffed into casings. Although this recipe will work for those adventurous enough to do so, the flavors are just as good with these free-form, rustic-style patties. They follow the style of Mexican chorizo sausage (not to be confused with the hard Spanish chorizo sausage). Note that at least 24 hours are needed for the pork mixture to marinate; 48 hours are even better. If the pear seems less ripe and sweet, sauté it with a little butter and sugar. This recipe makes the ultimate breakfast or brunch, but to save some time, serve toast instead of the corn pancakes.

FOR THE BREAKFAST SAUSAGE:
1/2 teaspoon black peppercorns
8 whole cloves
1 stick cinnamon (about 2 inches long), broken up
1/2 tablespoon cumin seeds
1/2 tablespoon dried oregano
2 dried ancho chiles, stemmed, seeded, toasted, and rehydrated (page 230)
2 dried New Mexico red chiles, stemmed, seeded, toasted, and rehydrated (page 230)
1 1/2 pounds high-quality ground pork, preferably pork butt, with fat
1 ripe firm pear, peeled, cored, and finely diced
1/2 cup finely diced onion
1 tablespoon minced garlic
1 teaspoon salt
1/4 cup red wine vinegar
2 tablespoons peanut or vegetable oil

FOR THE PANCAKES:
1/3 cup all-purpose flour
1/3 cup cornmeal
1/2 tablespoon ground cumin
1 teaspoon sugar
3/4 teaspoon kosher or sea salt
1/2 teaspoon baking powder
1/2 cup milk or buttermilk
2 eggs, beaten
1 tablespoon olive oil
1/2 cup fresh corn kernels
1/4 cup finely diced red bell pepper
1 tablespoon chopped fresh cilantro leaves
2 tablespoons finely sliced scallions

FOR THE EGGS:
2 tablespoons white wine vinegar
8 eggs

To prepare the sausages, place the peppercorns, cloves, cinnamon, cumin, and oregano in a dry skillet. Toast over medium heat for 1 or 2 minutes, shaking the pan continuously, until fragrant. Transfer to a mixing bowl. Chop the rehydrated chiles, and place them in a blender with enough of the rehydrating liquid to make puréeing possible. Purée until smooth and add to the mixing bowl. Add the pork, pear, onion, garlic, salt, and vinegar, and combine thoroughly. Cover the bowl and refrigerate for 24 hours, and up to 48 hours. When you are ready to cook, form the pork mixture into 12 patties. Heat the oil in a nonstick sauté pan and add the patties. Cook over medium heat for 8 to 10 minutes on each side, or until browned and cooked through, with the internal temperature reaching 160°F.

To prepare the corn pancakes, place the flour, cornmeal, cumin, sugar, salt, and baking powder in a food processor. In a mixing bowl, whisk together the milk, eggs, and oil and add to the dry ingredients. Blend to form a smooth batter, and return to a clean mixing bowl. Stir in the corn, bell pepper, cilantro, and scallions. Heat a large nonstick sauté pan and add the batter in batches to form 3-inch cakes. Cook over medium heat for about 2 to 3 minutes on each side, or until golden brown. Keep warm.

To prepare the eggs, bring a saucepan of salted water to a boil, add the vinegar, and reduce to a simmer. Gently break 1 egg into a saucer, and then slip it carefully into the pan. Cook until the egg white is set and firm, about 3 to 3 1/2 minutes. Remove with a slotted spoon and let drain. Repeat for the remaining eggs. Place 2 eggs on each warm serving plate and serve with 3 chorizo sausage patties and the corn pancakes.

SERVES 4

DOWN-HOME PORK HASH
WITH SAUTÉED FIDDLEHEAD FERNS

Here's a straightforward brunch recipe that marries a familiar American favorite—pork hash—with a decidedly elegant side dish. The intensely green fiddleheads are tightly curled young fern shoots that get their names from their resemblance to the head-end of a violin. In fresh form, they are available only in springtime, but they are also available frozen year-round at specialty food stores. Their unique flavor is somewhere between okra and asparagus, and they have an interestingly chewable texture. Wilted spinach (page 66) or chard (page 114) makes a fine alternative to the ferns.

Preheat the oven to 375°F. To prepare the hash, bring a saucepan of salted water to a boil. Add the potatoes and sweet potatoes, and blanch in the water for 8 minutes. Strain and transfer to an ice bath to stop the cooking process. Drain and transfer to a mixing bowl. Heat the butter in a large sauté pan, add the onion and bell pepper, and sauté over medium-high heat for 5 minutes. Add the ham, herbs, nutmeg, salt, and plenty of pepper, and stir together to thoroughly combine. Cook for 2 minutes longer, transfer to the mixing bowl with the potatoes, and gently mix all the ingredients together.

Transfer the mixture to a heavy cast-iron skillet, add the stock, and drizzle the top with the sugar. Bake in the oven for 15 minutes. Remove the skillet from the oven, stir, and sprinkle the cheese over the hash. Return to the oven for 10 more minutes, or until the cheese is golden and bubbling.

To prepare the fiddlehead ferns, heat the butter in a large sauté pan. Add the ferns and sauté over medium heat, stirring often, for 5 or 6 minutes, or until tender. Spritz with some lemon juice and season with salt and pepper. Serve with the hash.

SERVES 4

FOR THE PORK HASH:

12 ounces unpeeled red potatoes (about 3 potatoes), diced (about 2 cups)

12 ounces peeled sweet potato (about 1 small potato), diced (about 2 cups)

2 tablespoons butter (¼ stick)

1 cup finely diced onion

1 small red bell pepper, seeded and diced

1¼ pounds cooked ham, diced (about 3 cups)

2 teaspoons dried mixed herbs

½ teaspoon ground nutmeg

Salt and freshly ground black pepper to taste

½ cup Chicken Stock (page 225)

1 tablespoon granulated light brown sugar

¾ cup grated Gruyère cheese

FOR THE FIDDLEHEAD FERNS:

2 tablespoons butter (¼ stick)

10 ounces fiddlehead ferns, trimmed and washed

½ lemon

Salt and freshly ground black pepper to taste

BLACKBERRY AND BALSAMIC VINEGAR-
GLAZED PORK CHOPS
WITH WILTED CHARD

The fruity, sweet, and tangy glaze gives the pork chops a wonderful flavor. Balsamic vinegar is a natural partner for fruit, which in turn complements the sweet tones of the meat. By all means, use different preserves if you wish— raspberry or cherry jam will also work well, for example. Chard, a relative of beets, is not related to spinach, even though it is often used interchangeably. Chard is milder in flavor than spinach, which you can also substitute in this recipe. The ruby variety of chard, with its blood-red stalks, is preferred here for its striking color contrast. However, the white-stemmed Swiss chard can also be used.

FOR THE GLAZE AND PORK:

1 1/2 cups balsamic vinegar

3/4 cup blackberry jam

1/4 cup grape jelly

1 teaspoon minced garlic

1 teaspoon salt

4 center-cut, bone-in, pork rib loin chops
(about 8 ounces each and 3/4 inch thick),
trimmed of fat

Salt and freshly ground black pepper to taste

FOR THE CHARD:

1 pound ruby chard, washed

Juice of 1/2 lemon

3 tablespoons butter

2 shallots, minced

2 cloves garlic, minced

To prepare the glaze, place the vinegar, jam, jelly, garlic, and salt in a saucepan and bring to a boil. Reduce for about 10 minutes, or until about 1 1/2 cups remains, and then strain into a baking dish. Let cool and add the chops, turning to cover all sides with the marinade. Marinate in the refrigerator for 2 hours, turning once or twice.

Prepare the grill or preheat the broiler.

Meanwhile, prepare the chard. With a knife, cut each leaf from the rib; roughly shred the leaves and chop the ribs. Steam the chard ribs for 8 to 10 minutes, sprinkling them with lemon juice to prevent them from losing color. Melt the butter in a sauté pan, add the shallots and garlic, and sauté over medium heat for 2 minutes. Add the chard and sauté for about 2 minutes, until lightly wilted, stirring with tongs or 2 wooden spoons.

Remove the chops from the marinade, reserving the marinade in a saucepan, and drain any excess liquid from the chops. Season the chops with salt and pepper, and grill over direct medium-high heat for about 5 minutes per side for medium. If broiling, allow 6 to 7 minutes per side. Meanwhile, bring the marinade to a boil, and continue to boil for 3 minutes. Brush the chops with the marinade just before removing from the grill or broiler, and transfer to warm serving plates. Drizzle with about 1 tablespoon of the glaze, if desired, and serve with the chard.

SERVES 4

INDONESIAN MARINATED
PORK KABOBS
WITH A SPICY GREEN CABBAGE SAMBAL

The far-flung tropical archipelago that is now known as Indonesia is the original Spice Islands that drew explorers and traders long before the arrival of the first Europeans in medieval times. Some of the ingredients used in this dish—ginger, lemongrass, turmeric, and chiles (a New World import)—appear abundantly in Indonesia to season meats, fish, curries, salads, and sambals (popular condiments akin to salsas). This sambal recipe is large enough that you can offer it as a side salad. It can be made in advance and held for one or two days, but if you prefer crunchy cabbage salads (such as coleslaw), it's best made only an hour or so in advance. Serve this dish with Cilantro Rice (page 28) or plain white rice, if desired.

To prepare the marinade, combine the lime juice, soy sauce, peanut oil, ginger, garlic, sugar, lemongrass, red chiles, and turmeric in a large mixing bowl. Add the pork, toss to coat well, and marinate in the refrigerator for about 4 hours. Toss occasionally to make sure that all sides of the pork get coated with the marinade.

While the pork is marinating, prepare the cabbage sambal. Combine the lime juice, soy sauce, cilantro, fish sauce, chile sauce, ginger, garlic, and jalapeño in a large mixing bowl. Add the cabbage, pineapple, and onion, tossing well to combine. Keep refrigerated until ready to serve.

Soak eight 12-inch wooden skewers in water for 30 minutes to prevent them from burning on the grill. Prepare the grill.

To prepare the kabobs, drain the pork and pat it dry. Divide the pork, bell peppers, and onions evenly among the skewers. Thread them onto the skewers, alternating each ingredient. Grill the kabobs for 5 to 6 minutes on each side, or until the peppers start to blacken and the pork is cooked through. Transfer 2 skewers to each serving plate and serve with the cabbage sambal.

SERVES 4

FOR THE MARINADE:
1/4 cup freshly squeezed lime juice

2 tablespoons soy sauce

2 tablespoons peanut oil

2 tablespoons peeled and minced fresh ginger

1 tablespoon minced garlic

1 tablespoon light brown sugar

1 stick fresh lemongrass (bottom 6 inches only), thinly sliced

4 small dried red chiles, seeded and crumbled

1/2 teaspoon turmeric

FOR THE KABOBS:
2 pounds boneless pork loin, cut into 1 1/2-inch chunks

2 red bell peppers, seeded and cut into 1 1/2-inch pieces

2 onions, quartered and then cut in half crosswise

FOR THE SPICY GREEN CABBAGE SAMBAL:
1/4 cup freshly squeezed lime juice

2 tablespoons soy sauce

2 tablespoons chopped fresh cilantro leaves

1 tablespoon Asian fish sauce

1 teaspoon hot chile sauce

1 teaspoon peeled and minced fresh ginger

1 teaspoon minced garlic

1 jalapeño chile, seeded and minced

3 cups shredded green cabbage (about 1/4 head)

1 cup chopped fresh pineapple

1/2 red onion, diced

PORK

QINGDAO-STYLE
MOO SHU PORK
WITH THIN PEKING PANCAKES

"Moo shu" refers to the bright yellow color that the eggs give this dish. Stir-fried Chinese moo shu, featuring wood ear mushrooms, tiger lily buds, scrambled eggs, and pork, is served wrapped in thin pancakes, in the same manner as the classic Peking Duck. The delicate, long, thin lily buds (also sold as "golden needles") have a distinctive earthy, sweet flavor and are available in dried form at Asian grocery stores. If desired, prepare the pancakes ahead and steam for a few minutes before serving. For a shortcut, use lumpia wrappers or plain rice instead of making the pancakes.

FOR THE PANCAKES:

1 1/2 cups all-purpose flour

1/2 cup boiling water

1/4 cup cold water

2 teaspoons sesame oil

FOR THE MOO SHU PORK:

1/4 cup golden needles (dried tiger lily flower) (about 3/4 ounce)

1/4 ounce dried wood ear mushrooms

3 tablespoons peanut oil

1 tablespoon soy sauce

2 tablespoons rice wine or dry sherry

1 teaspoon arrowroot or cornstarch

10 ounces boneless pork shoulder or butt, trimmed of fat and julienned

3 eggs, beaten

1/2 teaspoon peeled and minced fresh ginger

2 cups shredded white cabbage

1/2 cup packed fresh bean sprouts

1/4 cup julienned canned bamboo shoots

3 scallions, finely sliced (white and green parts)

1/2 cup hoisin sauce

To prepare the pancakes, sift the flour into a mixing bowl and gradually stir in the boiling water. Mix to thoroughly incorporate, and then stir in the cold water and 1 teaspoon of the oil. Knead well until smooth and firm, cover with a damp towel, and let rest for 10 minutes. On a lightly floured work surface, roll out the dough into 2 long "sausages" about 2 inches across. Cut each "sausage" in half and then cut each half into 8 pieces. Using the palm of your hand, press each portion into a flat pancake. Lightly brush one side of each pancake with the remaining oil and place together in pairs, oiled-sides inward. Using a rolling pin, roll out each "double" pancake on both sides to form a thin 4- or 5-inch circle to make 16 "double" pancakes.

Heat 1 or 2 dry skillets or sauté pans over medium-high heat. When hot, cook the pancakes individually or in batches for about 20 seconds on the first side, or until air bubbles puff up, and 10 seconds on the second side, or until light brown spots begin to appear underneath. Immediately separate the pancake halves, fold in half, and stack. Cover with a damp cloth or foil and steam to warm through just before serving.

To prepare the pork, place the lily buds and dried mushrooms in a bowl of warm water and let rehydrate for 20 minutes, or until soft. Cut off the hard tips of the lily stems and cut the stems in half. Slice the mushrooms and set aside. Meanwhile, place 1 tablespoon of the oil, the soy sauce, rice wine, and arrowroot in a medium mixing bowl and combine. Add the pork, mix well, and let marinate for 15 minutes.

Heat 1 more tablespoon of the oil in a wok until hot. Add the eggs and lightly scramble over high heat until just set. Remove and set aside. Add the remaining tablespoon of oil to the wok. Add the ginger, sauté for 30 seconds, and then add the pork and marinating liquid. Stir-fry for 2 or 3 minutes, until browned, and then add the reserved lily buds and mushrooms. Stir-fry for 1 minute longer. Add the cabbage, bean sprouts, bamboo shoots, and scallions. Stir-fry for 2 minutes more, add the scrambled eggs, and stir-fry to heat through.

Transfer the moo shu pork to a serving bowl and place on the table. Serve the warmed pancakes in a basket covered with a cloth, and pour the hoisin sauce into a small bowl. Guests should serve themselves, spreading about $1/2$ or $3/4$ teaspoon of the hoisin sauce over each pancake, and spooning enough of the pork on top to allow the pancakes to be rolled up and eaten.

SERVES 4

PORK VINDALOO CURRY
WITH ORANGE-CUCUMBER RAITA AND OKRA BHAJI

118

The term "vindaloo" in Indian cuisine is synonymous with fiery heat. Vindaloo dishes are most commonly found in western and southwestern India, and they are typified by marinating the meat in a spicy vinegar mixture. In comparison, the raita provides a welcome cooling quality to this dish; for a shortcut, use canned mandarin orange sections. "Bhaji" is an Indian word for "dry curry," and this okra dish is a popular side in the subcontinent. Even if you are not an okra fan, you'll love the presentation here. The curry, rice, and raita make a filling meal on their own, so if you are short of time, omit the okra. Serve with naan bread (page 137), if you wish.

FOR THE PORK CURRY:

2 tablespoons ground coriander

2 tablespoons ground cumin

1 stick cinnamon (about 2 inches long), coarsely crushed

5 whole cloves

10 black peppercorns

1 onion, diced

2 tablespoons peeled and minced fresh ginger

1 tablespoon minced garlic

2 tablespoons cayenne, or to taste

½ tablespoon dried red pepper flakes

½ tablespoon turmeric

1 teaspoon salt

½ cup white wine vinegar

2 pounds boneless pork butt or pork loin, cubed

2 tablespoons clarified butter

2 teaspoons mustard seeds

FOR THE RAITA:

1 cup plain yogurt

¼ cup sour cream

½ English or hothouse cucumber, peeled and grated (about ¾ cup)

1 orange, peeled, sectioned, and diced

1 tablespoon minced fresh cilantro leaves

½ teaspoon ground cumin

¼ teaspoon salt

FOR THE BINDI BHAJI:

1 pound fresh okra

3 tablespoons vegetable oil

½ teaspoon cumin seeds

1 onion, diced

1 teaspoon ground coriander

½ teaspoon cayenne, or to taste

½ teaspoon turmeric

1 teaspoon freshly squeezed lemon juice

3 cups cooked basmati rice (page 227)

To prepare the curry, place the coriander, cumin, cinnamon, cloves, and peppercorns in a small, dry skillet, and toast over medium heat for 1 to 2 minutes, or until fragrant. Transfer to a food processor. Add the onion, ginger, garlic, cayenne, red pepper flakes, turmeric, salt, and the vinegar to the food processor. Blend to form a smooth paste, adding a little water if necessary. Transfer to a mixing bowl, add the pork, and mix to coat thoroughly. Marinate in the refrigerator for at least 3 hours.

To prepare the raita, mix the yogurt and sour cream in a serving bowl. Add the cucumber, tangerines, half the cilantro, the cumin, and salt. Stir to combine thoroughly, and then refrigerate. Garnish with the remaining cilantro just before serving.

To complete the curry, heat the clarified butter in a large saucepan and add the mustard seeds. Sauté over medium heat, and when they begin to jump and pop, add the pork and marinade. Bring to a simmer, cover, and reduce the heat to low. Simmer the curry for about 30 minutes, and then uncover the pan. Cook for 15 to 20 minutes longer, or until tender, stirring frequently. Add a little water as needed, although the curry should be served quite dry.

Prepare the rice according to the recipe on page 227.

While the curry is cooking, wash the okra and dry with paper towels. Trim at both ends and cut crosswise into ¼-inch slices. Heat the oil in a saucepan, and when hot, add the cumin seeds. Cook over medium heat for 30 seconds, and then add the onion, sliced okra, and 2 tablespoons water. Sauté for 3 minutes, stirring occasionally. Add the coriander, cayenne, and turmeric. Cover and reduce the heat to low. Cook for about 8 more minutes, stirring often; add the lemon juice about 3 minutes before the end.

Spoon the cooked rice onto serving plates and pour the curry over the top or to the side. Arrange the okra next to the curry. Serve the raita at the table.

SERVES 4

OMAHA STEAKS MEAT

THE ULTIMATE BLT PIZZA
WITH BALSAMIC-SHALLOT VINAIGRETTE

This is not your run-of-the-mill fast-food pizza. The title may sound exotic and distinctly unusual, and what we've cooked up here is indeed a bacon and tomato cheese pizza with a lettuce topping. You can use any greens you like for the garnish—a mesclun mix would be fine—but our preference is for something with a hint of pepperiness. For those with an architectural or artistic inclination, you might arrange sprigs of dressed watercress, baby romaine leaves, or long, thin lettuce leaves, such as mizuna, stuck upright in a slice of mozzarella in the center of the pizzas.

FOR THE PIZZA DOUGH:
3/4 cup lukewarm water (about 110°F.)

1/2 package active dry yeast

1 tablespoon honey

2 cups all-purpose flour, plus more for dusting

1/4 teaspoon salt

2 tablespoons olive oil

FOR THE PIZZA TOPPINGS:
1 1/4 pounds plum tomatoes

Salt and freshly ground black pepper to taste

12 slices bacon, cut in half

1 sweet onion, finely diced

2 tablespoons extra-virgin olive oil

4 teaspoons roasted garlic from 2 heads garlic (page 229)

2 cups shredded mozzarella cheese

FOR THE SALAD TOPPING:
1 cup torn romaine lettuce leaves, frisée, or mâche

1/2 packed cup arugula or watercress leaves

2 tablespoons Real French Vinaigrette (page 32)

To prepare the dough, pour the water in a mixing bowl and sprinkle in the yeast. Whisk in the honey and let sit in a warm place for 5 minutes. Sift the flour and salt into a large mixing bowl, stir in the liquid mixture, and mix until a soft dough forms. Add the oil and continue to mix until the dough forms a ball. Turn out onto a floured work surface and knead for 8 to 10 minutes, or until smooth; add more flour if necessary. Transfer the dough to a lightly oiled bowl, cover with a damp towel, and let rise in a warm place for 45 minutes, or until doubled in volume. Return the dough to a lightly floured work surface and divide into 4 portions. Knead each portion for 1 minute and form into balls. Place on a baking sheet, cover again, and let rise for 20 minutes. Roll each ball into 6-inch circles about 1/8 inch thick, sprinkling the dough and rolling pin with additional flour to prevent them from sticking together. Pinch the edges of the dough to create a raised brim. Set aside.

Meanwhile, prepare the toppings. Preheat the broiler and place the tomatoes on a rack in a roasting pan. Broil, turning often with tongs, until the skins are partly blackened and cracked, about 10 minutes. (Alternatively, grill the tomatoes.) Remove the seeds, roughly chop, and season with salt and pepper. Set aside.

Preheat the oven to 450°F. Place the bacon in a dry sauté pan and sauté over medium heat for about 5 minutes, until cooked through but not crispy. Remove the bacon, drain all but 2 tablespoons of the fat, and add the onion to the pan. Sauté for 5 or 6 minutes, until soft. Brush each pizza dough with the oil and spread the garlic on top. Top with the onion, then the bacon, and then the tomatoes. Sprinkle with the cheese, leaving a 1/2-inch border all around. Transfer to a pizza brick or pizza pans and bake in the oven for 12 to 15 minutes, or until the crusts are golden brown.

Just before removing the pizzas from the oven, place the romaine and arugula in a mixing bowl, and toss with the dressing. Place some of the dressed greens in a neat pile in the center of each pizza.

SERVES 4

CARNE ADOVADO:
MEXICAN PORK WITH ADOBO SAUCE AND NAVAJO FRY BREAD

Originating in Mexico and common on restaurant menus throughout the Southwest, carne adovado is pork (or beef) marinated and simmered in a blend of chiles and spices. In this recipe, we use the mild and flavorful ancho chiles (page 39). Note that the pork should marinate overnight, and up to 3 days. We serve the pork with fry bread, a traditional Southwestern Native American recipe that is quick and easy to prepare—even young children will find it fun. For a shortcut, serve the meat with warmed flour tortillas instead of the fry bread.

FOR THE CARNE ADOVADO:
6 dried ancho chiles, stemmed and seeded

3 cloves garlic, chopped

1 tablespoon cider vinegar

1 tablespoon ground cumin

2 teaspoons dried oregano

1 teaspoon salt, plus more to taste

1 teaspoon freshly ground black pepper, plus more to taste

2 cups Chicken Stock (page 225)

2 pounds pork butt

FOR THE NAVAJO FRY BREAD:
2 cups all-purpose flour

1/2 tablespoon baking powder

1 teaspoon salt

1 cup warm water

Vegetable oil, for frying

FOR THE GARNISH:
1/2 head romaine lettuce, shredded

3 plum tomatoes, chopped

1 onion, minced

Clean the chiles with a damp towel. Heat a dry cast-iron griddle or skillet over medium-high heat, and dry-roast the chiles for 30 to 60 seconds; do not allow them to blacken or scorch. Transfer the chiles to a bowl, cover with hot water, and soak for 20 minutes.

In a blender or food processor, combine the rehydrated chiles, the garlic, vinegar, cumin, oregano, salt, pepper, and 1 cup of the stock. Purée until relatively smooth. Place the pork in a nonreactive mixing bowl, and pour the marinade and the remaining cup of stock over the meat (or as much as necessary to cover the meat). Marinate in the refrigerator for at least 24 hours, and up to 3 days.

Place the pork and marinade in a large saucepan, and bring to a boil. Reduce the heat to a low simmer, cover, and cook about 2 hours, until the meat is fork tender. Remove the meat from the cooking broth, let cool slightly, and shred into thin strips. Scoop any fat from the pan with a spoon. Return the meat to the sauce, and reduce the liquid over medium-low heat until the meat is moist, but not soupy. Season with salt and pepper and keep warm.

To prepare the fry bread, combine the flour, baking powder, and salt in a large mixing bowl. Add the water and stir until all the dry ingredients are incorporated. Form into a mound and knead for about 2 minutes. Divide the dough into 4 portions and form into balls. Roll out the balls on a well-floured work surface into flat rounds at least 6 inches across and about 1/4 inch thick. Fill a large sauté pan with enough vegetable oil to come about 1 inch up the sides, and set over medium-high heat. When hot, fry the dough in the oil for 2 or 3 minutes on each side, until it puffs up and is golden brown. Drain on paper towels and serve immediately.

Place the carne adovado, lettuce, tomatoes, and onions in separate serving bowls. Place the fry bread in a cloth-lined basket covered with another cloth. Pass the dishes so that your guests can help themselves. For each serving, the carne adovado may be piled on the fry bread with the garnishes or folded like a taco.

SERVES 4

HERB-BRINED PORK ROAST
WITH GLAZED GINGERED CARROTS AND POTATO LATKES

Brining large cuts of meat helps them retain their moisture and juiciness and can also contribute interesting flavors. It's a technique that makes particular sense for preparing lean meat, such as pork loin. Latkes are a traditional Jewish side dish served at Hanukkah, and authentic latkes are made with matzo meal. Originally, before potatoes were introduced to Europe from the New World, they were made with buckwheat groats. Latkes are the prototypes for chic side dishes over the last few years as upscale restaurants have rediscovered and redefined potato fritters and potato pancakes; these now often include additional ingredients, such as corn, grated carrot, zucchini, and sun-dried tomatoes. You can try experimenting with these flavors if you like, but it's hard to beat a true classic.

FOR THE BRINE AND PORK ROAST:

2 cups warm water
1/2 cup sugar
1/4 cup white wine vinegar
1 onion, chopped
3 cloves garlic, sliced
2 tablespoons fresh thyme leaves
1 tablespoon fresh oregano leaves
1 tablespoon salt
1 tablespoons crushed black peppercorns
1 tablespoon dried red pepper flakes
1/2 tablespoon ground cumin
2 bay leaves, crumbled
1 double boneless pork loin roast
   (about 3 pounds), tied
1 tablespoon cornstarch
1 tablespoon cold water

FOR THE POTATO LATKES:

1 medium russet potato (about 12 ounces),
   peeled and coarsely grated
   (about 2 cups)
3 tablespoons matzo meal or fine fresh
   bread crumbs
2 eggs, beaten
1 tablespoon grated onion
1 teaspoon salt
1/2 teaspoon freshly ground black pepper
Pinch of nutmeg
1/4 cup vegetable oil
1 tablespoon minced fresh flat-leaf parsley,
   for garnish

Glazed Gingered Carrots (page 227)

To prepare the brine, place the water, sugar, vinegar, onion, garlic, thyme, oregano, salt, peppercorns, pepper flakes, cumin, and bay leaves in a mixing bowl; stir until the sugar has dissolved. Transfer to a large, resealable plastic bag or a nonreactive baking dish, and add the pork. Marinate in the refrigerator for at least 3 hours.

Preheat the oven to 450°F. Remove the roast from the brine, reserving the brine, and place fat-side up in a roasting pan. Pour enough of the brine into the pan to come 1/2 inch up the sides; reserve any remaining brine. Roast in the oven for 15 minutes. Reduce the oven to 350°F. and roast for about 1 1/4 more hours, or until the internal temperature reaches 150°F. Remove from the oven and let rest for 10 minutes before carving. (The internal temperature will rise to about 160°F.) Skim the fat from the pan juices and transfer the juices to a saucepan. Add enough of the reserved brine to make a total of 2 cups liquid. Combine the cornstarch and cold water, and stir into the brine. Bring to a boil, and boil for 3 minutes, stirring. Let cool; reheat just before serving.

To prepare the latkes, soak the potato in cold water for 20 minutes. Drain and place in a dish towel, wringing out as much liquid as possible. Place the matzo meal, eggs, onion, salt, pepper, and nutmeg in a mixing bowl, and whisk together. Add the potato and combine well. Heat the oil in a nonstick sauté pan or skillet. When hot, drop heaping tablespoons of the mixture into the oil, flattening each "cake" to a 1/4-inch thickness with the back of the spoon. Sauté over medium-high heat for 3 or 4 minutes per side, or until lightly browned. Cook in batches and keep warm.

Prepare the carrots according to the recipe on page 227.

Slice the roast pork and serve with the latkes and carrots. Spoon some of the sauce over the pork.

SERVES 4

MARINATED PORK SHOULDER STEAKS
WITH MUSHROOM AND SUN-DRIED TOMATO PASTA

An overlooked (an inexpensive) cut, pork shoulder steaks have just enough fat to produce a moist, flavorful steak. Marinating also helps to maximize their juiciness. By all means, use pork rib or loin chops for this recipe instead. The pasta side is simple, but full of flavor. It is a versatile dish that can also be served with veal or chicken, or enjoyed on its own. The spiral-shaped dried fusilli, resembling elongated springs, work well with either thin or thick sauces, or chunky ingredients, as here.

Place the water, vinegar, onion, garlic, thyme, cumin, peppercorns, bay leaves, cinnamon, and allspice in a mixing bowl, and thoroughly combine. Place the pork in a large baking dish or shallow bowl, cover with the marinade, and marinate in the refrigerator overnight.

Prepare the grill. Remove the pork from the marinade and bring to room temperature.

Meanwhile, prepare the pasta. Heat 2 tablespoons of the oil in a large saucepan, and add the onion. Sauté over medium-high heat for 3 or 4 minutes, until translucent. Add the remaining 2 tablespoons of oil and the mushrooms, season with salt and pepper, and sauté for 5 minutes longer. Add the wine and sun-dried tomatoes, cover, and simmer over low heat, until the liquid has been absorbed, about 20 minutes. Add the pine nuts and basil, if desired. Bring a saucepan of boiling salted water to a boil and add the fusilli. Cook al dente, according to the directions on the package; drain. Add the pasta to the saucepan and combine thoroughly.

While the pasta is cooking, grill the pork steaks over direct medium-high heat for 4 to 5 minutes per side for medium, or until the internal temperature reaches 155°F. Transfer to warm serving plates and serve with the pasta; sprinkle the Parmesan over the pasta.

SERVES 4

FOR THE MARINADE AND PORK:

4 cups warm water

$1/2$ cup white wine vinegar

1 onion, chopped

2 cloves garlic, minced

$1/2$ tablespoon dried thyme

$1/2$ tablespoon ground cumin

1 teaspoon black peppercorns

2 bay leaves

1 stick cinnamon

3 allspice berries

4 pork shoulder steaks or loin chops (about 8 ounces each and $3/4$ inch thick)

FOR THE PASTA:

4 tablespoons extra-virgin olive oil

1 cup sliced onion

8 ounces shiitake mushrooms, sliced

Salt and freshly ground black pepper to taste

$1/2$ cup dry white wine

$1/4$ cup diced sun-dried tomatoes (packed in oil)

$1/4$ cup pine nuts (optional)

$1/4$ cup chopped fresh basil leaves (optional)

1 pound fusilli pasta

6 tablespoons freshly grated Parmesan cheese

PORK

ROAST RACK OF PORK
WITH RED CABBAGE, APPLES, AND CRANBERRIES BRAISED IN RED WINE

This is a filling fall or winter recipe, especially if you choose to serve it with mashed potatoes. The cabbage side dish is adapted from a recipe by the late James Beard, who worked with Omaha Steaks for several years as a consultant. He enjoyed our steaks and wrote a number of recipes for us featuring them. It's best to use organically grown apples with the cabbage because we use them unpeeled in this recipe; alternatively, wash nonorganic apples as thoroughly as possible. Use any leftover pork for sandwiches.

FOR THE PORK:

2 tablespoons olive oil

1 tablespoon minced garlic

$\frac{1}{2}$ tablespoon dried rosemary

$\frac{1}{2}$ tablespoon dried thyme

$\frac{1}{2}$ tablespoon salt

1 teaspoon freshly ground black pepper

$2\frac{1}{2}$ pound rack of pork (4 ribs), chine bone removed and fat trimmed to $\frac{1}{8}$ inch

FOR THE BRAISED CABBAGE AND APPLES:

2 pounds red cabbage, outer leaves removed, cut in half, cored, and shredded

4 tablespoons butter ($\frac{1}{2}$ stick)

Salt and freshly ground black pepper to taste

1 cup red wine, such as Merlot

2 unpeeled, organic Granny Smith apples, diced, and cored

1 tablespoon red wine vinegar

2 tablespoons honey

$\frac{1}{2}$ cup dried cranberries

Preheat the oven to 450°F. To prepare the pork, place the oil, garlic, rosemary, thyme, salt, and pepper in a blender, and purée until smooth. Score the fat-side of the pork roast in a crosshatch pattern, and rub the pork roast all over with the puréed herb mixture. Place in a lightly oiled roasting pan and cover loosely with foil. Roast for 15 minutes. Reduce the oven to 350°F., and roast for about 1 hour longer, or until the internal temperature reaches 150°F. to 155°F. Remove the roast from the oven and let rest for 10 minutes before carving. (The internal temperature will rise to about 160°F.)

While the pork is roasting, soak the cabbage in a bowl of salted water for 5 minutes; drain well. Heat the butter in a large cast-iron skillet or heavy saucepan, add the cabbage, and wilt over medium-high heat for 5 minutes, tossing occasionally with wooden spoons as you would a salad. Season with salt and pepper and add the wine. Simmer over medium-low for 5 minutes. Add the apples, vinegar, and honey, stirring well. Cover and simmer over low heat for 20 minutes, add the cranberries, and stir well. Simmer for 25 to 30 minutes longer, until the cabbage and apple are tender.

Slice the pork roast, serving 1 rib chop per person. Serve with the braised cabbage and apples.

SERVES 4

LAMB

Lamb, described effusively by French King Louis XVI as "walking cutlets," is one of the most popular meats in the world, outside the United States (where Texans dismiss it as "wool on a stick"). It is true that in this country, lamb is the meat of choice for certain ethnic groups—such as those from the Middle East, the Mediterranean Basin, and the Indian subcontinent—but it has never struck a chord with the vast majority of Americans. The average American eats less than 2 pounds of lamb a year, compared with about 80 pounds of beef and 60 pounds of pork. In *The Great American Meat Book*, author Merle Ellis makes the interesting point that in "the rest of the world, lamb is one of the very few meats against which there are almost no prejudices. Beef is not consumed in India because of religious taboos. Pork is not eaten by followers of the traditional Jewish faith, nor are the hindquarters of beef. Moslems do not eat pork. But fewer prejudices exist against lamb than against any other meat. Lamb is, to some, a symbol of purity."

Many people have a bias against lamb because they think the flavor is "gamey." While this was sometimes true in the past of mutton (meat from older sheep), improvements in breeding and the predominance of younger, leaner animals on the market nowadays make this a non-issue. By definition, lamb is defined as meat from an animal less than a year old, unless it is labeled as "spring lamb," in which case it is three to five months old. Meat from sheep older than two years old goes by "mutton," a meat rarely seen in the United States, but much enjoyed elsewhere.

A great deal of lamb sold in stores in the United States is imported frozen from New Zealand (where sheep outnumber the human population twenty-fold) or Australia. Some sheep are raised domestically, dating as far back as the churros brought by the Spanish from Mexico in the 1600s. English breeds were introduced later on, sparking the Range Wars of the mid-1800s in the American West when cattle ranchers resisted the encroachment of sheep, which they viewed as a threat to limited grasslands. Some of the highest quality flocks these days are raised in the Northwest and in the high country of Colorado, where the climate allows grass to grow prolifically.

Try to find fresh lamb: it should have soft, white fat; stay away from any meat with hard or yellow fat. Trim most or all of the external fat before cooking because, unlike beef or pork, it is inedible. Lamb has little internal fat, or marbling—keeping it low in calories and cholesterol. But for the meat to retain its succulence, we recommend cooking it somewhere between medium-rare and medium. Overcooked lamb will become dry and tough. The delicately robust flavor of lamb has a hint of sweetness that combines magnificently with most seasonings and ingredients, especially herbs like rosemary and mint; spices, such as cumin; and that great flavor-enhancer, red wine.

GRILLED LAMB CHOPS
WITH TERRY'S GREEN BEAN SALAD AND LEMON-THYME VINAIGRETTE

The key to this simple and delicious dish is to buy the best quality lamb you can and to use really fresh beans. The onion and tomatoes are not essential in terms of flavoring the salad, but they do add a striking visual element. The same goes for the yellow wax beans, so if they are unavailable, just increase the amount of green beans. For best results, make the salad just before grilling the lamb and serve at room temperature. However, you can prepare it up to a few hours in advance and keep it chilled. This recipe is one of our favorites developed by Terry Finlayson, a talented New York–based food writer and former associate cookbook editor at the Culinary Institute of America. Serve with Garlic Oven Fries (page 34) or Herbed Roasted Potato Chips (page 111), if you like.

To prepare the glaze, put the mustard, honey, rosemary, and garlic in a bowl, and combine thoroughly. Set aside.

To prepare the vinaigrette, put the lemon juice, parsley, thyme, and garlic in a mixing bowl, and whisk together. Drizzle in the oil in a steady stream, whisking continuously until emulsified. Season with salt and pepper and keep refrigerated.

Prepare the grill.

Place both the green and wax beans in a steamer basket set over a saucepan of boiling salted water. Cover tightly and steam for 4 or 5 minutes, or until just tender. Drain in a colander and rinse under cold running water to stop the cooking process. Add the onion and tomatoes, if desired, and toss with the vinaigrette. Serve at room temperature.

Season the lamb chops with salt and pepper. Grill on the first side over direct medium-high heat for about 4 minutes. Turn the chops over, brush with the glaze, and grill for 4 to 5 minutes longer for medium-rare, about 6 minutes for medium, or to the desired doneness. Brush again with the glaze just before removing the chops from the grill. Transfer to warm serving plates and serve with the bean salad.

SERVES 4

FOR THE MUSTARD-ROSEMARY GLAZE:
¼ cup Dijon mustard

1 tablespoon honey

1 teaspoon minced fresh rosemary leaves

½ teaspoon minced garlic

FOR THE LEMON-THYME VINAIGRETTE:
3 tablespoons freshly squeezed lemon juice

1 tablespoon minced fresh flat-leaf parsley

2 teaspoons minced fresh thyme leaves

1 clove garlic, minced

½ cup olive oil

Salt and freshly ground black pepper to taste

FOR THE GREEN BEAN SALAD:
1 pound green beans, cut into 1½-inch lengths

8 ounces wax beans, cut into 1½-inch lengths

¼ red onion, thinly sliced (optional)

½ pint teardrop or cherry tomatoes, cut in half (optional)

FOR THE LAMB CHOPS:
4 lamb loin chops (about 6 ounces each and 1 inch thick), Prime or Choice grade

Salt and freshly ground black pepper to taste

ADOBO-ROASTED
MEXICAN LEG OF LAMB
WITH REFRIED BLACK BEANS AND MIXED GREEN
SALAD WITH CILANTRO-AVOCADO VINAIGRETTE

"Adobo" is a paste or sauce made with chiles, vinegar, and spices, and it's used in Mexico both as a sauce and a marinade—canned chipotle chiles, for example, are packed in an adobo sauce. It is more common to cook pork with adobo in Mexico, but lamb works at least as well. A bone-in leg of lamb can be used instead of boneless, but allow a little more time for the roast to cook. Expect leftover lamb for sandwiches, always a bonus when it comes to roasts.

FOR THE REFRIED BLACK BEANS:

1 pound dried black beans, soaked overnight and drained

3 tablespoons vegetable oil or lard

1 onion, diced

Salt and freshly ground black pepper to taste

4 ounces fresh goat cheese, crumbled

FOR THE ADOBO SAUCE AND LAMB:

3 dried ancho chiles, stemmed and seeded

3 dried guajillo chiles, stemmed and seeded

1 piece canela stick (about $1\frac{1}{2}$ inches long), or 1-inch stick cinnamon

1 bay leaf

3 cloves garlic, chopped

1 tablespoon cider vinegar

2 teaspoons ground cumin

1 teaspoon dried Mexican oregano

1 teaspoon salt

1 teaspoon freshly ground black pepper

$\frac{1}{2}$ cup Chicken Stock (page 225)

4 pounds boneless leg of lamb, Prime or Choice grade

FOR THE CILANTRO-AVOCADO VINAIGRETTE:

$\frac{1}{2}$ cup olive oil

$\frac{1}{4}$ cup freshly squeezed lime juice

$\frac{1}{4}$ cup fresh cilantro leaves

2 teaspoons grated lime zest

1 clove garlic, chopped

1 avocado, peeled, pitted, and cut into chunks

Salt and freshly ground black pepper to taste

FOR THE SALAD:

1 head romaine, thinly sliced crosswise

1 head radicchio, thinly sliced crosswise

2 pink grapefruit, peeled, sectioned and halved

1 red onion, thinly sliced

Place the beans in a large saucepan, and add enough water to cover by 2 to 3 inches. Simmer the beans $1\frac{1}{2}$ to 2 hours, until tender, skimming occasionally. Drain the beans, reserving both the beans and their cooking broth. About 20 minutes before serving, heat the oil in a cast-iron skillet and sauté the onion over medium heat for 6 or 7 minutes, until golden. Add half of the beans with about $\frac{1}{2}$ cup of their cooking liquid, season with salt and pepper, and mash with a potato masher until coarse. Gradually add more beans and cooking liquid, adding more liquid as necessary, until all of the beans are mashed. Continue cooking until the beans become fairly dry and season with salt and pepper to taste. Pour into a warmed serving bowl and garnish with the goat cheese.

To prepare the adobo sauce, heat a cast-iron skillet over medium-high heat, and dry roast the chiles for about 1 minute. Do not allow them to blacken or scorch. Place the chiles in a stainless-steel or glass bowl, cover with hot water, and let them soak for about 20 minutes. Grind the canela and bay leaf in a spice mill or coffee grinder, and transfer to a food processor. Add the chiles, garlic, vinegar, cumin, oregano, salt, pepper, and stock. Purée until smooth and paste-like, adding more stock if necessary. Press the mixture through a fine mesh strainer and set aside.

Preheat the oven to 400°F. Season the lamb with salt and pepper. Place in a roasting pan and roast in the oven for 10 minutes. Remove from the oven and reduce the heat to 325°F. Spread the adobo sauce over the entire leg of lamb, return the lamb to the oven, and continue to roast for 25 to 30 minutes for medium-rare, 35 to 40 minutes for medium, or to the desired doneness. Cover loosely with foil and let rest for 10 minutes before carving.

To prepare the vinaigrette, place the oil, lime juice, cilantro, zest, garlic, and half of the avocado in a blender, and purée until smooth. Season with salt and pepper. Place the romaine, radicchio, grapefruit, red onion, and remaining avocado in a salad bowl, and toss with the vinaigrette. Serve the lamb with the beans and salad.

SERVES 4

OMAHA STEAKS MEAT

The Noones of County Mayo's
Lamb Stew
and Irish Soda Bread with Golden Raisins

Call this a family recipe. Lamb is the most commonly cooked meat around the world, although you wouldn't know this living in the United States, where beef is king. Lamb stews, in particular, are common to most cuisines, including Ireland. Traditional Irish Soda Bread contains only flour, a little sugar, salt, baking soda, and buttermilk; this recipe is more of a typical American-Irish version—a little sweeter, and more scone-like, with the addition of raisins. A pint of Guinness would be an excellent choice of beverage to have on hand with this meal.

To prepare the stew, season the lamb with salt and pepper. Heat the butter and oil in a large Dutch oven or casserole over medium heat. Add the lamb and sauté for 8 to 10 minutes, stirring occasionally, until browned on all sides. (To avoid overcrowding the pan, you may wish to do this in 2 or 3 batches.) Remove the meat with a slotted spoon and set aside. Add the onions and sauté for about 5 minutes, until light golden. (Add a little olive oil to prevent them from sticking, if necessary.) Add the garlic and cook for 2 minutes longer. Add the sugar and toss lightly to coat the onion and garlic. Caramelize the onions and garlic over medium heat for 3 or 4 minutes, stirring occasionally. Return the lamb to the pan, sprinkle in the flour, and cook for 4 or 5 minutes longer, stirring continuously. Add the tomatoes, beef stock, and wine, and stir to deglaze the pan. Add the rosemary and bay leaves, cover, and simmer for about 1 hour, skimming the surface occasionally. Add the carrots, potatoes, and pearl barley and continue to simmer for 45 minutes to 1 hour, or until the lamb is fork tender. Add the peas in the last 5 minutes of cooking. Remove the rosemary sprigs and bay leaves before serving.

While the stew is cooking, prepare the bread. Preheat the oven to 350°F. Coat an 8-inch square baking pan or pie tin with 1 tablespoon of the melted butter and set aside. Combine the flour, sugar, baking powder, baking soda, and salt in a large mixing bowl. Add the raisins and toss to coat. In a separate mixing bowl, beat together the eggs, buttermilk, and 3 tablespoons of the remaining butter. Add to the flour mixture, beating well to combine. Pour the batter into the prepared pan and bake in the oven for about 1 hour, or until golden brown.

Remove the bread and brush the remaining tablespoon of butter over the surface. Ladle the lamb stew into serving bowls. Cut the warm bread into portions and serve immediately with the stew.

SERVES 4

For the Stew:
2 pounds high-quality lamb stew meat cut from the leg or shoulder, cubed

Salt and freshly ground black pepper to taste

2 tablespoons butter ($\frac{1}{4}$ stick)

1 tablespoon olive oil

2 onions, chopped

3 cloves garlic, minced

1 tablespoon sugar

2 tablespoons all-purpose flour

2 cups canned chopped tomatoes

1$\frac{1}{2}$ cups Beef Stock (page 225)

$\frac{1}{2}$ cup red wine

2 sprigs fresh rosemary

2 bay leaves

3 carrots, peeled and sliced

2 small russet potatoes (about 1 pound), peeled and cubed

$\frac{1}{2}$ cup pearl barley

1 cup frozen peas

For the Soda Bread:
5 tablespoons butter, melted

2$\frac{1}{2}$ cups all-purpose flour

$\frac{1}{4}$ cup sugar

2 teaspoons baking powder

$\frac{3}{4}$ teaspoon baking soda

1 teaspoon salt

1 cup golden raisins

2 eggs, beaten

1$\frac{1}{4}$ cups buttermilk

LAMB

RACK OF LAMB
WITH SPICY HOISIN GLAZE AND SAUTÉED GINGERED LONG BEANS

This unusual and delightful dish is one of our favorites. Although rack of lamb may not be common to Asian households, the flavor of lamb holds up well with the sweet-hot flavor of the traditional Chinese hoisin sauce and the gingered beans. Hoisin sauce (also known as Peking sauce) is found in many supermarkets and in Asian specialty stores. The tender, foot-long Chinese (or Thai) green beans make a striking presentation if cooked whole, but if they are unavailable, use haricots verts. For an additional side dish, serve rice or rice noodles.

To prepare the glaze, place the hoisin sauce, honey, soy sauce, sake, vinegar, chile sauce, and ginger in a small saucepan and bring to a simmer. Cook for about 15 minutes over low heat, until thickened. Keep warm.

To prepare the lamb, preheat the oven to 425°F. If you didn't buy the racks already frenched, do it yourself by trimming away a bit of the meat from the end of each rib for an attractive presentation. Season the racks with salt and pepper. Heat a large nonstick sauté pan over medium-high heat and sear the racks for 2 or 3 minutes on each side, or until browned. Transfer to a roasting pan, rib-side down, and brush with the warm glaze. Roast in the oven for 15 to 20 minutes for medium-rare, 20 to 25 minutes for medium, or to the desired doneness, glazing occasionally. When the roast is ready, remove from the oven, cover with foil, and let rest for about 10 minutes before slicing. Cut between the bones and serve 3 chops per person.

While the lamb is roasting, prepare the beans. Place the beans in a vegetable basket set over a saucepan of boiling water, cover tightly, and steam for about 5 minutes, or until just tender. Drain in a colander and rinse under cold running water to stop the cooking process. Heat the peanut oil in a large sauté pan and add the shallots, garlic, and ginger. Sauté over medium heat for 2 or 3 minutes, until softened. Add the beans, season with salt, and toss to combine. Cover and cook over low heat to just reheat the beans. Serve immediately.

Layer the lamb chops on one side of a warm serving plate. Drizzle some of the warmed hoisin glaze over the chops. Pile the green beans beside the chops.

SERVES 4

FOR THE SPICY HOISIN GLAZE:
$1/2$ cup hoisin sauce

$1/4$ cup honey

$1/4$ cup soy sauce

$1/4$ cup sake

2 tablespoons rice vinegar

2 tablespoons Asian (or other) chile sauce with garlic

$1 1/2$ tablespoons peeled and minced fresh ginger

FOR THE LAMB:
2 racks of lamb with 6 ribs each (3 to $3 1/2$ pounds total), Prime or Choice grade, trimmed of fat and frenched

Salt and freshly ground black pepper to taste

FOR THE GINGERED LONG BEANS:
$1 1/2$ pounds Chinese long beans, left whole or cut into $1 1/2$-inch pieces, or haricots verts, trimmed

$1 1/2$ tablespoons peanut oil

2 shallots, minced (about $1/4$ cup)

2 cloves garlic, minced

2 teaspoons peeled and minced fresh ginger

NAVAJO LAMB FAJITAS
WITH MINT AND TOMATO SALSA

132

Ever since the 17th century when early Spanish settlers moved northward from Mexico into the American Southwest, the livestock they brought with them—cattle, sheep, and hogs—have remained the backbone of the region's cuisine. The Navajo people of the Four Corners territory took up sheep farming extensively, and while it is rare to see fajitas made with lamb in restaurants, this recipe draws on the classic Tex-Mex tradition of fajitas and proves that it is our loss. The mint in the familiar tomato salsa gives the classic flavor combination of lamb and mint a new dimension. Serve with Refried Black Beans (page 128) or white rice, if you wish.

FOR THE MARINADE AND LAMB:
¼ cup red wine vinegar
2 tablespoons olive oil
1 tablespoon Worcestershire sauce
4 cloves garlic, minced
1 jalapeño chile, seeded and minced
½ teaspoon salt
½ teaspoon freshly ground black pepper
½ teaspoon ground cumin
½ teaspoon dried oregano
½ teaspoon minced fresh rosemary leaves
1½ pounds lamb loin, Prime or Choice grade, cut into thin strips about 3 inches long and ½ inch wide

FOR THE MINT SALSA:
2 cups seeded and diced plum tomatoes
¼ cup minced onion
1 jalapeño chile, seeded and minced
½ cup thinly sliced fresh mint leaves
2 teaspoons freshly squeezed lemon juice
Salt to taste

FOR THE FAJITAS:
2 tablespoons olive oil
2 onions, thinly sliced lengthwise
1 red bell pepper, seeded and sliced lengthwise
1 green bell pepper, seeded and sliced lengthwise
Salt and freshly ground black pepper to taste
Juice of 1 lime
8 large flour tortillas

To prepare the marinade, place the red wine vinegar, olive oil, Worcestershire sauce, garlic, jalapeño, salt, pepper, cumin, oregano, and rosemary in a nonreactive mixing bowl, and combine thoroughly. Add the lamb and toss to coat well. Cover the bowl and marinate in the refrigerator for at least 4 hours, and preferably overnight.

Meanwhile, prepare the salsa. Place the tomatoes, onion, chile, mint, lemon juice, and salt in a mixing bowl, and toss gently to combine. If necessary, season with additional salt and lemon juice to taste. Keep refrigerated.

To prepare the fajitas, remove the lamb from the marinade, drain, and let sit at room temperature for about 30 minutes. Heat the oil in a large cast-iron skillet. Pat the meat dry with paper towels, and then sauté over medium-high heat for 2 to 3 minutes, stirring frequently, until browned. Remove and keep warm. Add the onions and bell peppers to the pan, season with salt and pepper, and sauté 5 or 6 minutes, until softened. Return the meat to the pan, stir in the lime juice, cover, and keep warm.

Warm the tortillas on a griddle or in a dry skillet. Place in a basket and cover with a towel to keep warm. Place the meat and vegetables on a warm serving platter (or on a heated cast-iron fajita pan) and let your guests help themselves by filling 2 tortillas each and rolling them up. Pass the tortillas and mint salsa on the side.

SERVES 4

OMAHA STEAKS MEAT

SOUTH AFRICAN
LAMB MEATBALLS
WITH APRICOT SAUCE AND CINNAMON COUSCOUS

South Africa has a sizable Indian community, dating back to the earliest trading days. The combination of flavors in this simple dish typify the culinary influence of this ethnic group. Asian stores carry such ingredients as curry powder, garam masala, and turmeric. Try Bulghur Pilaf (page 92) or basmati rice as an alternative to the couscous—also an African dish, albeit from the other (northern) end of the continent. The meatballs also make a great dish for buffets and parties, or as an appetizer, served with the sauce.

To prepare the lamb meatballs, heat 1 tablespoon of the olive oil and the butter in a sauté pan, and sauté the onion over medium heat about 5 minutes, or until light golden. Add the garlic, ginger, chile, curry powder, garam masala, turmeric, cayenne, salt, and pepper, and sauté while stirring for 2 or 3 minutes longer, until fragrant. Remove from the heat and let cool slightly. Gently combine the mixture with the ground lamb and form into 16 meatballs. Heat the remaining tablespoon of olive oil in a large sauté pan over medium heat. Add the meatballs (in batches if necessary) and sauté for about 5 minutes, or until browned on all sides. Remove and drain on paper towels.

To prepare the sauce, heat the olive oil and butter in a small sauté pan, and sauté the onion over medium heat about 5 minutes, or until golden. Add the coriander, cumin, curry powder, and cayenne, and sauté for 2 minutes longer, until fragrant. Add the stock, lemon juice, jam, sugar, lemon zest, and dried apricots, and simmer for 5 minutes. Add the meatballs, cover, and simmer for about 20 minutes, or until cooked through, stirring occasionally. Season with salt and pepper and keep warm. If necessary, skim any fat from the surface of the sauce before serving.

To prepare the couscous, bring the chicken stock to a boil in a saucepan. Reduce the heat to low and add the couscous and cinnamon stick. Cover and cook for 5 minutes. Turn off the heat and let the couscous stand for 10 minutes. Remove the cinnamon stick, fluff the couscous with a fork, add the lemon zest, and season with salt and pepper. Transfer to warm serving plates and serve the meatballs and sauce over the couscous.

SERVES 4

FOR THE LAMB MEATBALLS:
2 tablespoons olive oil
1 tablespoon butter
2 onions, diced
4 cloves garlic, minced
2 tablespoons peeled and grated fresh ginger
1 serrano chile, seeded and minced
2 tablespoons curry powder
2 tablespoons garam masala
2 teaspoons turmeric
1/4 teaspoon cayenne
Salt and freshly ground black pepper to taste
2 pounds high-quality ground lamb

FOR THE APRICOT SAUCE:
1 tablespoon olive oil
1 tablespoon butter
1 onion, chopped
1 teaspoon ground coriander
1 teaspoon ground cumin
1 teaspoon curry powder
1/4 teaspoon cayenne
1/2 cup Chicken Stock (page 225)
1/4 cup freshly squeezed lemon juice
1/4 cup apricot jam
2 tablespoons light brown sugar
1 teaspoon minced lemon zest
8 dried apricots, chopped

FOR THE COUSCOUS:
1 1/4 cups Chicken Stock (page 225)
1 1/2 cups couscous
1 stick cinnamon
1 teaspoon minced lemon zest
Salt and freshly ground black pepper to taste

LAMB

JIM COLEMAN'S FENNEL-DUSTED
ROAST LAMB RIB-EYE
WITH FRESH SAUERKRAUT AND ASPARAGUS

Here is a simple and delicious low-fat, low-sodium, and heart-healthy recipe from Jim Coleman, Executive Chef at Philadelphia's famous Rittenhouse Hotel. Jim is the author of The Rittenhouse Cookbook *(Ten Speed Press), as well as the host of a nationally syndicated radio show and a PBS television series, both about food. It's a good thing he has energy to spare! Jim's inspiration for this recipe came from the natural affinity of lamb for fennel, and the fact that sauerkraut is his favorite way of cooking cabbage. You can substitute green or white cabbage for the red, if you prefer. "Lamb loin can sometimes be hard to find," says Jim. "So ask your butcher to do it for you, or buy a rack of lamb and trim the loin* rib-eye section from the bone.*"*

FOR THE LAMB:

1 1/2 pounds boneless rack of lamb rib-eye, Prime or Choice grade, trimmed of fat

1 tablespoon finely ground fennel seed

1 tablespoon olive oil

FOR THE SAUERKRAUT:

5 cups cored and shredded red cabbage (1 small red cabbage)

1 cup white wine vinegar

1 tablespoon caraway seed

1 tablespoon finely ground fennel seed

1 tablespoon sugar

32 spears asparagus

4 sprigs fresh oregano, for garnish

Preheat the oven to 400°F. Cut the lamb into 4 equal portions and dust with the fennel. Heat the olive oil in an ovenproof sauté pan or skillet, and when hot, sear the lamb for 1 or 2 minutes on each side, until brown. Transfer the pan to the oven and roast for about 10 minutes for medium-rare, about 12 minutes for medium, or to the desired doneness.

Meanwhile, to prepare the sauerkraut, place the cabbage, vinegar, caraway, fennel, and sugar in a saucepan and bring to a simmer over medium heat. Cover and cook for 8 to 10 minutes, or until the cabbage is tender. Place the asparagus in a vegetable basket set over a saucepan of boiling salted water, cover tightly, and steam for 8 to 10 minutes, or until tender.

Arrange 8 asparagus spears across each serving plate, with the tips at the edge of the plate. Place the sauerkraut in a mound in the center of each plate, covering the stem-ends of the asparagus. Slice each portion of lamb loin and arrange the slices against the sauerkraut so that the lamb is leaning a little against it. Garnish with the oregano.

SERVES 4

Although you can buy red pepper jelly at gourmet food stores or Southwestern food markets and mail-order sources, it is well worth the effort of making your own. It will keep for two or three months if refrigerated in a jar or airtight container, and can be used as a sandwich spread, as well as an all-purpose condiment. Its sweetness and heat contrast well with the herbed lamb and the plain, delicately nutty quinoa; for notes on quinoa, see page 50.

FOR THE RED PEPPER JELLY:

2 fresh New Mexico or Anaheim red chiles, or 6 red jalapeño chiles, roasted, peeled, seeded, and chopped (page 228)

2 red bell peppers, roasted, peeled, seeded, and chopped (page 228)

1 cup cider vinegar

2 cups sugar

Juice of 1 small lime

2 teaspoons dry pectin

1 tablespoon warm water

FOR THE QUINOA SALAD:

1 1/2 cups quinoa, rinsed and drained

1/2 tablespoon olive oil

1 1/2 tablespoons extra-virgin olive oil

1 1/2 tablespoons balsamic vinegar

1/2 cup pine nuts, toasted (page 229)

2 tablespoons minced fresh oregano leaves

2 tablespoons minced fresh basil leaves

Salt and freshly ground black pepper to taste

FOR THE HERB-CRUSTED LAMB:

1/4 cup minced fresh flat-leaf parsley

3 tablespoons minced fresh thyme leaves

2 tablespoons minced fresh rosemary leaves

1 1/2 tablespoons finely sliced chives

1 cup fresh bread crumbs

1/3 cup plus 3 tablespoons olive oil

2 racks of lamb with 8 ribs each (about 4 pounds total), Prime or Choice grade, trimmed of fat and cut in half

Salt and freshly ground black pepper to taste

3 tablespoons Dijon mustard

To prepare the jelly, place the chiles, bell peppers, and 1/4 cup of the vinegar in a blender. Purée until smooth and transfer to a saucepan. Add the remaining vinegar, the sugar, and lime juice, and bring to a boil. Reduce the heat to medium-low and simmer for 20 minutes. Mix the pectin with the water and stir to dissolve. Add to the saucepan, stir well, and return to a boil. Remove from the heat immediately and let cool. Keep refrigerated.

Dry the rinsed quinoa on paper towels. Heat the olive oil in a saucepan, add the quinoa, and stir over medium heat for 1 minute, until coated. In a separate saucepan, bring 2 3/4 cups of water to a boil and pour over the quinoa. Return to a boil, partially cover the pan, and reduce the heat to low. Simmer for 12 minutes, until al dente, and then drain any excess water. Transfer to a mixing bowl and let cool. Combine the extra-virgin olive oil and vinegar, and add to the bowl. Add the pine nuts, oregano, and basil, combine thoroughly, and season with salt and pepper. Chill in the refrigerator.

Preheat the oven to 425°F. To prepare the crust, place the parsley, thyme, rosemary, and chives in a mixing bowl, and combine well. Add the bread crumbs and 1/3 cup of the oil, and mix thoroughly. Heat 2 tablespoons of the remaining oil in a cast-iron skillet and season the lamb racks with salt and pepper. Sear one lamb rack over medium-high heat for 5 or 6 minutes, until browned on all sides; use tongs to hold the rack upright to sear the ends. Remove the lamb and let cool. Add the remaining tablespoon of oil to the skillet and repeat for the other lamb rack. Spread the mustard over the meat side of the racks and press the crust into the mustard so it adheres. Place the lamb racks in a large roasting pan, bone-side down, and roast in the oven for 20 to 25 minutes for medium-rare, until the internal temperature reaches 140°F., or about 30 minutes for medium, reaching a temperature of 150°F. Remove from the oven, loosely cover with aluminum foil, and let rest for 5 minutes.

Cut the lamb into double chops and serve 2 per plate. Spoon some of the jelly next to the lamb and serve with the salad.

SERVES 4

Roghan Josh (literally "red stew") is a traditional dish from the Kashmir region of northwestern India. It is rich and usually prepared for special occasions, such as weddings or other celebratory feasts. Its distinctive color and aromatic flavor is given by the spice paste called "masala" in Indian cuisine. Naan bread is the large, puffy wheat bread traditionally baked on the sides of special tandoori (hot clay) ovens, but a version of the real thing can also be made in a home oven. For a shortcut, serve the curry with basmati rice (page 227) instead of the naan bread.

To prepare the naan bread, place both flours, the salt, baking powder, baking soda, and sugar in a mixing bowl, and form a well in the center. In a separate bowl, combine the egg and yogurt, and then add to the dry ingredients. Begin by mixing with a wooden spoon and then work together with your hands until a dough forms. Knead by hand for 5 minutes, work in the diced butter, and knead for 5 minutes longer, or until smooth and satiny. Form into a ball, transfer to a lightly oiled bowl, and cover with a damp towel. Let rise in a warm place for about 1 1/2 hours. Preheat the oven to 475°F. Divide the dough into 4 balls and let rise again for 30 minutes.

About 10 to 15 minutes before you are ready to serve, bake the naan. Place 2 baking sheets in the oven to warm. Sprinkle flour on a work surface and flatten each piece of dough into a circle about 6 inches across and about 1/8 inch thick. Pull one side so it forms a teardrop shape, about 8 or 9 inches in length. Place the naan on the hot baking sheets, and bake in the oven for about 5 minutes, or until puffy. Keep warm.

To prepare the spice paste, place the almonds, ginger, garlic, chile powder, paprika, cumin, coriander, fennel, cinnamon, peppercorns, cardamom, cloves, and bay leaves in a blender, and add enough water to form a paste. Purée until smooth and set aside.

To prepare the lamb, heat the oil and butter in a saucepan, and add the onion. Sauté over medium-high heat for 5 minutes, or until soft. Add the reserved spice paste and mix well. Add the lamb and sauté, while stirring, for 3 or 4 minutes, until browned. Add the tomatoes, salt, and 1/2 cup of water, and reduce the heat to medium. Cook for 15 minutes, uncovered, stirring occasionally. Cover, reduce the heat to low, and simmer for about 45 minutes, or until the lamb is completely tender. Add a little more water if necessary. Just before serving, remove the pan from the heat, and stir in the yogurt. Garnish with the cilantro and serve with the naan bread.

SERVES 4

FOR THE NAAN BREAD:
1 1/4 cups all-purpose flour
6 tablespoons whole-wheat flour
1/2 teaspoon salt
1/2 teaspoon baking powder
1/2 teaspoon baking soda
1/4 teaspoon sugar
1 egg, beaten
1/2 cup plain yogurt
1 tablespoon diced butter

FOR THE SPICE PASTE:
1/4 cup blanched almonds
1 tablespoon peeled and chopped fresh ginger
2 teaspoons chopped garlic
1 tablespoon cayenne or pure red chile powder
1 tablespoon paprika
2 teaspoons ground cumin
1/2 tablespoon ground coriander
1 teaspoon ground fennel seeds
1/2 teaspoon ground cinnamon
1/4 teaspoon black peppercorns, crushed
6 cardamom pods, crushed
3 whole cloves
2 bay leaves, crumbled

FOR THE LAMB:
2 tablespoons olive oil
2 tablespoons butter (1/4 stick)
1 onion, diced
1 1/2 pounds boneless leg of lamb or shoulder meat, Prime or Choice grade, cubed
1 1/2 cups canned crushed tomatoes
Salt to taste
2 cups plain yogurt
2 tablespoons minced cilantro, for garnish

LAMB

MUSHROOM-STUFFED AND JUNIPER-MARINATED
LEG OF LAMB
WITH CREAMED BUTTERNUT SQUASH AND CRANBERRIES

Here is an ideal, comforting recipe for fall or winter. The elongated pear-shaped butternut squash—a winter variety with sweet, orange-colored flesh—makes for an attractive presentation. No mention of this recipe would be complete without acknowledging the contribution of Lynn Gagné. Lynn is a freelance Chicago-based food stylist who works with food photographer Tim Turner, and her suggestions and fine-tuning helped make a great recipe even better.

For the marinade, place the wine, juniper, peppercorns, allspice, rosemary, and bay leaves in a large baking dish. Add the butterflied lamb (unrolled) and marinate in the refrigerator for 6 to 8 hours, and preferably overnight; turn occasionally.

To prepare the stuffing, heat the oil in a sauté pan, and sauté the garlic and scallions over medium-high heat for 2 minutes. Add the mushrooms and sauté for 3 or 4 minutes longer, stirring often. Add the wine and cook for 3 minutes, or until the mushrooms are tender. Season with salt and pepper and add the rosemary. Let cool. Remove the lamb from the marinade; strain the marinade into a saucepan and bring to a boil. Reduce the heat, simmer for 3 or 4 minutes, and set aside. Season the inside of the leg with salt and pepper, add the stuffing evenly, roll up the meat, and tie it.

Preheat the oven to 350°F. Heat the 1 tablespoon of oil in a roasting pan set over high heat. Add the lamb and sear until browned on all sides. Transfer to the oven and roast for 50 to 60 minutes, or until the internal temperature reaches 125°F., basting with the marinade often. Raise the oven temperature to 450°F. for 10 to 15 minutes to brown the exterior, or until the lamb is medium-rare (140°F.); cook for about 10 minutes longer for medium (150°F.), or to the desired doneness. Remove the lamb from the oven and let rest for 10 minutes before carving.

Rehydrate the cranberries in warm water for 20 minutes. Cut the squash into chunks and place in a vegetable basket set over a large saucepan of boiling water. Cover tightly and steam for 25 to 30 minutes, or until tender. Place the milk, butter, and sugar in a saucepan and heat through, stirring to dissolve the sugar. (Do not let boil.) Transfer the cooked squash to a mixing bowl and mash, adding the heated milk mixture in increments. Add the nutmeg and season with salt and pepper. Drain the cranberries and stir in.

Spoon the squash onto serving plates and serve with the lamb and potato galette, if desired. Spoon the pan juices over the lamb.

SERVES 4

FOR THE MARINADE AND LAMB:

1 bottle red wine, preferably Cabernet Sauvignon

8 juniper berries, crushed

8 black peppercorns, crushed

1/8 teaspoon ground allspice

1 sprig fresh rosemary

2 bay leaves

4 pounds boneless leg of lamb, Prime or Choice grade, butterflied and trimmed of fat

1 tablespoon olive oil

FOR THE STUFFING:

1 tablespoon olive oil

3 cloves garlic, minced

2 tablespoons finely sliced scallions

8 ounces shiitake mushrooms, finely diced

1/4 cup white wine

Salt and freshly ground black pepper to taste

1/2 tablespoon chopped fresh rosemary leaves

FOR THE CREAMED BUTTERNUT SQUASH AND CRANBERRIES:

3 tablespoons dried cranberries or dried sour cherries

1 butternut squash (about 2 pounds), peeled, cut in half, and seeded

2 tablespoons milk

2 tablespoons butter (1/4 stick), softened

1 teaspoon light brown sugar

1/3 teaspoon ground nutmeg

Salt and freshly ground black pepper to taste

Potato Galette (page 73) (optional)

LAMB

LAMB MOUSSAKA
WITH MIXED GREEN GARDEN SALAD AND FRENCH DRESSING

140

Moussaka, the casserole-style dish made with layers of ground lamb, eggplant, and cheese sauce, is popular in a number of countries in the eastern Mediterranean. Although associated with Greece in particular, moussaka was inherited from the Ottoman Turks who ruled the country for several centuries. Buy eggplants that feel heavy for their size, and make sure the skin is not wrinkled—a sign of age (which will make them more bitter). Sprinkling the eggplant with salt makes them "sweat" and draws out any bitterness they may have; it also reduces the amount of oil they can absorb.

FOR THE MOUSSAKA:

2 large eggplants (about 14 ounces each), sliced crosswise

Salt to taste

10 tablespoons olive oil

1 large onion, diced

1 1/2 pounds high-quality ground lamb

1 1/2 cups diced tomatoes

2 tablespoons tomato paste

1/2 cup red wine, preferably Merlot or Cabernet Sauvignon

1/2 teaspoon ground cinnamon

1 teaspoon Herbes de Provence or dried mixed herbs

Freshly ground black pepper to taste

FOR THE CHEESE SAUCE:

2 cups milk

1/2 cup chopped onion

2 cloves garlic, minced

1 stick butter (8 tablespoons)

1/4 cup all-purpose flour

1 teaspoon Dijon mustard

1 cup grated Cheddar cheese (about 4 ounces)

2 eggs, beaten

1/4 teaspoon ground nutmeg

Salt and freshly ground black pepper to taste

Julia's Green Summer Salad with Papa's Real French Vinaigrette (page 32) (optional)

To prepare the moussaka, place the eggplant in layers in a colander, sprinkling each layer with salt. Cover with plastic wrap and let sit over a plate for 30 minutes. Rinse the eggplant under cold running water and drain. Heat 2 tablespoons of the olive oil in a large saucepan, add the onion, and sauté over medium-high heat for 7 or 8 minutes, or until lightly golden brown. Add the ground lamb, tomatoes, tomato paste, red wine, cinnamon, and herbs, and season with salt and pepper. Cook for 10 minutes longer, stirring often.

Heat 2 tablespoons more of the oil in a large sauté pan and add one-quarter of the eggplant slices in a single layer. Sauté over medium heat for 3 or 4 minutes on each side, or until just tender and light brown. Remove with a slotted spoon and drain on paper towels. Add another 2 tablespoons of the oil and repeat with one-quarter more of the eggplant. Repeat with the remaining eggplant and oil. Set aside.

To prepare the sauce, heat the milk in a saucepan, add the onion and garlic, and bring just to a boil. Turn off the heat and let sit for 30 minutes. Strain, reserving the milk. Preheat the oven to 350°F. Melt the butter in a saucepan and add the flour, stirring constantly over low heat for 2 minutes. Gradually add the infused milk and continue to stir. When completely blended in, bring to a boil over medium heat, stirring continuously. When the sauce thickens, remove from the heat and stir in the mustard and cheese. Whisk in the eggs and season with the nutmeg, salt, and pepper.

Line a large, lightly oiled, ovenproof baking dish with one-third of the cooked eggplant and arrange one-third of the meat mixture on top. Cover with one-third of the sauce. Repeat these layers twice, ending with the sauce. Cover the baking dish, and if using foil, make sure it is not touching the moussaka. Transfer to the oven and bake for 45 minutes. Remove the cover and bake for 15 minutes more. Remove from the oven and let cool for 5 minutes. Serve on warm plates, with the salad served in bowls on the side, if desired.

SERVES 4

HUBERT'S WHOLE-GRAIN MUSTARD–GLAZED LAMB LOIN WITH TARRAGON INFUSION

Hubert Keller, the owner/chef of San Francisco's acclaimed four-star Fleur de Lys restaurant, finds that lamb is one of his most popular entrées. This recipe pairs lamb with tarragon—an herb like rosemary and thyme—to which the meat is particularly well suited. French cuisine calls for tarragon far more extensively than other types of cooking. In his cookbook, The Cuisine of Hubert Keller *(Ten Speed Press), Hubert explains that the technique of marinating meat by seasoning and sealing in plastic wrap requires less oil than the traditional method, and he believes the direct contact of the meat with the herbs and spices results in a more intense flavor.*

Place the lamb on a large piece of plastic wrap and brush with the oil. Rub the tarragon between your fingers to bruise it and release the oils. Place half of the tarragon on the bottom of the lamb, half on the top. Enclose the lamb tightly in the plastic wrap and refrigerate for at least 6 hours, and preferably overnight.

To prepare the glaze, whisk the cream in a chilled bowl until stiff peaks form. Fold in the egg yolk and mustard, and refrigerate.

Preheat the oven to 425°F. Unwrap the lamb and bring to room temperature. Discard the tarragon sprigs and season the lamb with salt and pepper. Heat the olive oil in a large, ovenproof skillet set over high heat. Add the lamb, sear for about 2 minutes on each side, remove from the skillet, and reserve.

To prepare the sauce, heat the oil in a large sauté pan, and add the onion, carrots, garlic, and thyme. Sauté over medium-high heat for 3 to 4 minutes. Place the seared lamb on top of the vegetables, using them as a bed. Transfer the skillet to the oven for 7 to 8 minutes for medium-rare. Remove from the oven and place the lamb on a small plate inverted onto a larger plate, so the juices run off and the lamb stays crisp. Cover with aluminum foil and keep warm. Return the skillet and vegetables to the stovetop and add the wine. Reduce the liquid over high heat until almost dry. Combine the stock and cornstarch in a bowl. Add the stock, half of the sliced tarragon, and any lamb juices from the plate to the skillet. Adjust the seasonings if necessary and keep the infusion warm.

Preheat the broiler. Slice each lamb loin into 6 slices, place on a baking sheet, and top each slice with 1/2 teaspoon of the mustard glaze. Place under the broiler for 1 1/2 minutes, or until the glaze turns golden brown. Place 3 lamb slices in the center of each warm serving plate, and spoon the infusion around the lamb. Serve with the orzo, if desired.

SERVES 4

FOR THE LAMB:

2 lamb loins or rib-eyes (about 12 ounces each) from 2 racks, Prime or Choice grade, trimmed of fat

1 tablespoon olive oil

4 large sprigs fresh tarragon

FOR THE GLAZE:

3 tablespoons heavy cream

1 egg yolk

1/2 tablespoon whole-grain mustard

Salt and freshly ground black pepper to taste

1 tablespoon olive oil

FOR THE TARRAGON SAUCE:

2 tablespoons olive oil

1 onion, cut in half lengthwise and then cut into 1/2-inch slices

2 carrots, cut into 1/2-inch slices

2 cloves garlic, lightly crushed

1 sprig fresh thyme

1/2 cup red wine, such as Merlot or Cabernet Sauvignon

2 cups Chicken Stock (page 225) or Veal Stock (page 225)

2 teaspoons cornstarch

1 1/2 tablespoons sliced fresh tarragon

Orzo (page 97) (optional)

LAMB

This combination of lamb and rosemary, sweet parsnips, and a picante-herbed tomato sauce stands as a winner. Even if you already love parsnips, you'll find these roasted ones outrageously good. Parsnips, relatives of carrots, were cultivated by the Romans. They were popular as a staple starch because of their natural sugars during medieval times—an era when sweeteners were scarce and the potato had not yet been discovered in the New World. The zesty tomato sauce is similar to the one that accompanies veal (page 57), but the heat comes from a different type of chile, and the addition of herbs here adds more complex flavor tones.

To prepare the lamb, pour the olive oil into a baking dish and add the rosemary and garlic. Mix well and add the lamb chops. Rub both sides of the lamb with the mixture and marinate in the refrigerator for 2 hours, turning occasionally.

To prepare the sauce, heat the oil in a sauté pan and add the onion and garlic. Sauté over medium heat for 3 minutes and add the pepper flakes. Sauté for 2 minutes longer. Add the tomatoes, basil, oregano, and lemon juice; season with salt and pepper. Reduce the heat to low and simmer for 10 minutes, stirring occasionally. Add a little more lemon juice or water if necessary. Let cool; reheat just before serving.

Preheat the oven to 350ºF. To prepare the parsnips, pour the oil into a large roasting pan and heat in the oven for 2 or 3 minutes, until the oil is warm. Remove the pan from the oven and add the parsnips, turning to coat thoroughly with the oil. Return to the oven and roast for 30 minutes. Remove from the oven and pour the honey over the parsnips. Using tongs, turn the parsnips so they are coated, and return to the oven for 5 to 10 minutes longer. Remove from the oven, season with salt and pepper, and keep warm.

Prepare the grill. Remove the lamb from the marinade, draining any excess oil and rosemary leaves, and season with salt and pepper. If using a charcoal grill, add 4 of the rosemary sprigs to the fire just before grilling. Place the lamb chops over direct medium-high heat, and cover the grill for 2 minutes to allow the chops to be infused with the aroma of the smoldering rosemary. Uncover the grill and cook for about 4 or 5 minutes longer on the first side. Turn over and cook for about 4 minutes on the other side for medium-rare, about 5 minutes for medium, or to the desired doneness. Transfer 2 chops to each serving plate and serve with the warm sauce. Arrange the parsnips next to the lamb, and garnish them with the remaining rosemary sprigs, placed upright.

SERVES 4

FOR THE LAMB:

1/2 cup extra-virgin olive oil

1 tablespoon fresh rosemary leaves or 1 teaspoon dried

1 teaspoon minced garlic

8 bone-in lamb loin chops (about 5 ounces each and 1 1/2 inches thick), Prime or Choice grade

Salt and freshly ground black pepper

FOR THE SPICY TOMATO SAUCE:

2 tablespoons olive oil

1/4 cup minced white onion

1/2 tablespoon minced garlic

1 teaspoon dried red pepper flakes

1 1/2 pounds plum tomatoes, blanched, peeled, seeded, and chopped (page 228)

1/2 tablespoon minced fresh basil leaves

1/2 tablespoon minced fresh oregano leaves

2 tablespoons freshly squeezed lemon juice

Salt and freshly ground black pepper to taste

FOR THE HONEY-ROASTED PARSNIPS:

3 tablespoons olive oil

1 1/2 pounds parsnips, peeled and cut into 1-inch chunks

2 tablespoons honey

Salt and freshly ground black pepper to taste

8 fresh rosemary sprigs, for garnish

LAMB

FOUR CORNERS LAMB STEW
WITH CAMPFIRE SKILLET CORN BREAD

Native American communities raise large flocks of sheep and cattle in the Four Corners region, an area that encompasses parts of Utah, Arizona, New Mexico, and Colorado. This recipe incorporates many distinctive ingredients that have been staples of the region for centuries, such as corn, chiles, and squash. Jerusalem artichokes (also called sunchokes) are tubers in the sunflower family and native to North America. Available mainly through the winter, they have a slightly sweet, nutty flavor and a crisp texture. You can substitute potatoes (another native to the Americas) and turnips. Adding some soaked wood chips to the coals on the grill will convince anyone that this stellar corn bread was cooked over a campfire!

FOR THE LAMB STEW:

1 cup all-purpose flour
2 tablespoons pure red chile powder
1 teaspoon salt
$\frac{1}{2}$ teaspoon freshly ground black pepper
$1\frac{1}{2}$ pounds high-quality stewing lamb, cut into 1-inch chunks
5 tablespoons olive oil
1 onion, diced
2 carrots, peeled and diced
4 Jerusalem artichokes, peeled and diced
1 cup fresh corn kernels (about 2 small ears)
$\frac{1}{2}$ cup diced zucchini
5 plum tomatoes, diced
1 tablespoon chopped fresh rosemary leaves
1 tablespoon chopped fresh thyme leaves
1 tablespoon chopped fresh oregano or marjoram leaves
$3\frac{1}{2}$ cups Lamb Stock, Veal Stock, or Beef Stock (page 225), or water
1 cup dry white wine

FOR THE CORN BREAD:

2 small ears fresh corn, husked
2 teaspoons olive oil
2 cups cornmeal
1 cup all-purpose flour
2 teaspoons salt
$\frac{1}{2}$ tablespoon baking powder
1 teaspoon baking soda
3 large eggs
1 cup buttermilk
1 cup half-and-half
$\frac{1}{2}$ cup melted butter, plus 1 tablespoon chilled butter
3 tablespoons chopped fresh cilantro leaves

To prepare the lamb, place the flour on a large plate and mix in the chile powder, salt, and pepper. Dredge the lamb in the mixture and shake off any excess. Heat 3 tablespoons of the oil in a large saucepan set over medium-high heat. When hot, add the lamb and, stirring occasionally, sear for 5 minutes, until browned. In a large sauté pan, heat the remaining 2 tablespoons of oil, and add the onion, carrots, and Jerusalem artichokes. Sauté over medium heat for 5 minutes. Stir in the corn, zucchini, tomatoes, rosemary, thyme, and marjoram. Transfer to the saucepan containing the reserved lamb, add the stock and wine, and reduce the heat to low. Cover the pan and simmer for 45 to 50 minutes, or until the meat is tender. Adjust the seasonings.

While the stew is cooking, prepare the grill. To prepare the corn bread, brush the corn with the oil, and grill over indirect medium heat for about 15 minutes, turning frequently, until lightly browned on all sides. Remove from the grill, and when cool enough to handle, cut the kernels from the cobs. (Alternatively, see instructions on roasting corn in a pan on page 229.) Place the cornmeal, flour, salt, baking powder, and baking soda in a mixing bowl, and combine well. In a separate bowl, whisk together the eggs, buttermilk, half-and-half, and the $\frac{1}{2}$ cup of butter, and pour into the cornmeal mixture. Fold in the grilled corn and cilantro. Set a dry cast-iron skillet over medium-high heat for 2 minutes to heat through. Add the remaining tablespoon of butter, let melt, and then pour in the batter. Place the skillet on the grill over indirect medium heat. Cook for 30 to 35 minutes, or until golden brown and a toothpick inserted in the center comes out clean. Cut into wedges.

Serve the lamb stew in serving bowls, with the corn bread on side plates.

SERVES 4

SPICE-RUBBED LAMB STEAKS
WITH BROWN RICE AND CUCUMBER SALAD AND POMEGRANATE SAUCE

Here's an intriguing idea: a sauce containing pomegranate juice and brewed coffee! The combination may sound strange, but the deep fruity and roasty tones balance the spiced lamb to perfection. The unassertively flavored salad provides the ideal foil for both. The sauce is inspired from a recipe created by Jimmy Schmidt, the award-winning chef at The Rattlesnake Club in Detroit. Pomegranates are native to Iran, where they symbolize fertility, and they were much prized in ancient Egypt and Greece. It's too bad they are so difficult to peel and eat, otherwise their juiciness and sweet-tart flavor would make them a far more popular fruit. Brown rice is highly nutritious due to the high-fiber bran coating that gives it color—also the same part that is removed to make white rice.

To prepare the salad, place the rice and 2¹/₂ cups of water in a saucepan, and bring to a boil. Reduce the heat to a simmer, cover, and cook for about 45 minutes, until the rice is tender and has absorbed the water. (Add a little more water if necessary.) Transfer to a mixing bowl and let cool. Add the cucumber, carrot, bell pepper, scallions, lemon juice, parsley, oil, and cumin to the cooled rice. Season with salt and pepper and combine thoroughly. Chill in the refrigerator and serve cold.

To prepare the sauce, place the stock, pomegranate juice, shallots, orange juice, honey, sugar, peppercorns, parsley, and marjoram in a saucepan. Bring to a boil and reduce over medium heat for about 50 to 60 minutes, or until ³/₄ cup remains. Strain the sauce through a fine-mesh strainer into a clean saucepan. Bring the sauce to a simmer over medium-high heat and season with salt and pepper. Reduce the heat to low and keep warm.

To prepare the steaks, place the thyme, peppercorns, allspice, and chile powder in a spice mill and grind finely. Season the lamb with salt to taste, and rub with the ground spice mixture. Heat the oil in a sauté pan, and sauté over medium-high heat for 4 to 5 minutes per side for medium-rare, about 6 minutes per side for medium, or to the desired doneness. Remove the lamb and keep warm. Add the wine, stir to deglaze the pan, and bring to a boil. Reduce the liquid by one-half and add the reserved pomegranate sauce and the coffee. Reduce the sauce for 8 to 10 minutes, or until thick enough to coat the back of a spoon.

Spoon about 2 tablespoons of the sauce onto one side of each serving plate. Place a lamb steak next to the sauce and garnish with a thyme sprig. Serve the rice salad on the other side of the lamb.

SERVES 4

FOR THE SALAD:
1 cup short-grain brown rice
¹/₂ cup finely diced, peeled, and seeded cucumber
¹/₄ cup peeled, grated, and chopped carrot
¹/₃ cup finely diced yellow bell pepper
2 scallions, sliced (about ¹/₃ cup)
2 tablespoons freshly squeezed lemon juice
1 tablespoon minced fresh flat-leaf parsley
1 tablespoon extra-virgin olive oil
¹/₂ teaspoon ground cumin
Salt and freshly ground white pepper to taste

FOR THE POMEGRANATE SAUCE:
1 cup lamb stock or Beef Stock (page 225)
1¹/₂ cups pomegranate juice
¹/₄ cup minced shallots
¹/₄ cup freshly squeezed orange juice
1 tablespoon honey
1 tablespoon light brown sugar
1 teaspoon crushed black peppercorns
1 tablespoon minced fresh flat-leaf parsley
1 teaspoon minced fresh marjoram leaves
Salt and freshly ground black pepper to taste

FOR THE LAMB STEAKS:
1 tablespoon fresh thyme leaves
¹/₂ tablespoon black peppercorns
¹/₄ teaspoon ground allspice
¹/₂ tablespoon pure red chile powder
1 tablespoon safflower or vegetable oil
4 lamb sirloin or round steaks (6 or 7 ounces each and about 1 inch thick), Prime or Choice grade, trimmed of fat
¹/₄ cup dry red wine
2 tablespoons freshly brewed coffee
4 fresh thyme sprigs, for garnish

LAMB MEDALLIONS
NIÇOISE-STYLE WITH A ZUCCHINI, TOMATO, AND RICE CASSEROLE

The cuisine of the Nice area and the Mediterranean coastal region of Provence is famous for its bright, clean flavors, due in part to the use of fresh herbs, olives, tomatoes, zucchini, and, of course, wine. This dish incorporates many ingredients from that region for a highly flavorful and easy-to-prepare meal. You can make the sauce and casserole in advance and cook the lamb loin at the last minute, if preferred. This recipe works equally well with the more readily available lamb chops instead of boneless lamb rib-eye (see also the introductory note on page 134).

FOR THE ZUCCHINI, TOMATO, AND RICE CASSEROLE:

2 tablespoons olive oil

2 cloves garlic, minced

1 pound zucchini, sliced into ¼-inch-thick rounds

1 tablespoon minced fresh flat-leaf parsley

1 tablespoon minced fresh basil leaves

½ teaspoon minced fresh thyme leaves

Salt and freshly ground black pepper to taste

2 cups cooked long-grain white rice (page 227)

6 plum tomatoes, peeled and sliced into ¼-inch-thick rounds

¼ cup freshly grated Parmesan cheese

¼ cup Chicken Stock (page 225)

¼ cup heavy cream

FOR THE LAMB MEDALLIONS:

1½ pounds boneless rack of lamb rib-eye, Prime or Choice grade, trimmed of fat

Salt and freshly ground black pepper to taste

2 tablespoons olive oil

1 onion, thinly sliced

3 cloves garlic, minced

6 plum tomatoes, peeled, seeded, and diced

2 sprigs fresh rosemary leaves

1 sprig fresh thyme leaves

½ cup Chicken Stock (page 225)

½ cup dry red wine

¼ cup niçoise olives, pitted

Preheat the oven to 350°F. To prepare the casserole, heat the olive oil in a sauté pan, add the garlic, and sauté over medium heat for 3 minutes. Add the zucchini, parsley, basil, thyme, and season with salt and pepper. Cook for 4 or 5 minutes, or until softened. Lightly oil an 8-inch baking or gratin dish. Season the rice with salt and pepper, and spread half over the bottom of the dish. Place half of the zucchini mixture in an even layer over the rice. Top with half of the tomatoes in an even layer. Sprinkle with half of the Parmesan cheese, and repeat the layers of rice, zucchini, tomatoes, and cheese. Combine the stock with the cream, pour over the casserole, and bake in the oven for 30 minutes.

While the casserole is baking, prepare the medallions. Slice the lamb loin into 8 equal portions and flatten them so that they are approximately the same size. Season with salt and pepper. Heat 1 tablespoon of the olive oil in a skillet and sauté the medallions over medium-high heat for about 2 minutes on each side for medium-rare or 2½ to 3 minutes on each side for medium. Remove the lamb and keep warm. Reduce the heat to medium, add the remaining olive oil to the skillet, and sauté the onion and garlic for about 5 minutes, or until light golden. Add the tomatoes, rosemary, and thyme, and cook for 2 or 3 minutes, until almost dry. Add the stock, wine, and olives, and stir to deglaze the pan. Add any juices from the sautéed lamb to the sauce. Season with salt and pepper and cook for about 15 minutes, until slightly thickened. Return the lamb to the pan and cook for about 1 minute, or until thoroughly warmed. Remove the rosemary and thyme from the sauce before serving.

To serve, pool the sauce on one side of each warm serving plate and top with 2 lamb medallions. Slice the casserole and place a helping next to the sauce.

SERVES 4

MUSTARD-HONEY
RACK OF LAMB
WITH ROASTED ROSEMARY POTATOES AND MINT SAUCE

This is a simple rendition of a timeless, comforting, yet elegant classic. It should serve to remind us that 20 miles can be an enormous distance in culinary terms: while the French have been known to look down their noses at mint sauce as an accompaniment for lamb, across the Channel in Britain, lamb and mint sauce are inseparable. This is not, it should be said, the only difference between the two cuisines! The potatoes make a wonderfully fragrant side dish for most meats. Serve with glazed carrots (page 227), ratatouille (page 26), or steamed asparagus, if desired.

To prepare the lamb, place the mustard, honey, molasses, white wine, and garlic in a bowl, and thoroughly combine. Score the lamb between each chop with a sharp knife and place in a baking dish. Cover with the marinade and rub in. Let marinate in the refrigerator for 3 or 4 hours, turning occasionally.

Preheat the oven to 350°F. Place the potatoes in a baking dish or roasting pan with at least a 1-inch rim. Toss with the garlic, olive oil, and rosemary, and season with salt and pepper. Roast on the top shelf in the oven for about 1 hour, tossing occasionally, or until the potatoes are golden and crisp.

Meanwhile, remove the lamb from the refrigerator and scrape off the marinade. Transfer to a roasting pan and bring to room temperature, about 30 minutes. Roast the lamb on the center rack in the oven for about 30 minutes, until the internal temperature reaches 140°F. for medium-rare, about 35 minutes for medium or 150°F., or to the desired doneness. Remove from the oven and let rest for 5 minutes, loosely covered with aluminum foil. (The internal temperature will rise by about 5°F.)

To prepare the sauce, chop the mint and sugar together and transfer to a bowl. Add the vinegar, water, and oil, and whisk until the sugar is dissolved. Pour into a serving boat.

Cut the lamb racks into chops and serve 3 or 4 per plate. Serve with the potatoes and pass the mint sauce at the table.

SERVES 4

FOR THE MUSTARD-HONEY RACK OF LAMB:
3/4 cup Dijon mustard

6 tablespoons honey

2 tablespoons dry white wine

3 cloves garlic, minced

2 racks of lamb with 6 ribs each (3 to 3 1/2 pounds total), Prime or Choice grade, trimmed of fat and cut in half

FOR THE ROSEMARY ROASTED POTATOES:
1 1/2 pounds small, unpeeled Yukon Gold or red potatoes, quartered

1 tablespoon minced garlic

3 tablespoons extra-virgin olive oil

2 teaspoons dried rosemary

Salt and freshly ground black pepper to taste

FOR THE MINT SAUCE:
2 cups packed fresh mint leaves

1/4 cup sugar

1/3 cup white wine vinegar

3 tablespoons hot water

2 tablespoons olive oil

Tagine is the name not only for this type of spiced Moroccan lamb dish, but also for the special covered pot in which it is traditionally cooked. Tagines have come into vogue lately, and there are unlimited versions. Their common essence is the slow braising method, the aromatic spice mixture, and the addition of dried fruit for sweetness and texture. Some of the ingredients here have assertive flavors, but they combine very well and become mellowed by the braising process. You can substitute couscous for the rice, if you prefer. (See the recipe on page 133.)

FOR THE TAGINE-BRAISED LAMB:

3 tablespoons olive oil

1 onion, finely diced

1 tablespoon minced garlic

1 teaspoon ground coriander

1 teaspoon ground cumin

$1/2$ teaspoon ground dried ginger

$1/2$ teaspoon salt

$1 1/2$ teaspoons freshly ground black pepper

1 stick cinnamon

1 cup all-purpose flour

$1 1/2$ pounds boneless lamb shoulder, Prime or Choice grade, trimmed of fat and cubed

2 cups Beef Stock (page 225)

1 cup pitted prunes

$1/2$ cup dried apricots

$1/2$ cup pitted green olives

$1/4$ cup pine nuts

2 apples, such as Granny Smith, peeled, cored, and cut into wedges

1 tablespoon chopped lemon zest

1 tablespoon honey

1 tablespoon finely sliced fresh mint leaves

FOR THE RAISIN-CINNAMON RICE:

1 cup white long-grain rice

2 tablespoons butter ($1/4$ stick)

$1/2$ white onion, finely diced

1 carrot, peeled and finely diced

$1/2$ stalk celery, finely diced

$1/4$ teaspoon salt

2 teaspoons ground cinnamon

$1/4$ cup raisins

4 fresh mint sprigs, for garnish

To prepare the lamb, heat the olive oil in a large saucepan and add the onion and garlic. Sauté over medium-high heat for 2 minutes. Add the coriander, cumin, ginger, salt, $1/2$ teaspoon of the pepper, and the cinnamon. Combine the flour and the remaining teaspoon of pepper on a plate, and dredge the lamb in this mixture. Shake off any excess, and add the lamb to the pan, stirring well. Sauté until the lamb is well coated by the ingredients in the pan. Add the stock and stir to deglaze the pan. Bring to a boil, cover, and reduce the heat to low. Simmer the tagine for 45 minutes. Remove the lid and stir in the prunes, apricots, and olives. Cover and continue to simmer for 15 minutes. Add the pine nuts, apples, lemon zest, honey, and mint, and simmer for 15 minutes longer, or until the lamb is completely tender.

Place the rice in a strainer and rinse under cold running water until the water no longer looks milky. Drain and set aside. Heat 1 tablespoon of the butter in a saucepan, and sauté the onion, carrot, and celery over medium-low heat for 8 minutes, stirring occasionally. Add the rice, salt, cinnamon, raisins, and $2 1/2$ cups of water, and bring to a boil over high heat. When the water is reduced to the level of the rice, reduce the heat to low, and cover the pan. Simmer for about 15 minutes, or until the water is absorbed, stirring occasionally. Remove the pan from the heat and let sit for 5 minutes. Add the remaining tablespoon of butter and fluff with a fork just before serving. Spoon a bed of the rice onto warm serving plates and serve the tagine on top of, or next to, the rice. Garnish with the mint.

SERVES 4

SHASHLIK: MIDDLE EASTERN
LAMB SHISH KABOBS
WITH CURRIED RICE

"Shashlik" is the southern Russian word for "shish kabob." In turn, "shish" is the Turkish word for skewer, with "kabob" or "kebab" referring to the main ingredient: meat. As the etymology suggests, this dish is a specialty of the region that includes Armenia, the Russian Caucasus, and Turkey. Shish kabobs invariably are marinated, and there are many variations on the marinade for the lamb. Some prefer a red wine, oil, and herb mixture; others, yogurt; and more modern, if less authentic, recipes call for a mixture of soy sauce and oil. Substitute button mushroom caps, eggplant cubes, cherry tomatoes, or apple slices for any of the vegetables called for in this recipe. Serve with a salad, if desired. You can also broil the kabobs.

FOR THE SHISH KABOBS:

1/2 cup olive oil

Juice of 1 large lemon

2 cloves garlic, minced

1/2 tablespoon minced fresh oregano leaves

1/2 teaspoon salt

1/2 teaspoon freshly ground black pepper

1 1/2 pounds boneless leg of lamb meat or lamb shoulder, Prime or Choice grade, trimmed of fat and cut into 24 cubes (about 1 inch each)

1 green bell pepper, cut in half and seeded

1 orange, peeled and quartered

16 pearl onions

FOR THE CURRIED RICE:

2 tablespoons butter (1/4 stick)

2 tablespoons olive oil

1 1/2 cups basmati rice

2 tablespoons curry powder, or to taste

1 cup Chicken Stock (page 225) or water

1 cup canned coconut milk

1/3 cup raisins

1/4 teaspoon salt

4 sprigs fresh oregano, for garnish

Place the olive oil, lemon juice, garlic, oregano, salt, and pepper in a mixing bowl, and whisk together. Add the lamb and marinate for at least 4 hours, and preferably overnight.

Prepare the grill. Soak 8 bamboo skewers (preferably 12 inches long) in water for at least 10 minutes so they won't burn up on the grill, and then drain. (Alternatively, use metal skewers.)

Meanwhile, prepare the rice. Heat the butter and oil in a large saucepan, and when the butter is melted, add the rice and curry powder. Cook the rice over medium-low heat, stirring frequently, for 5 minutes, or until translucent. Add the 1 cup of water, the stock, coconut milk, raisins, and salt, and bring to a boil. Reduce the heat to low, cover, and simmer for about 15 minutes, until the rice has absorbed the liquid. Remove from the heat, keep covered, and let sit for 5 minutes. Fluff with a fork before serving.

While the rice is cooking, remove the lamb from the marinade and set aside, reserving the marinade. Cut the bell pepper halves into 8 pieces and cut each orange quarter crosswise into 2 wedges. Add the bell pepper, orange, and onions to the marinade. Gently distribute to make sure each ingredient is coated in the marinade, and let sit only until the lamb reaches room temperature. Thread the ingredients onto each skewer, alternating them in the following order: lamb, pearl onion, lamb, bell pepper, orange, lamb, pearl onion, bell pepper, lamb. (Each skewer should have 4 pieces of lamb, 2 pieces of bell pepper, 2 pearl onions, and 1 piece of orange.) Grill the kabobs over medium heat for about 5 or 6 minutes on each side, until the lamb is cooked and the onions begin to brown.

Spoon the rice onto warm serving plates. Place 2 skewers on each plate next to the rice and garnish with the oregano.

SERVES 4

BLACK MESA SHEPHERD'S PIE
WITH RED CHILE–MASHED POTATO TOPPING

We have already mentioned the little-known tradition of raising sheep in the Southwest, a legacy of the Spanish settlement centuries ago (see page 132). In this modern interpretation of an English classic, the mashed potato topping is given a tingling twist with the addition of a little red chile. We included a similar recipe, only using beef instead of lamb, in our earlier book, Beef for All Seasons. *Because we have received such glowing reports about that recipe, we feel we would be depriving you if we didn't present this version. Traditionally, Shepherd's Pie is an ideal recipe for using leftover lamb that is then minced. For a more traditional, plainer topping, mash boiled potatoes with butter and milk and sprinkle in $1/2$ cup of grated Cheddar cheese. Spread the potatoes over the lamb and bake in the oven for 30 minutes.*

Heat the olive oil in a saucepan, and sauté the garlic, onion, leeks, and carrots over medium-high heat for 5 minutes. Add the lamb and sauté for 7 or 8 minutes longer, stirring frequently, or until the lamb is well browned on all sides. Season with salt and pepper. Add the flour and cook for 1 more minute. Add the stock, wine, tomato paste, Worcestershire sauce, and dried herbs. Reduce the heat to medium and cook, uncovered, for 30 minutes, stirring occasionally. Stir in the peas and remove from the heat. Transfer the mixture to a large, ovenproof, glass baking dish, preferably 9 or 10 inches square, and let cool while preparing the mashed potatoes.

Place the potatoes in a saucepan of salted water and bring to a boil. Reduce the heat and simmer for about 20 minutes, until tender. Drain and transfer to a mixing bowl. Meanwhile, melt the butter with the milk in a sauté pan, and bring to a boil. Add the garlic and corn. Reduce the heat and simmer for 3 minutes. Sprinkle in the chile powder and stir. Strain the mixture, reserving the corn separately from the liquid. With an electric mixer or a wire whisk, whip the potatoes while drizzling in the reserved cooking liquid, adding a little more milk as needed. Stir in the reserved corn, the cilantro, and honey, and season with salt.

While the potatoes are cooking, preheat the oven to 350°F.

With a fork, spread the mashed potatoes evenly over the lamb mixture, making a ridged pattern on the top of the potatoes with the fork. Bake in the oven for 25 minutes. Place under the broiler and broil the top of the potatoes until golden brown, about 2 to 3 minutes. Let cool slightly before serving.

SERVES 4 TO 6

FOR THE SHEPHERD'S PIE:
2 tablespoons olive oil

2 cloves garlic, minced

1 large onion, sliced

2 leeks, white and green parts, sliced and chopped (about 2 cups)

2 carrots, sliced

$1/2$ pounds high-quality ground lamb

Salt and freshly ground black pepper to taste

1 tablespoon all-purpose flour

1 cup Chicken Stock (page 225) or vegetable stock

$1/2$ cup white wine

3 tablespoons tomato paste

2 teaspoons Worcestershire sauce

1 teaspoon Herbes de Provence or dried mixed herbs

1 cup frozen peas

FOR THE RED CHILE–MASHED POTATO TOPPING:
$1/2$ pounds potatoes, peeled and chopped

2 tablespoons butter ($1/4$ stick)

1 cup milk

3 cloves garlic, minced

$1/2$ cups fresh corn kernels (about 2 ears)

$1/2$ tablespoon pure red chile powder

$1/2$ tablespoon chopped fresh cilantro leaves

1 teaspoon honey

Salt to taste

LAMB

MACADAMIA NUT-COCONUT
CRUSTED LAMB CHOPS
WITH BLACK BEAN SALSA AND STAR ANISE-RED WINE SAUCE

One of the most delicious preparations we have ever enjoyed for lamb chops was created by Honolulu's Alan Wong, and here we have adapted the crusting recipe that he uses at his restaurant. If ever you needed an excuse to visit Hawaii, then his restaurant (conveniently called Alan Wong's) is it. You can find more of his acclaimed recipes in his cookbook, The New Wave Luau *(Ten Speed Press). Alan serves the lamb with an Asian-accented ratatouille, and if you prefer to go in that direction instead of the salsa, try our ratatouille recipe on page 26. Star anise is a Chinese seed unrelated to anise, though both remarkably share the same distinctive essential oil. In this sauce, it perfectly accents the tropical flavors of other ingredients.*

To prepare the salsa, place the beans, mango, bell pepper, lime juice, pepper flakes, and salt in a mixing bowl, and gently combine. Chill in the refrigerator.

Preheat the oven to 325°F.

To prepare the sauce, heat the butter in a small saucepan and add the onion. Sauté over medium heat for 3 minutes, or until translucent. Add the peppercorns and star anise, and sauté for 2 minutes longer. Add the wine and reduce until 1/4 cup remains. Add the stock and reduce until 1/2 cup remains. Strain the sauce into a clean saucepan and keep warm.

To prepare the lamb chops, spread the coconut flakes and macadamias on a baking sheet, and toast in the oven for 4 minutes, or until lightly golden, stirring occasionally. Let cool. Prepare the broiler. In a mixing bowl, combine the honey and mustard, and add the toasted coconut, garlic, thyme, and pepper. Heat the oil in a sauté pan and add the chops. Sauté over medium-high heat for 3 minutes per side, or until almost medium-rare. Remove from the pan and spread the crust on one side of each chop. Transfer to a roasting pan and broil for 2 to 3 minutes, or to the desired doneness.

Serve the potatoes in the center of warm serving plates. Lean the chops against the potatoes, with the rib-ends up. Spoon 2 tablespoons of the sauce around the chops on each plate and serve with the salsa.

SERVES 4

FOR THE SALSA:
1 1/2 cups drained cooked black beans (page 226) or canned
1 cup diced mango (about 2 small mangoes)
1/4 cup finely diced red bell pepper
Juice of 1 lime
1 teaspoon dried red pepper flakes
Salt to taste

FOR THE SAUCE:
2 tablespoons butter (1/4 stick)
1/2 cup finely diced onion
12 black peppercorns
3 star anise
1 cup red wine, preferably Cabernet Sauvignon
2 cups Lamb Stock or Beef Stock (page 225)

FOR THE LAMB CHOPS:
1/2 cup dried coconut flakes
1/2 cup macadamia nuts, finely chopped
1/2 cup honey
2 tablespoons Dijon mustard
3/4 teaspoon minced garlic
1/2 tablespoon minced fresh thyme leaves
1/2 teaspoon freshly ground white pepper
1 tablespoon vegetable oil
12 lamb rib chops (2 to 3 ounces each), Prime or Choice grade

Roasted Garlic Mashed Potatoes (page 49) (optional)

VENISON AND RED GAME MEAT

Game was the first meat enjoyed by humans millennia ago, and it seems ironic that today, it is underused, little understood, and exotic or mysterious to most people. As a consequence, many individuals are missing out on a wonderful range of flavors and textures, and we hope this chapter goes a little way to redress this balance. We include here recipes for venison (deer and elk), wild boar, ostrich, rabbit, buffalo, and goat. Venison, ostrich, and buffalo are finding their way onto more and more American restaurant menus. Rabbit, like deer, was hunted by Native Americans centuries ago for clothing and tools as well as food. Goat is particularly favored by certain ethnic groups, such as West Indians, Mexicans, and Greeks, for whom Easter is incomplete without a celebratory roast.

Wild game in general is associated by many people with a "gamey" flavor—strong and unpleasant. But with proper harvesting, cleaning, storing, and aging techniques, good-quality game shows fairly robust, yet understated, flavor tones, and little or no gameyness. It is also very healthful—typically, game meat contains no additives or hormones, is lean and generally low in cholesterol, and can be cooked in just the same way as other meats.

Venison—derived from the Latin, "venare," to hunt—is a finely grained, dense, dark-red meat with a subtle yet intense flavor that includes herbaceous tones from open-range grazing. Most of the venison available in stores or restaurants is farm-raised, as it is illegal to sell privately hunted meat unless inspected by the United States Department of Agriculture (USDA). Significant amounts of Axis venison are imported from New Zealand. Years ago, venison was considered a fall or winter meat, reflecting the hunting season, but domesticated herds now mean that it is available year-round.

Marinades are important for tenderizing wild (as opposed to farm-raised) animals and for minimizing any assertive meaty flavor. Because some of the venison we used for recipe testing was privately hunted, we call for overnight marinating, but by all means, minimize the time to 2 or 3 hours if using the farm-raised product. Tender cuts of venison should be cooked only to medium-rare at most, otherwise this already lean meat will dry out and turn gray. Any fat should be trimmed, if it isn't already, as it may have an unpleasant taste.

For notes on other types of game meat used in this chapter, see the individual recipe introductions. For those not fond of the idea of game meat, or who live in parts of the country where it is hard to find in stores, the good news is that you can substitute other red meats for all of the recipes in this chapter. Beef can be substituted for venison, ostrich, and buffalo. Pork can replace wild boar, chicken is interchangeable with rabbit, and lamb makes a fine alternative to goat. Of course, the flavors will not be exactly the same, but with these substitutions, you will not go far wrong.

VENISON STEAKS
WITH WILD RICE AND ROASTED CORN–SERRANO SALSA

This recipe uses Denver leg of venison, a boned and trimmed portion of the hind leg that is every bit as tender as a traditional steak cut. It is often available prepackaged at butchers that offer game meats. This marinade works well with any venison steak, and if using wild game rather than farm-raised, we recommend marinating the meat overnight. Note that the wild rice should also soak overnight. If you choose not to or you are short of time, the rice will need to cook for at least double the length of time called for here.

To prepare the marinade, place the oil, vinegar, shallots, peppercorns, garlic, cumin, salt, and cayenne in a shallow baking dish and add the venison. Marinate in the refrigerator for 4 to 5 hours or overnight, turning once or twice.

To prepare the salsa, cut the kernels from the ears of corn and transfer to a mixing bowl. Add the chiles, bell pepper, cilantro, olive oil, lime juice, garlic, onion, salt, and pepper, and thoroughly combine. Let chill.

Prepare the grill.

To prepare the rice, place 4 cups of water in a saucepan. Drain and rinse the rice under cold running water, and add to the pan. Bring to a boil, cover, and reduce the heat to a low. Simmer for 15 to 20 minutes, or until the rice has burst open and is soft. (The exact cooking time will depend on the freshness of the rice.) Drain the rice and season with the salt and pepper. Add the butter and fluff with a fork until the butter is melted.

While the rice is cooking, remove the venison steaks from the marinade, shaking off any excess, and grill over direct medium-high heat for 3 to 4 minutes per side for medium-rare, 4 to 5 minutes per side for medium, or to the desired doneness. Transfer to warm serving plates, garnish the venison with the chiles, and serve with the wild rice and salsa.

SERVES 4

FOR THE MARINADE AND VENISON:
- 3/4 cup olive oil
- 1/4 cup sherry vinegar
- 2 tablespoons finely diced shallots
- 1 tablespoon crushed black peppercorns
- 1 teaspoon minced garlic
- 1 teaspoon ground cumin
- 1 teaspoon salt
- 1/2 teaspoon cayenne
- 4 venison steaks (Denver leg) (5 ounces each and about 3/4 inch thick)

FOR THE ROASTED CORN–SERRANO SALSA:
- 3 ears corn, roasted (page 229)
- 2 serrano chiles or 1 jalapeño, seeded and minced
- 2 tablespoons finely diced red bell pepper
- 2 tablespoons minced fresh cilantro leaves
- 2 tablespoons extra-virgin olive oil
- 1 1/2 tablespoons freshly squeezed lime juice
- 1 1/2 tablespoons roasted garlic (page 229)
- 1 1/2 tablespoons minced red onion
- Salt and freshly ground black pepper to taste

FOR THE WILD RICE:
- 3/4 cup wild rice, soaked overnight and drained
- 1 teaspoon salt
- 1/2 teaspoon freshly ground black pepper
- 1 tablespoon butter, diced
- 4 red serrano or other small fresh red chiles, for garnish

VENISON PEPPER STEAKS
WITH DRIED CHERRY COMPOTE AND
ROASTED GARLIC HASH BROWNS

This recipe makes a great campfire meal if you prepare the compote ahead and bring it with you. Although you would lose some of the peppercorns, the venison would taste wonderful grilled or cooked over a fire. It is very important that you use a tender cut of venison. If you have any doubt about the tenderness, marinate the meat overnight and pound it gently before cooking; use the recipe from the Marinated Grilled Venison (page 157) or the Venison Goulash (page 158). If you like, add some chopped Granny Smith apples, raisins, or cranberries to the cherries.

FOR THE DRIED CHERRY COMPOTE:

2 tablespoons vegetable oil

$1/2$ cup chopped sweet onion

$3/4$ cup dried cherries (about 3 ounces), cut in half

$1/2$ cup apple cider

$1/4$ cup apple cider vinegar

2 tablespoons applejack brandy or Calvados (optional)

1 tablespoon minced orange zest

FOR THE ROASTED GARLIC HASH BROWN POTATOES:

2 pounds russet potatoes, peeled and coarsely diced

3 tablespoons olive oil

$1/2$ onion, diced

Salt and freshly ground black pepper to taste

1 tablespoon butter

16 cloves roasted garlic (page 229)

FOR THE VENISON PEPPER STEAKS:

4 venison loin steaks (about 8 ounces each and $3/4$ inch thick)

Salt to taste

$1/4$ cup coarsely ground black pepper

2 tablespoons olive oil

To prepare the compote, heat the oil in a small saucepan and sauté the onion over medium heat for about 5 minutes, until softened. Add the cherries, cider, vinegar, brandy, and orange zest and simmer for about 15 minutes, until the cherries are soft and the compote has thickened. Remove from the heat and let cool to room temperature.

To prepare the hash browns, bring a saucepan of lightly salted water to a boil. Add the cubed potatoes and blanch for 5 minutes. Drain and set aside. Heat the oil in a large skillet and sauté the onion over medium heat for 4 minutes. Add the blanched potatoes, season with salt and pepper, and sauté about 3 minutes longer, stirring often. Reduce the heat to medium-low, add the butter and roasted garlic cloves, and cover the pan. Continue to sauté for about 12 to 15 minutes, until the potatoes are softened, stirring often. Raise the heat to medium and sauté for about 5 minutes longer, or until dark golden brown. Adjust the seasonings and serve immediately.

While the potatoes are cooking, pat the steaks dry, season with salt, and rub the pepper into the steaks. Cover with cheesecloth or plastic wrap and pound them lightly with the flat side of a meat cleaver or a rolling pin for about 30 seconds to ensure that the pepper adheres. Heat the olive oil in a large heavy skillet and sear the steaks over medium-high heat for about 2 minutes on each side, or until browned. Reduce the heat to medium, and continue to sauté for about 2 minutes on each side for medium-rare, about 3 minutes on each side for medium, or to the desired doneness.

Place each steak to one side of a warm serving plate. Pour any pan juices over the steaks and top with a spoonful of the cherry compote. Pile the hash browns next to the steaks and pass the remaining compote at the table.

SERVES 4

MARINATED GRILLED VENISON
WITH BACON-BARLEY PILAF

Barley, an important crop since the dawn of man, is probably best known as the primary ingredient of beer. It's also used in soups and grain breads, and its nutty flavor and crunchy texture really emerge when used as a primary ingredient, as it is in this recipe. Pilaf (also called pilau) is a Middle Eastern dish whose main component is rice, although other grains, such as bulghur wheat or barley, are sometimes used. Vegetables and/or meats are also usually added to pilafs. The essential technique in preparing pilafs is to heat the grain through in butter or oil, thoroughly coating it before adding the cooking liquid. When selecting the venison, be sure to select a tender cut—loin or a tender section of the leg works best for grilling.

To prepare the marinade, combine 1 cup of water with the vinegar, Worcestershire sauce, onion, garlic, bay leaves, thyme, cloves, salt, and pepper in a large nonreactive bowl or baking dish. Add the venison steaks and marinate overnight.

Prepare the grill.

To prepare the pilaf, bring the stock to a boil in a saucepan, reduce the heat, and keep at a low simmer. Meanwhile, in another saucepan, sauté the bacon and garlic over medium heat for about 3 minutes, or until all the fat is released from the bacon. Drain the bacon and garlic, and set aside, reserving 1 tablespoon the bacon fat in the pan. Add the onion to the bacon fat and sauté over medium heat for about 5 minutes, until golden. Add the barley and stir for about 2 minutes, until all the grains are coated. Add the stock and a pinch of salt, cover, and cook over low heat for about 40 minutes, or until the barley is tender. Remove the pan from the heat and let it rest, covered, for about 10 minutes. Add the bacon and garlic, fluff with a fork, and season with salt and pepper.

While the barley is cooking, remove the steaks from the marinade and pat dry. Rub or brush the olive oil over each steak, and season with salt and pepper. Grill the steaks for about 3 minutes on each side for medium-rare, about 4 minutes per side for medium, or to the desired doneness. Serve immediately with the barley pilaf.

SERVES 4

FOR THE MARINADE AND VENISON:
1 cup white wine vinegar

2 tablespoons Worcestershire sauce

1 onion, chopped

2 cloves garlic, chopped

4 bay leaves, crumbled

2 fresh thyme sprigs

4 whole cloves

Salt and freshly ground black pepper to taste

4 venison loin steaks (about 8 ounces each and ¾ inch thick)

2 tablespoons olive oil

FOR THE BARLEY AND BACON PILAF:
4 cups Chicken Stock (page 225)

4 slices bacon, chopped

2 cloves garlic, minced

1 onion, chopped

1 cup pearl barley

Salt and freshly ground black pepper to taste

VENISON AND RED GAME MEAT

DURANGO
VENISON GOULASH
WITH YELLOW FINN POTATOES

Although goulash is a national dish of Hungary (where it is more properly known as gulyás), it takes the form there of a meat soup. Instead, what we call goulash is known as paprikás in Hungary, the key element being paprika, the ground dried powder of the pimiento chile. Like all chiles, pimientos originated in the New World. After they were brought to Europe, the Hungarians developed different varieties, not all of which are mild and sweet. Indeed, those with heat-tolerant palates should consider adding hot paprika or even some cayenne to the dish. Pasta, such as egg noodles, is often the accompaniment of choice, but buttery Yellow Finn potatoes are our preference here to complement the texture and flavor of the goulash. The dish goes very nicely with a mixed green salad.

FOR THE MARINADE AND VENISON:

2 cups red wine, preferably Cabernet Sauvignon

1 onion, sliced

1 clove garlic, chopped

2 bay leaves

2 sprigs fresh flat-leaf parsley

1 sprig fresh thyme

2 pounds venison shoulder, rib, or neck, cut into 1 1/2-inch cubes

FOR THE GOULASH:

Salt and freshly ground black pepper to taste

2 tablespoons olive oil

2 onions, coarsely chopped

2 cloves garlic, minced

3 tablespoons mild paprika

1 tablespoon tomato paste

1 cup Beef Stock (page 225)

2 bay leaves

3 carrots, sliced into 1/2-inch rounds

1 tablespoon minced fresh flat-leaf parsley

1 teaspoon minced fresh marjoram leaves

1/2 cup sour cream

FOR THE YELLOW FINN POTATOES:

2 pounds Yellow Finn or Yukon Gold potatoes

1 teaspoon salt

2 tablespoons melted butter

1 clove garlic, minced

1 tablespoon minced fresh flat-leaf parsley

Salt and freshly ground black pepper to taste

Combine 2 cups of water with the wine, onion, garlic, bay leaves, parsley, and thyme in a large nonreactive bowl. Add the venison and marinate overnight in the refrigerator.

Remove the meat from the marinade and pat dry. Strain the marinade, reserving the liquid and discarding the solids. Pour the liquid into a saucepan and bring to a boil. Cook over medium-high heat until reduced to about 2 cups.

To prepare the goulash, season the venison with salt and pepper. Heat the oil in a large Dutch oven or flameproof casserole over medium heat. Adding the venison in batches, sauté for about 8 minutes, stirring occasionally, until browned on all sides. Remove with a slotted spoon and set aside. Add the onion and sauté for about 5 minutes, until light golden. Add the garlic, paprika, and tomato paste, and cook for 2 minutes longer. Add the reduced marinade, the venison, stock, and bay leaves, and stir to deglaze the pan. Bring to a simmer, cover, and cook over medium-low heat for 1 hour, stirring occasionally.

Add the carrots and cook for 30 minutes longer. Add the parsley and marjoram and simmer, uncovered, for another 15 minutes, or until the venison and carrots are tender and the goulash begins to thicken. Add the sour cream, adjust the seasonings, and cook for about 2 minutes, stirring to completely incorporate. Remove the bay leaves before serving.

While the goulash is cooking, place the potatoes in a large saucepan and cover with cold water. Add the salt and bring to a boil. Cook for 15 to 20 minutes, or until just tender. Drain the potatoes and return them to the saucepan. Add the melted butter, garlic, and parsley. Season with salt and pepper, and toss gently to coat. Serve with the goulash.

SERVES 4

MUSTARD AND BEER-BRAISED VENISON
WITH CAULIFLOWER GRATIN

Braising meat—especially beef and game—in beer is a hallmark of cooking in parts of northern France and Belgium, and the results can be spectacular. For best results, use a bottled ale or dark beer, such as a bock or wheat beer. Although you can use a stout (such as Guinness), the heavy roasting of the barley can give a bitter edge to the marinade and compete with the venison in terms of flavor. Cauliflower, a member of the mustard family, pairs well with the mustard and beer in the braising liquid, especially when combined with the sharp, nutty flavor of the Gruyère. You can substitute broccoli for the cauliflower. Serve this dish with rice or potatoes.

To prepare the marinade, combine the beer, mustard, onion, and garlic in a large bowl or baking dish. Add the venison, cover, and marinate overnight in the refrigerator.

Remove the venison and strain the beer marinade, reserving the liquid; discard the onions and garlic. Pat the venison dry and season with salt and pepper. Heat the oil in a flameproof casserole over medium-high heat. Add the venison and sauté for 2 or 3 minutes per side, until browned. Remove and set aside. Reduce the heat to medium, add the onion, and sauté for about 5 minutes, until lightly golden. Add the garlic and sauté 2 minutes longer. Stir in the beer marinade and the beef stock. Return the venison to the casserole and bring to a simmer. Cover and cook for 1½ to 2 hours, or until tender. Add the mustard and horseradish to the sauce, season with salt and pepper, and simmer, uncovered, for about 15 minutes longer, until the sauce has thickened.

While the venison is cooking, prepare the cauliflower. Preheat the broiler. Place the cauliflower in a vegetable basket set over a saucepan of salted water and bring to a boil. Cover tightly and steam for 6 to 8 minutes, until tender or to the desired doneness, and then drain. Place the cauliflower in an oiled gratin or baking dish. (Stand the florets up as much as possible, so that the stems are on the bottom and the "flowers" are on the surface.) In a bowl, combine the grated cheese, bread crumbs, and cayenne, and sprinkle over the cauliflower. Place under the broiler and cook for 3 to 5 minutes, or until golden brown. Transfer to warm serving plates and serve with the venison.

SERVES 4

FOR THE BEER MARINADE AND VENISON:

12 ounces dark beer

2 tablespoons Dijon mustard

1 onion, coarsely chopped

2 cloves garlic, chopped

2 pounds venison top round steak (about ¾ inch thick), cut into 4 portions

FOR THE BRAISE:

Salt and freshly ground black pepper to taste

2 tablespoons olive oil

1 onion, diced

3 cloves garlic, minced

1 cup Beef Stock (page 225)

1 tablespoon Dijon mustard

2 teaspoons prepared horseradish

FOR THE CAULIFLOWER GRATIN:

1 cauliflower (about 1½ pounds), trimmed and cut into large florets

½ cup grated Gruyère or Swiss cheese

¼ cup fresh bread crumbs

¼ teaspoon cayenne (optional)

VENISON AND RED GAME MEAT

ROASTED LOIN OF VENISON
WITH CRANBERRY-MARSALA SAUCE AND WILD MUSHROOM CHILAQUILES

This recipe adapts the classic saddle of venison, the tender cut of meat that includes both sides of the loin. Using a single loin is easier and less expensive, and this recipe is a natural for special elegant occasions. The sauce is a simpler version of Cumberland Sauce (page 221), a classic accompaniment with venison, and which can be substituted here. We have matched the venison with chilaquiles (pronounced "chee-lah-key-lehs"), a Mexican casserole based on tortilla strips that are fried to prevent them from becoming soft and mushy. Although this recipe describes the easiest option for preparing the chilaquiles in a single dish, you can also prepare them in individual gratin dishes, as shown in the photograph.

FOR THE MARINADE AND VENISON:

2 cups buttermilk

5 juniper berries, crushed

5 black peppercorns, crushed

2 bay leaves

Juice of 1 lemon

2 pounds venison loin

1 tablespoon olive oil

Salt and freshly ground black pepper to taste

FOR THE WILD MUSHROOM CHILAQUILES:

Vegetable oil, for frying

10 corn tortillas, cut into 1/2-inch-wide strips

3 tablespoons olive oil

1/2 cup diced sweet onion

1 teaspoon minced garlic

1 pound wild mushrooms, such as chanterelles, morels, or oyster mushrooms, sliced

2 cups heavy cream

Salt and freshly ground black pepper to taste

1/2 cup grated Parmesan cheese

FOR THE CRANBERRY-MARSALA SAUCE:

1/2 cup cranberry jelly

1/4 cup Marsala wine

3 tablespoons freshly squeezed orange juice

To prepare the venison, place the buttermilk, juniper, peppercorns, bay leaves, and lemon juice in a shallow baking dish, and add the venison. Let marinate in the refrigerator for at least 8 hours, and preferably overnight.

Preheat the oven to 350°F. Remove the venison from the marinade, pat dry with paper towels, and bring to room temperature. Rub the venison with the oil, season generously with salt and pepper, and transfer to a roasting pan. Roast in the oven for about 25 minutes for medium-rare, about 30 minutes for medium, or to the desired doneness, basting occasionally with the drippings or a little more olive oil. Let rest for 5 minutes before slicing.

While the venison is roasting, prepare the chilaquiles. Heat enough vegetable oil over medium heat to come 1/2 inch up the sides of a large heavy skillet. When lightly smoking, add the tortilla strips in batches, and fry until crisp, about 1 minute. Remove with a slotted spoon and drain on paper towels. Add more oil as necessary for each batch and repeat. Heat 1 tablespoon of the olive oil in a sauté pan, and add the onion and garlic. Sauté over medium-high heat for 3 minutes. Add the remaining 2 tablespoons of oil, heat through, and add the mushrooms. Sauté for 5 minutes longer. Add the cream, warm through, and season with salt and pepper. Evenly spread the tortilla strips in a large ovenproof baking dish and pour with the mushroom mixture. Sprinkle the cheese over the mushrooms. Transfer to the oven and bake for about 25 minutes, until the cheese is bubbly and golden brown.

For the sauce, heat the jelly and Marsala in a saucepan and bring to a boil. Remove from the heat and add the orange juice. Spoon the sauce onto warm plates and arrange the sliced venison on top of the sauce. Serve the chilaquiles next to the venison.

SERVES 4

ROASTED
HERB-RUBBED VENISON
WITH CORN-SCALLION PANCAKES AND PORT GRAVY

Spend any time in the mountains of Colorado during hunting season, and you will find venison on the menu in many upscale restaurants. However, the USDA does not monitor or grade wild game or approve its use commercially, so restaurants usually import farm-raised venison to meet the demand. Wild venison typically contains intense herbal flavor tones reminiscent of the land on which they graze, but the milder farm-raised meat benefits greatly from a rub containing herbs and spices, as in this recipe. Either wild or farm-raised would work great here.

FOR THE HERB RUB:
1/2 tablespoon garlic powder
1/2 tablespoon fennel seed
1/2 tablespoon hot paprika
1/2 tablespoon dried rosemary
1/2 tablespoon dried thyme
1/2 tablespoon freshly ground black pepper
1 teaspoon dried oregano
1 teaspoon salt
1 teaspoon cayenne

FOR THE VENISON:
3 pounds venison rib roast
3 cloves garlic, cut into slivers
3 tablespoons olive oil

FOR THE CORN-SCALLION PANCAKES:
1 1/2 cups fresh corn kernels (about 2 ears)
1 cup milk
3 eggs
1/2 cup heavy cream
1 teaspoon salt
Freshly ground black pepper to taste
1 1/2 cups all-purpose flour
1/2 cup finely sliced scallions
6 tablespoons safflower oil or peanut oil

FOR THE GRAVY:
2 tablespoons butter (1/4 stick), if needed
1 tablespoon all-purpose flour
1 cup Beef Stock (page 225)
2 tablespoons port
2 fresh thyme sprigs
Salt and freshly ground black pepper to taste

Preheat the oven to 425°F. To prepare the herb rub, place the garlic powder, fennel, paprika, rosemary, thyme, pepper, oregano, salt, and cayenne in a spice mill, and roughly grind. Transfer to a plate. Using a sharp paring knife, make incisions in the venison roast and insert the garlic slivers. Rub about 1/2 tablespoon of the oil over the meat and then dredge all sides in the herb rub. Heat the remaining oil in a heavy sauté pan and sear the venison on all sides over medium-high heat, about 5 minutes. Transfer to a roasting pan and place in the oven. Roast for 15 minutes and then reduce the oven temperature to 350°F. Roast for 45 to 50 minutes longer for medium-rare, about 1 hour for medium, or to the desired doneness. Remove from the oven, cover loosely with aluminum foil, and let rest for 10 minutes before carving.

While the venison is roasting, prepare the pancakes. Place the corn and milk in a blender and roughly purée. Whisk together the eggs and cream in a mixing bowl, add the corn mixture, and season with salt and pepper. Place the flour in a separate mixing bowl, make a well in the center, and whisk in the egg-corn mixture. Stir in the scallions. Heat 1 tablespoon of the oil in a nonstick sauté pan over medium heat. When the oil is hot, add enough batter (about 1/4 cup per pancake) to make 2 pancakes about 4 inches across. Cook for about 3 minutes on each side, until golden brown. Keep warm and repeat for the remaining batter.

While the venison is resting, prepare the gravy. Pour 2 tablespoons of the drippings from the roasting pan into a saucepan set over medium heat. (If you do not have any drippings, use butter instead.) Gradually whisk in the flour and cook for 1 or 2 minutes. Add the stock, port, and thyme, and bring just to a boil, stirring continuously. Simmer for 2 or 3 minutes, continuing to stir, and season with salt and pepper.

Slice the venison roast between the bones. Transfer to warm serving plates and serve with the pancakes and gravy.

SERVES 4

VENISON CHILI
WITH PUEBLO BLUE CORN BREAD

It is easy to be confused about the different spellings of chili (spelled with an "i") and chile (with an "e"). The former (sometimes spelled chilli) refers to the spicy dish, while the latter is properly used to signify the spicy plant and seasoning also—but erroneously—known as the hot pepper. Chili, short for chili con carne, is believed to have originated in Texas in the early 1800s. Later in the same century, the dish was popularized by the "chili queens" of San Antonio, elaborately dressed women who sold their fare from cauldrons and brightly lit carts set up around the main plazas and along the main streets. From these humble local beginnings sprang a food that is now the state dish of Texas and hugely popular all over the United States and beyond. Venison makes a wonderful chili, although beef or buffalo can certainly be substituted. As with many chilis and stews, this dish tastes even better the next day, after the flavors have a chance to marry.

To prepare the chili, heat the oil in a large heavy saucepan or Dutch oven and add the onion, bell peppers, and garlic. Sauté over medium-high heat for about 5 minutes, or until softened. Add the venison and sauté for 10 minutes longer, stirring occasionally, until the meat is browned. Add the tomato paste, chile powder, oregano, and cumin and stir for another 2 minutes. Add the stock, wine, tomatoes, and chiles. Season with salt and pepper, and bring to a simmer. Reduce the heat to low and simmer for about 1 hour, stirring occasionally.

Preheat the oven to 425°F. While the chili is cooking, prepare the corn bread. Pour 1 tablespoon of the melted butter into a large cast-iron skillet or 9-inch baking pan and place in the oven to warm. Combine the cornmeal, sugar, baking powder, and salt in a large mixing bowl. Whisk in the remaining 4 tablespoons of melted butter, the egg yolks, half-and-half, and crumbled goat cheese. Beat the egg whites to soft peaks in another mixing bowl and fold into the corn bread batter. Pour into the heated skillet and bake for about 25 minutes, or until a knife inserted into the center of the bread comes out clean.

Cut the roasted corn from the ears (there should be about 1 cup) and add to the chili. Add the beans to the chili and adjust the seasonings. Ladle the chili into soup bowls and garnish with the cilantro. Serve with the corn bread.

SERVES 4

FOR THE CHILI:
3 tablespoons olive oil
1 onion, diced
1 red bell pepper, seeded and diced
1 green bell pepper, seeded and diced
3 cloves garlic, minced
2 pounds ground venison
1/4 cup tomato paste
2 tablespoons pure red chile powder
1 tablespoon minced fresh oregano leaves
2 teaspoons ground cumin
2 cups Beef Stock (page 225)
1 cup dry red wine
1 (14-ounce) can chopped tomatoes
3 red New Mexico or Anaheim chiles, roasted, peeled, seeded, and diced (page 228)
Salt and freshly ground black pepper to taste

FOR THE CORN BREAD:
5 tablespoons butter, melted and cooled slightly
1 1/2 cups stone-ground blue cornmeal
1/4 cup sugar
1 tablespoon baking powder
1/2 tablespoon salt
2 eggs, separated
1 cup half-and-half
4 ounces mild goat cheese, crumbled
2 small ears corn, roasted (page 229)
2 cups cooked black beans (page 226) (optional)
1 tablespoon chopped cilantro leaves, for garnish

VENISON AND RED GAME MEAT

HUBERT KELLER'S HORSERADISH-CRUSTED VENISON CHOPS
AND CURRANT SAUCE WITH THE REVEREND MARTIN'S EGGPLANT PUFF PASTRIES

Hubert is, without doubt, one of our favorite chefs anywhere. His restaurant, Fleur de Lys, is a jewel in San Francisco's crown, and has not only a reputation as one of the most romantic dining spots but also as one of the very best French restaurants in the United States. Hubert is originally from Alsace in eastern France, an area well known for its wild game. The horseradish crust in his recipe perfectly complements both the venison and the fruity sauce. The puff pastry accompaniment is a wonderful example of how a home cook can excel at his craft. Martin Preston is an English "man of the cloth" whom we met while he was on a parish exchange in Hawaii. His repertoire is wide and impressive, and these morsels are worthy of sharing the plate with Chef Keller's creation.

FOR THE MARINADE AND VENISON:

1 tablespoon olive oil

1 small carrot, chopped

1 small onion, chopped

2 cloves garlic, chopped

1 stalk celery, chopped

2 tablespoons red wine vinegar

$2^1/_2$ cups Cabernet Sauvignon, Pinot Noir, or other robust red wine

12 juniper berries, lightly crushed

1 Bouquet Garni (page 226)

12 freshly cracked black peppercorns

4 venison loin chops (8 ounces each and about 1 inch thick)

Salt and freshly ground black pepper to taste

FOR THE PUFF PASTRIES:

6 ounces puff pastry dough

1 egg yolk

$1/_2$ teaspoon water

3 tablespoons olive oil

1 eggplant (about 10 ounces), diced

1 leek, sliced

1 red bell pepper, seeded and diced

1 jalapeño chile, seeded and minced

$1/_2$ tablespoon peeled and minced fresh ginger

1 teaspoon sugar

Salt and freshly ground black pepper to taste

To prepare the marinade, heat the olive oil in a large skillet and sauté the carrot, onion, garlic, and celery over medium-high heat for 6 to 8 minutes. Stir in the vinegar, red wine, juniper berries, bouquet garni, and peppercorns, and bring to a boil. Reduce the heat and simmer for 10 minutes. Transfer the marinade to a large bowl and let cool. Season the venison with salt and pepper, and place in the marinade. Cover and refrigerate for at least 4 hours or overnight.

Preheat the oven to 400°F. Roll out the puff pastry dough to a thickness of $1/_8$ inch. With a cookie cutter or a sharp knife, cut out 4 rounds about 4 inches in diameter, and transfer to a baking sheet moistened with a little water. Whisk together the egg yolk and $1/_2$ teaspoon of water in a bowl and brush it over the pastry rounds. Score the top of the rounds with a fork and bake in the oven for 8 to 10 minutes, or until golden brown. Remove from the oven and let cool. Carefully cut the top of the rounds to make the lids. With a fork, hollow out the interior of the baked rounds; set aside.

Heat 2 tablespoons of the olive oil in a sauté pan and add the eggplant, leek, bell pepper, and chile. Sauté over medium-high heat for about 5 minutes, or until softened. Transfer to a plate. Add the remaining tablespoon of oil to the pan, and when hot, add the ginger and sugar. Sauté for 1 minute, and then stir in the eggplant mixture. Cook for 4 minutes longer, or until cooked through. Season with salt and pepper and keep warm.

(CONTINUED ON PAGE 166)

FOR THE CURRANT SAUCE:

1 tablespoon dried currants

1 large tomato, blanched, peeled, seeded, and chopped (page 228)

2 cups Beef Stock (page 225)

Salt and freshly ground black pepper to taste

1½ tablespoons olive oil

2 teaspoons drained prepared horseradish

¼ cup fresh bread crumbs

To prepare the sauce, place the currants in a bowl and add warm water to cover well. Rehydrate for 10 minutes, drain well, and set aside. Remove the venison from the marinade, dry well with paper towels, and keep refrigerated. Strain the marinade into a saucepan and bring to a boil. Add the tomato and reduce to 1 cup. Add the stock and reduce the liquid to ½ cup. Strain the mixture through a fine-mesh sieve into a small saucepan, add the currants, and return to a boil. Reduce the heat and simmer for 2 to 3 minutes. Remove from the heat, cover, and keep the sauce warm. (Alternatively, let cool and reheat to serve.)

Preheat the oven to 375°F. Pat the venison chops dry and season with salt and pepper. Heat 1 tablespoon of the olive oil in a large skillet, add the venison, and sear over medium-high heat for 2 to 3 minutes on each side, or until brown. Transfer to a baking sheet and spread a thin layer of the horseradish on top of each chop. Sprinkle generously with the bread crumbs and drizzle the remaining ½ tablespoon of olive oil over the chops. Place the baking sheet on the top oven rack and roast for 4 minutes, or until the crust is golden brown and the meat is pink and juicy. Arrange the venison on warm serving plates and spoon the currant sauce around the chops. Place one puff pastry cup on each plate, pile the vegetables in the cup, and lean the puff pastry top against the vegetables. Serve immediately.

SERVES 4

SANTA FE-STYLE
CHIPOTLE-BRAISED VENISON
WITH MASHED SWEET POTATOES

Travel to New Mexico in late fall or winter to visit the "City Different," and you will be dazzled by the quality of the high-desert light and entranced by the adobe wonderland. As you enjoy another spectacular sunset and detect the evocative aroma of piñon wood smoke curling up from fireplace chimneys, nothing ends the day more perfectly than this colorful and warming dish. It contains the pleasing kick of chipotle chiles, which are smoked dried jalapeños, but if you prefer to cut the heat a little, reduce or eliminate the amount of adobo sauce. Alternatively, stir in some sour cream at the end. You might want to "dress up" the sweet potatoes by using, for example, the recipe on page 108, but we think plain sweet potatoes complement the delicious stew best.

Season the venison with salt and pepper. Heat the oil in a large flameproof casserole or Dutch oven and add the venison. Sauté over medium-high heat for about 5 minutes, stirring occasionally, until browned on all sides. (To avoid overcrowding the pan, you may wish to do this in 2 or 3 batches.) Remove with a slotted spoon and set aside. Reduce the heat to medium, add the onion, and sauté for about 5 minutes, until light golden brown. (If necessary, add a little more olive oil to prevent the onion from sticking.) Add the garlic and sauté for 2 minutes longer. Stir in the tomato paste, chipotle, and adobo sauce, and cook for 1 minute. Add the stock and stir to deglaze the pan. Add 1 cup of water, the wine, and oregano. Return the venison to the pan, bring to a simmer, cover, and cook for 1 1/2 hours, skimming the surface occasionally.

Blanch the corn in a small saucepan of boiling water for 2 minutes. Drain and add to the casserole. Add the beans and cilantro, season with salt and pepper, and continue cooking, uncovered, for about 15 minutes, until the venison is tender and the sauce has thickened.

While the venison is cooking, place the sweet potatoes in a saucepan of salted water and bring to a boil. Continue to boil for about 20 minutes, or until tender, and then drain. Add the butter, milk, salt, and pepper, and mash with a potato masher until smooth.

To serve, spoon the mashed potatoes in the center of warm soup plates. Spoon the venison stew around the potatoes.

SERVES 4

FOR THE CHIPOTLE-BRAISED VENISON:

2 pounds venison top round, cut into 1 1/2-inch cubes

Salt and freshly ground black pepper to taste

2 tablespoons olive oil

1 onion, diced

2 cloves garlic, minced

1 tablespoon tomato paste

1 canned chipotle chile in adobo, minced

1 tablespoon adobo sauce (from the canned chipotles)

1 cup Beef Stock (page 225)

1/4 cup red wine, such as Merlot or Cabernet Sauvignon

1 teaspoon minced fresh oregano leaves

1/2 cup fresh corn kernels (about 1 ear)

1/2 cup cooked black beans (page 226) or canned

2 tablespoons chopped fresh cilantro leaves

FOR THE MASHED SWEET POTATOES:

2 pounds sweet potatoes, peeled and quartered

2 tablespoons butter (1/4 stick)

2 tablespoons milk

Salt and freshly ground black pepper to taste

VENISON AND RED GAME MEAT

OSTRICH STEAKS
WITH ROY'S RED CURRANT–CABERNET SAUCE AND PESTO POTATOES

The ostrich is the largest bird in the world—an adult can weigh more than 300 pounds. It yields a flavorful red meat that The National Culinary Review *has described as "the premier red meat of the new century." Ostrich tastes rather like slightly sweet beef, with an agreeable texture similar to tender steak. Because there is very little fat, it is best to cook it like a very lean meat, such as filet mignon, and to serve it with a sauce, preferably something sharp and fruity, as we have done here. You could also pair the sauce and potatoes in this recipe—the creation of Hawaii-based chef and cookbook author Roy Yamaguchi—with venison or filet mignon, if you prefer. For sources of ostrich, see page 172.*

To prepare the sauce, heat the oil in a saucepan. Add the onion, carrot, celery, garlic, bay leaves, and peppercorns, and sauté over medium heat for 5 or 6 minutes, or until light golden. Add the sugar and caramelize for about 2 minutes, while stirring. Add 4 cups of the wine, and stir to deglaze the pan. Reduce the liquid by two-thirds to about 1 1/2 cups, about 20 minutes. Add the stock and reduce again by two-thirds, about 25 minutes. Strain through a fine sieve into a clean saucepan and continue to reduce for 5 or 10 minutes, until the sauce is thick enough to coat the back of a spoon. Set aside. In another saucepan, heat the remaining 1/4 cup of wine and the red currant preserves. Bring to a boil and reduce over medium-high heat for 3 or 4 minutes, stirring constantly, or until the sauce is thick enough to coat the back of a spoon. Stir in the strained wine mixture and warm through just before serving. If desired, whisk in the butter a little at a time, and incorporate thoroughly for a velvety finish.

To prepare the pesto, place the basil, oil, pine nuts, garlic, cheese, salt, and pepper in a blender or food processor, and purée until smooth. Cover and use at room temperature; to store, keep in the refrigerator.

(CONTINUED ON PAGE 170)

FOR THE SAUCE:
2 tablespoons olive oil

1 onion, chopped

1 carrot, chopped

1 stalk celery, chopped

8 cloves garlic, chopped

4 bay leaves

5 cracked black peppercorns

2 tablespoons sugar

4 1/4 cups Cabernet Sauvignon wine (about 1 1/3 bottles)

4 cups Veal Stock (page 225)

1/4 cup red currant preserves

4 tablespoons butter (1/2 stick), diced (optional)

FOR THE PESTO:
1 cup tightly packed fresh basil leaves (about 2 ounces), julienned

2 tablespoons extra-virgin olive oil

1 tablespoon pine nuts

1 clove garlic, chopped

2 tablespoons freshly grated Parmesan cheese

Salt and freshly ground black pepper to taste

VENISON AND RED GAME MEAT

FOR THE POTATOES:

2 pounds potatoes, peeled and chopped
1/2 tablespoon salt
2 tablespoons butter (1/4 stick)
1/2 teaspoon minced garlic
1 cup milk
Salt and freshly ground black pepper to taste

FOR THE STEAKS:

4 ostrich loin steaks (6 ounces each and about 5/8 inch thick)
3 tablespoons olive oil
Salt and freshly ground black pepper to taste

Preheat the oven to 300°F. Place the potatoes in a saucepan of salted water and bring to a boil. Reduce the heat and simmer for about 20 minutes, or until tender. Drain the potatoes and transfer to an ovenproof bowl. Whisk with an electric mixer until smooth and fluffy. Transfer to the oven for 2 to 3 minutes so the excess moisture evaporates. Melt the butter in a small saucepan, and sauté the garlic over low heat for 30 seconds. Add the milk, bring to a boil, and stir into the potatoes. Whisk until thoroughly combined and smooth. Season with salt and pepper, and then gently fold in the pesto so that the potatoes are not uniformly green but a mixture of green and white. Keep warm in the oven while preparing the steaks.

To prepare the ostrich steaks, heat the olive oil in a large nonstick sauté pan over medium-high heat. Season the steaks with salt and pepper, and sear for 1 minute on each side, until browned. Reduce the heat to medium, and sauté quickly for 2 to 3 minutes longer on each side for medium-rare, 3 to 4 minutes per side for medium, or to the desired doneness. Transfer the steaks to warm serving plates. Spoon the sauce around the steaks and spoon the potatoes next to them. Pass the remaining sauce at the table.

SERVES 4

WILD BOAR SAUSAGE
WITH CARAMELIZED APPLES AND BUTTERMILK-CORNMEAL WAFFLES

Wild boar has a rich flavor that is more herbaceous than pork. You can buy wild boar from specialty butchers or from mail-order sources, such as Native Game in Spearfish, South Dakota, or the Texas Wild Game Cooperative in Ingram, Texas. In this recipe, we use wild boar leg meat and grind with a food processor. Because boar has so little fat, this recipe uses additional ground pork. These patties pair well with the flavor and texture of the cornmeal waffles. We serve them here with caramelized apples and pecans for a Southern-style brunch or Sunday supper. The caramelized apples can be prepared ahead of time and served warm or at room temperature.

To prepare the sausage, gently combine the wild boar, pork, garlic, sage, marjoram, chile powder, salt, cumin, pepper, and cayenne in a large mixing bowl. Cover and let chill in the refrigerator for at least 4 hours or overnight so the flavors blend.

Preheat the oven to 300°F. Prepare the waffle batter. Combine the cornmeal, flour, baking powder, and salt in a large mixing bowl. In a separate mixing bowl, whisk together the buttermilk, sour cream, butter, egg yolks, and corn. Whisk the liquid ingredients into the dry ingredients until incorporated. In another bowl, whisk the egg whites to soft peaks and fold into the waffle batter. Let sit while preparing the sausage patties and apples.

Heat 1 tablespoon of the oil in a large sauté pan. Form the sausage meat into 12 patties of about 2 tablespoons each. Sauté in 2 or 3 batches over medium heat for 3 or 4 minutes on each side, until browned and the internal temperature reaches 160°F. Add the remaining oil for the second or third batch. Keep the patties warm in the oven.

To prepare the apples, melt the butter in a large sauté pan over medium heat. Add the apples and cook about 5 minutes, until lightly golden, but still slightly firm. Stir in the sugar and caramelize for about 2 minutes. Reduce the heat to medium-low, stir in the orange zest and pecans, and cook for 1 minute longer. Serve warm.

Heat a waffle iron over high heat and generously coat or spray with oil before adding the waffle batter each time. (If using a nonstick waffle iron, no oil is needed.) Cook the waffles for 3 to 5 minutes, depending on the waffle iron, or until golden brown. Transfer to serving plates and serve with the apples and sausage patties.

SERVES 4

FOR THE WILD BOAR SAUSAGE:
1 pound ground wild boar
8 ounces ground pork
2 cloves garlic, minced
2 teaspoons minced fresh sage leaves
2 teaspoons minced fresh marjoram leaves
2 teaspoons pure red chile powder
1/2 tablespoon salt
1 teaspoon ground cumin
1/2 teaspoon freshly ground black pepper
1/8 teaspoon cayenne

FOR THE CORNMEAL WAFFLES:
1 1/2 cup stone-ground white cornmeal
1/2 cup all-purpose flour
2 teaspoons baking powder
1 teaspoon salt
1 1/4 cups buttermilk
1/2 cup sour cream
4 tablespoons butter (1/2 stick), melted
3 eggs, separated
1/2 cup blanched fresh corn kernels (page 229) (optional)
2 tablespoons olive oil

FOR THE CARAMELIZED APPLES:
2 tablespoons butter (1/4 stick)
3 Granny Smith apples, peeled and chopped
1 tablespoon sugar
1 teaspoon minced orange zest
1/3 cup chopped pecans, toasted (page 229)

VENISON AND RED GAME MEAT

TERRY'S OSTRICH BURGERS
WITH CHIPOTLE POTATO SALAD

Burgers can be made with most types of meat, and they are certainly a fine way to use ground ostrich meat. Sure, you will enjoy their novelty value, but you will quickly come to appreciate the flavorful qualities of ostrich. In addition, it is lean enough that adding cheese and avocado to the burger shouldn't make anyone feel too guilty! Ostrich is available at specialty foods and gourmet stores, or you can contact the American Ostrich Association in Texas at (817) 626-3523. The burgers can be grilled, as well as sautéed. Use this zesty potato salad with any of the other burger recipes in this book or with your favorite cookout dishes.

FOR THE CHIPOTLE POTATO SALAD:

2 pounds unpeeled Red Bliss potatoes

1/2 cup olive oil

1/4 cup apple cider vinegar

1/2 tablespoon freshly squeezed lemon juice

1/2 cup minced shallots

2 teaspoons minced canned chipotle chiles in adobo

1 teaspoon minced garlic

Salt and freshly ground black pepper to taste

FOR THE OSTRICH BURGERS:

1 teaspoon olive oil

1 red bell pepper, seeded and diced

3 scallions, chopped

1 clove garlic, minced

1 1/2 pounds ground ostrich steak

1 tablespoon soy sauce

2 teaspoons Asian fish sauce

Salt and freshly ground black pepper to taste

2 tablespoons vegetable oil

4 slices Monterey Jack cheese

4 sesame seed hamburger buns

1 avocado, pitted, peeled, and diced

Place the potatoes in a saucepan of salted water, bring to a boil, and cook for about 20 minutes, or until just tender. Drain, cut the potatoes into quarters, and transfer to a mixing bowl. While the potatoes are cooking, whisk together the olive oil, vinegar, lemon juice, shallots, chipotle, and garlic in a mixing bowl. Season with salt and pepper, toss with the potatoes, and chill (or serve at room temperature).

To prepare the burgers, heat the olive oil in a sauté pan, add the bell pepper, and sauté over medium heat for 4 minutes. Add the scallions and garlic and sauté for 2 minutes longer. Transfer to a mixing bowl and let cool. Add the ostrich meat, soy sauce, and fish sauce to the mixing bowl, and season with salt and pepper. Divide the mixture into 4 equal portions and form into patties. Heat the vegetable oil in a large nonstick sauté pan and sear the burgers over medium-high heat for 1 or 2 minutes on each side. Reduce the heat to medium, and continue to cook for 3 more minutes. Turn the patties over and cook for 1 minute. Place the cheese slices on top of the patties and cook for about 2 minutes longer, or until the internal temperature reaches 160°F. Split the buns open and toast briefly in a toaster or under the broiler, until golden brown. Place the burgers on the bottom half of each bun and top with the sliced avocado. Serve open-faced with the potato salad.

SERVES 4

JEAN ALBERTI'S
KOKKARI BRAISED RABBIT
WITH BRAISED OKRA

In the winter of 1998, Kokkari, an upscale Greek restaurant, opened in downtown San Francisco to rave reviews. Jean Alberti, the Executive Chef at Kokkari, refers to his style of cooking as "contemporary Hellenic cuisine," and he successfully incorporates fresh, local seasonal ingredients and his classical French training into the traditions of rustic Greek cooking. Rabbit has long been an important food source in the United States, as well as in Europe, and the flavor and texture of commercial rabbit taste similar to chicken. Watch out for the small bones in the meat. For notes on okra, see page 22.

Preheat the oven to 300°F. To prepare the rabbit, combine the nutmeg, cinnamon, and allspice in a bowl, and rub over the rabbit pieces. Heat the oil in a flameproof casserole set over medium-high heat, add the rabbit pieces, and cook for 4 or 5 minutes, until browned on all sides. Transfer to a plate and set aside. Reduce the heat to medium and add the carrot, onion, celery, and garlic to the casserole. Cook, stirring often, for about 10 minutes, or until the vegetables are well browned. Add the wine and bring to a boil. Cook for 12 to 15 minutes, or until 1/4 cup of liquid remains. Return the rabbit to the casserole, and add 4 cups of water, the stock, thyme, bay leaf, rosemary, peppercorns, cinnamon, tomato paste, and vinegar. Season with salt, cover, and transfer the casserole to the oven. Braise for about 1 1/4 hours, or until the rabbit is very tender and falling from the bone.

Meanwhile, place the okra in a large mixing bowl and sprinkle with the vinegar and salt. Let sit for 30 minutes and rinse under cold running water. Heat the oil in a large sauté pan and sauté the onion over medium-high heat for 4 or 5 minutes, until translucent. Add the okra, tomatoes, parsley, and sugar, and season with salt and pepper. Add just enough water to cover the okra, and bring to a simmer. Reduce the heat to low and cook for 30 minutes.

When cooked, remove the rabbit from the casserole and keep warm. Strain the braising liquid into a clean saucepan. Over medium heat, reduce the liquid by half, or until it reaches a syrupy consistency. Place the rabbit on warm serving plates and pour the reduced sauce over it. Serve with the braised okra.

SERVES 4 TO 6

FOR THE BRAISED RABBIT:

1 tablespoon ground nutmeg

1 tablespoon ground cinnamon

1 tablespoon ground allspice

2 rabbits (about 3 pounds each), cut into serving pieces

2 tablespoons extra-virgin olive oil

1 carrot, peeled and chopped

1 onion, peeled and chopped

1 stalk celery, peeled and chopped

2 heads garlic, split

1 cup red wine

8 cups Veal Stock (page 225)

1 sprig fresh thyme

1 bay leaf

1 sprig fresh rosemary

3 black peppercorns

1 stick cinnamon

1 tablespoon tomato paste or ketchup

1 tablespoon balsamic vinegar

Salt to taste

FOR THE BRAISED OKRA:

1 1/2 pounds fresh okra, trimmed and rinsed

2 tablespoons red wine vinegar

Salt to taste

1/2 cup extra-virgin olive oil

1 large onion, sliced

2 tomatoes, blanched, peeled, seeded, and chopped (page 228)

1 tablespoon chopped fresh flat-leaf parsley

Pinch of sugar

Freshly ground black pepper to taste

VENISON AND RED GAME MEAT

MARINATED
BUFFALO STRIP STEAKS
WITH WILD MUSHROOM RAGOUT AND POLENTA

There is something about boneless strip steaks that sets the mouth watering. They are less refined than the filet, yet substantial and elemental, juicy and tender. In these regards, buffalo meat is no different that beef. Wild game, which is more sinewy that farm-raised game, benefits from marinating overnight, and although buffalo is ranch-raised these days, a marinade can provide subtle flavor as well as contribute to tenderness. Cumin especially has an earthy quality that enhances red meats, while oregano and other herbs reinforce the natural flavors that come, in part, from the grazing diet of wild animals. The deep, complex flavors and meaty texture of wild mushrooms make them a natural partner with game.

FOR THE MARINADE AND BUFFALO STEAKS:

1/2 cup olive oil

1/4 cup red wine vinegar

2 teaspoons minced garlic

1 teaspoon ground cumin

1 teaspoon dried oregano

1 teaspoon salt

1/2 teaspoon freshly ground black pepper

1/2 teaspoon dried red pepper flakes

4 buffalo strip steaks (about 10 ounces each and 1 inch thick)

FOR THE WILD MUSHROOM RAGOUT:

1 tablespoon olive oil

1 tablespoon butter

1 small onion, finely chopped

4 ounces chanterelle, cremini, or shiitake mushrooms, sliced (about 2 cups)

1 teaspoon minced garlic

1 cup Beef Stock (page 225)

1/2 cup dry red wine

3 sprigs fresh thyme

2 sun-dried tomatoes (packed in oil), minced

1/2 cup tomato purée

1/2 teaspoon chipotle purée or adobo sauce from canned chipotle chiles

Salt and freshly ground black pepper to taste

Polenta (page 21)

4 sprigs fresh flat-leaf parsley, for garnish

4 cherry tomatoes, cut in half, for garnish

To prepare the marinade, combine the olive oil, vinegar, garlic, cumin, oregano, salt, pepper, and red pepper flakes in a baking dish. Add the buffalo steaks and turn to coat thoroughly. Marinate in the refrigerator for 2 to 3 hours, turning occasionally.

Prepare the grill. Remove the steaks from the marinade, reserving the marinade, and bring them to room temperature. Strain the marinade into a saucepan, bring to a boil, and simmer for 3 or 4 minutes. Set aside and warm through just before grilling the steaks.

To prepare the ragout, heat the oil and butter in a large sauté pan and sauté the onion over medium-high heat for about 5 minutes, until softened. Add the mushrooms and cook for 10 minutes, stirring frequently, until dry. Add the garlic and sauté for 2 more minutes. Add the stock, wine, thyme, and sun-dried tomatoes, and cook for about 10 minutes, or until the liquid is reduced by half. Add the tomato purée and chipotle purée, return to a simmer, and cook until thickened to a sauce-like consistency. Remove the thyme sprigs, season with salt and pepper, and keep warm.

Prepare the polenta according to the recipe on page 21.

Grill the steaks over direct medium-high heat for 4 or 5 minutes for medium-rare, 5 to 6 minutes for medium, or to the desired doneness. Baste frequently with the reserved marinade. Transfer to warm serving plates and spoon the ragout over and around the steaks. Serve with the polenta and garnish with the parsley and tomatoes.

SERVES 4

BUFFALO STEW
WITH GREEN CHILE SPOONBREAD

Buffalo—or more strictly speaking, bison—are making a comeback on American ranches, with about one-quarter of a million head currently being raised for breeding stock or meat. Buffalo is also becoming increasingly popular in restaurants, as the "endangered species" tag has become a thing of the past and patrons appreciate its organic, healthful qualities. With flavor similar to beef, if not a little more pronounced, buffalo cooks slightly faster because of its leanness. (You can substitute beef or venison in this recipe.) The term spoonbread is believed to originate from the Native American word for porridge—suppawn or suppone—or may simply derive from the fact that it is usually eaten with a spoon. In any case, the custardy version we are most familiar with originated in the South, probably Virginia.

FOR THE BUFFALO STEW:

2 pounds buffalo stew meat (from the shoulder), cut into 1-inch chunks

Salt and freshly ground black pepper to taste

3 tablespoons olive oil

1 large onion (about 12 ounces), diced

3 cloves garlic, minced

¼ cup tomato paste

2 cups Beef Stock (page 225)

1 (14-ounce) can chopped tomatoes

12 ounces dark beer, such as Dos Equis or Negra Modelo

8 fresh sage leaves, chopped

2 bay leaves

1 tablespoon butter

8 ounces parsnips, halved lengthwise and sliced into half-moons ½ inch thick

8 ounces carrots, halved lengthwise and sliced into half-moons ½ inch thick

6 ounces green beans, cut into 1-inch pieces

8 ounces domestic mushrooms, quartered

1 tablespoon minced fresh flat-leaf parsley

FOR THE SPOONBREAD:

1 cup stone-ground white cornmeal

4 cups milk

4 eggs, beaten

3 tablespoons butter, softened

3 poblano or green New Mexican or Anaheim chiles, roasted, peeled, seeded, and diced (page 228)

Salt to taste

Season the buffalo with salt and pepper. Heat 2 tablespoons of the oil in a large flameproof casserole or Dutch oven and add the buffalo. Sauté over medium-high heat for about 5 minutes, stirring occasionally, until browned on all sides. (To avoid overcrowding the pan, you may wish to do this in 2 or 3 batches.) Remove with a slotted spoon and set aside. Reduce the heat to medium, add the onion, and sauté for about 5 minutes, until light golden. (If necessary, add a little olive oil.) Add the garlic and sauté for 2 minutes longer. Stir in the tomato paste and cook for 1 minute. Add the stock and stir to deglaze the pan. Add the tomatoes, beer, sage, and bay leaves, and season lightly with salt and pepper. Return the buffalo meat to the pan and bring to a simmer. Cover and cook for 1 hour, skimming the surface occasionally.

Heat the butter and the remaining tablespoon of olive oil in a large sauté pan. Sauté the parsnips and carrots over medium heat for about 5 minutes, or until light golden. Transfer to the stew and add the green beans. Continue to cook for 1 hour longer. Add the mushrooms and parsley and cook for about 30 more minutes, or until the buffalo is tender. Season with salt and pepper, and remove the bay leaves before serving.

About 1 hour before serving, prepare the spoonbread. Preheat the oven to 350°F. and butter a 9-inch casserole or soufflé dish. In a large nonstick saucepan, combine the cornmeal and 1 cup of the milk, whisking to incorporate. Whisk in the remaining milk, and cook over medium heat until thickened, 7 or 8 minutes. Remove from the heat and let cool slightly. Add the eggs, butter, and chiles, and season with salt. Stir to combine, pour into the prepared casserole, and bake for 35 to 40 minutes, or until lightly browned and a knife inserted into the center comes out clean.

SERVES 4 TO 6

BUFFALO BURGERS
WITH MUSHROOMS AND SWEET POTATO FRIES

This starting point for this recipe was the buffalo burgers on chef Waldy Malouf's menu when he was at New York's Rainbow Room restaurant. Those burgers outsold the restaurant's regular hamburgers two to one, no doubt in part because of their novelty value. It also speaks volumes for the flavor and texture of buffalo meat. Ground chuck is our preference if you plan on buying a cut and processing the meat yourself, and because buffalo meat is so lean, it's best to cook the burgers medium-rare to prevent them from becoming dry. The slaw recipe on page 22 makes a good accompaniment with this dish.

Preheat the oven to 350°F. Prepare the grill.

To prepare the fries, place the sweet potatoes in a roasting pan and bake in the oven for 20 minutes. Remove and let cool. (While they are cooling, prepare the burgers). Leaving the potatoes unpeeled, cut them neatly into thin sticks. Heat the vegetable oil in a deep fryer or large saucepan to 350°F. and fry the potatoes for 3 or 4 minutes, until golden brown. Remove with a slotted spoon and drain on paper towels. Season with salt and pepper and keep warm.

To prepare the burgers, heat 2 tablespoons of the olive oil in a sauté pan set over medium-high heat. When hot, add the sliced mushrooms and sauté for 4 or 5 minutes, until golden brown. Keep warm. Place the buffalo meat in a mixing bowl, add the sage, salt, pepper, Worcestershire sauce, and Tabasco sauce, and mix thoroughly. Shape the mixture into 4 patties and brush with the remaining tablespoon of oil. Grill over direct medium-high heat for about 3 minutes on each side for medium-rare.

Split open the onion rolls and toast briefly on the grill until golden brown. Place the burgers on the bottom half of each bun and top with the sautéed mushrooms and the remaining bun. Serve with the sweet potato fries.

SERVES 4

FOR THE SWEET POTATO FRIES:
3 large sweet potatoes
3 cups vegetable oil
   Salt and freshly ground black pepper to taste

FOR THE BURGERS:
3 tablespoons olive oil
6 ounces cremini mushrooms or small portobellos, stemmed and sliced (about 2 cups)
1 1/2 pounds ground buffalo meat
1/2 teaspoon dried sage
   Salt and freshly ground black pepper to taste
   Dash of Worcestershire sauce (optional)
   Dash of Tabasco sauce (optional)
4 onion rolls or hamburger buns

VENISON AND RED GAME MEAT

SPICE-RUBBED ELK CHOPS
WITH GINGERED BRUSSELS SPROUTS AND PORT-PRUNE SAUCE

Elk, a large species of deer, provides another highly nutritious and flavorful dark red meat, with slightly different, milder flavor tones than venison. Elk meat is most usually available frozen, unless you have friends who hunt. As with venison and other game meats, elk is low in fat, so be sure not to overcook it. We recommend medium-rare, or the meat may dry out. You can substitute elk steaks or venison for the elk chops in this recipe. The rub is a hot spice blend, well complemented by a sweet rich sauce.

FOR THE SPICE RUB AND ELK:

1 tablespoon pure red chile powder

1/2 tablespoon sugar

1 teaspoon hot paprika

1 teaspoon ground coriander, toasted

1 teaspoon ground cumin, toasted

1 teaspoon salt

1/2 teaspoon freshly ground black pepper

1/3 teaspoon cayenne

1/3 teaspoon dried thyme

FOR THE SAUCE:

1 cup pitted prunes (about 6 ounces)

1 cup port

2 tablespoons butter (1/4 stick)

1/4 cup minced onion

1 cup Beef Stock (page 225)

1 teaspoon freshly squeezed lemon juice

Salt to taste

FOR THE ELK:

4 elk chops (about 6 ounces each and 1 inch thick)

1 tablespoon olive oil

FOR THE SPROUTS:

2 tablespoons peanut oil

1/4 cup diced onion

1 pound Brussels sprouts, trimmed and quartered

1 tablespoon peeled and minced fresh ginger

1/2 cup Chicken Stock (page 225) or water

1/2 teaspoon dried red pepper flakes

Salt and freshly ground black pepper to taste

To prepare the rub, place the chile powder, sugar, paprika, coriander, cumin, salt, pepper, cayenne, and thyme in a bowl, and thoroughly combine.

To prepare the sauce, place the prunes and port in a bowl, and let soak for 30 minutes. Transfer the prunes and liquid to a blender, roughly purée, and set aside. Melt 1 tablespoon of the butter in a saucepan, and sauté the onion over medium heat for 3 to 4 minutes, until translucent. Add 1 teaspoon of the spice rub and stir for 1 minute. Add the prune mixture and stock, and bring to a simmer. Cook for about 10 minutes longer, until the liquid is reduced by half and the sauce has thickened. Stir in the lemon juice and remove from the heat. Add the remaining tablespoon of butter and season with salt. Keep warm.

While the prunes are soaking, prepare the grill. Rub the elk chops with the olive oil and sprinkle generously with the remaining spice rub. Grill over medium-high heat for about 4 minutes on each side for medium-rare, about 5 minutes per side for medium, or to the desired doneness.

While the steaks are grilling, prepare the sprouts. Heat the oil in a sauté pan, add the onion, and sauté over medium-high heat for 2 minutes, stirring often. Add the sprouts and ginger, and sauté for 5 minutes longer. Add the stock and pepper flakes, reduce the heat to medium, and cook for another 5 minutes, or until the liquid is evaporated and the sprouts are tender. Season with salt and pepper.

Transfer the sprouts to warm serving plates. Spoon the sauce next to the sprouts and serve the elk chops over the sauce.

SERVES 4

JAMAICAN CURRIED GOAT
WITH APRICOT CHUTNEY

This quintessentially Caribbean dish is probably most popular in Jamaica. Goats were introduced by the early Western explorers and they have remained an important source of meat on many of the islands. Goats adapted so well to their new environment that, in some places, feral animals are something of a problem. If goat is unavailable, or if it does not appeal to you, substitute lamb or chicken in this recipe. The closely related habanero and Scotch bonnet chiles are believed to be the hottest chiles in existence, so we advise you to use gloves when handling them and to wash your hands thoroughly afterwards. The volatile oils they contain are more intensely strong than you can imagine. Note that both the goat and apricots require marinating or soaking overnight.

To prepare the chutney, place the apricots in a bowl and cover with $1/2$ cup of water. (Add a little more water if necessary.) Let rehydrate overnight. Transfer the rehydrated apricots and rehydrating liquid to a saucepan and simmer for about 10 minutes, until tender. Transfer to a blender and purée. In a clean saucepan, heat the vinegar, sugar, ginger, garlic, red pepper flakes, and salt over medium heat. Stir to dissolve the sugar, and continue stirring until syrupy, about 5 minutes. Stir in the apricot purée and simmer for 10 minutes. Let cool.

To prepare the curry, place the goat meat in a mixing bowl. Add the curry powder, chiles, scallions, garlic, onions, allspice, salt, pepper, and 2 tablespoons of the oil. Mix well, cover the bowl, and let sit in the refrigerator overnight.

Heat the remaining 2 tablespoons of the oil in a large saucepan or Dutch oven, and add the butter. When melted, add the goat mixture and raisins, and sauté over medium-high heat for 10 minutes, until the meat is browned and the vegetables are softened. Stir in the tomatoes, coconut milk, and 2 cups of water, and simmer for about 1 hour, stirring occasionally, or until the meat is tender. Add a little more water if necessary. Season with salt and pepper.

While the curry is cooking, prepare the rice. Spoon the rice onto warm serving plates and serve the curry over the rice. Drizzle some of the chutney over the curry, and pass the remainder at the table.

SERVES 4

FOR THE APRICOT CHUTNEY:
$3/4$ cup dried apricots (about 5 ounces)
$1/4$ cup cider vinegar
$1/2$ cup sugar
$1/2$ tablespoon peeled and minced fresh ginger
$3/4$ teaspoon minced garlic
$1/4$ teaspoon dried red pepper flakes
$1/4$ teaspoon salt

FOR THE CURRIED GOAT:
2 pounds lean boneless goat stewing meat, cut into $1 1/2$-inch cubes
3 tablespoons medium-hot curry powder
2 fresh habanero or Scotch bonnet chiles, seeded and finely minced
2 scallions, sliced
2 cloves garlic, minced
2 onions, diced
1 teaspoon ground allspice
1 teaspoon salt, plus more to taste
1 teaspoon freshly ground black pepper, plus more to taste
4 tablespoons peanut oil
2 tablespoons butter ($1/4$ stick)
$1/2$ cup raisins
14 ounces canned chopped tomatoes
1 cup canned unsweetened coconut milk

Long-Grain White Rice (page 227)

VENISON AND RED GAME MEAT

The popularity of poultry (domesticated birds) and fowl (wild ones) in the United States has gone from strength to strength ever since the commercial poultry industry geared up at the end of the 19th century. The growth has been particularly spectacular for chicken since the introduction of large-scale operations over the last 50 years, combined with improved breeding and husbandry programs. (Some would say that the advent of Kentucky Fried Chicken and other fast-food chains has helped too!) These developments have meant that the supply has kept up with the surging demand for the low-fat, juicy, white meat of the ubiquitous chicken—to such an extent that, taking account of inflation, chicken costs less today than it did 30 years ago.

Chickens are descended from wild red fowl that originally roamed the jungles of India. They were domesticated in Asia more than 4,000 years ago and became popular for their meat in Europe in medieval times. Up until then, chickens were kept mainly for their eggs. Today, there are more chickens on the planet than humans, a testament to their ability to fend for themselves and survive in all kinds of climates and locations, and to their affordability—even in poorer countries. Unlike many meats, chicken is not restricted on religious grounds in hardly any country.

Chicken is a highly versatile meat, and it can be cooked with virtually any technique. It is high in protein and some minerals, such as iron, and compared with other meats, chicken is relatively low in calories, especially cuts such as skinless breast. We recommend free-range, hormone- and antibiotic-free chickens, usually available at health-food stores and specialty butchers, as they have more flavor and better overall quality, as do kosher birds. However, our recipes do not assume that free-range birds are available, and consequently, many of the recipes in this chapter add distinctive flavors and textures by means of marinades, sauces, and glazes to enhance the perfect "vehicle" of chicken meat. As the famed late 18th- and early 19th-century French gourmet and writer, Brillat-Savarin, wrote, "Chicken for the cook is what canvas is for the painter."

Wild turkey is native to the New World, and the bird was revered and prized by successive cultures in South and Central America, where it was domesticated centuries ago. However, the reason the bird carries the name of an eastern Mediterranean country is because of a misnomer that originated in the 1600s. The Spanish took birds ("Indian chickens") back to Europe, where they rapidly multiplied and became a popular meat. Turkish traders took some birds from Spain to sell in England, where they were marketed as "turkie cocks." There, they eventually replaced goose as the traditional Christmas centerpiece. The significance of turkey as a food in the United States is enhanced by the fact that the Indians brought it to the famished pilgrims of the Plymouth Colony for the first Thanksgiving feast in the 1620s. Benjamin Franklin believed that this alone should qualify the bird as the national symbol, rather than the belligerent eagle. Domesticated turkey is now the second most popular bird in this country after chicken.

Note that background information on the other fowl included in this chapter—duck, quail, pheasant, and squab—are contained in the appropriate recipe introductions.

In terms of buying and cooking, all poultry is inspected by the USDA and graded from "A" (highest quality) to "C" (lowest). Most wholesale and retail chicken and turkey is the meaty, well-finished "A" grade, the rest being used for processed products. Flavor and tenderness, however,

are qualities not covered by grading. They instead depend on the bird's age, with the youngest being the most tender. (See the recipe introduction on page 216 for more details on definitions.) If at all possible, buy fresh poultry and fowl rather than frozen, and avoid buying birds that have bruised or blotchy skins or a strange aroma. As with other meats, be careful to refrigerate poultry and fowl promptly.

When preparing whole birds, rinse them under cold running water inside and out and be sure the giblets are removed. Pat dry with paper towels before proceeding with the recipe. Poultry should be cooked through until the internal temperature reaches 175°F., or 180°F. for whole birds. At these temperatures, salmonella and other harmful bacteria are killed. For fowl, follow the directions in the recipes. With skin-on pieces of poultry or fowl, we recommend starting the cooking process skin-side down in order to keep the meat as moist as possible.

182

Chicken noodle soup is not only a satisfying comfort food, but most likely an immune system booster too. Of course, grandmas across the country have always known this, but recent research suggests that amino acids contained in chicken may ease the symptoms of colds and flu. You can add up to $1/4$ cup of tomato paste and a little chile sauce to the soup, if you like, and add some chopped yellow potatoes or squash.

6 cups Chicken Stock (page 225)

3 boneless, skinless chicken breast halves (about 4 ounces each)

2 carrots, peeled and diced

2 stalks celery, diced

3 cloves garlic, minced

1 teaspoon peeled and finely minced fresh ginger

1 bay leaf

Salt to taste

4 ounces dried short fusilli pasta or orzo

2 tablespoons olive oil

1 onion, chopped

$1/4$ cup diced red bell pepper

$1/4$ cup diced green bell pepper

2 cups fresh corn kernels (about 3 ears)

2 tablespoons freshly squeezed lime juice

Freshly ground white pepper to taste

1 tablespoon minced fresh flat-leaf parsley, for garnish

Pour the stock into a saucepan and add the chicken, carrots, celery, garlic, ginger, bay leaf, and salt. Bring to a boil, cover, and reduce the heat to a simmer. Cook for 30 to 35 minutes, or until the chicken is cooked through.

Meanwhile, cook the fusilli noodles in a saucepan of boiling salted water according to the directions on the package. Drain and let cool. When cooked through, remove the chicken from the soup and let cool. Heat the oil in a sauté pan and add the onion and bell peppers. Sauté for 5 minutes, until softened. Add to the soup, stir in the corn, cover, and simmer for 5 minutes longer. Roughly shred the chicken, return to the pan with the cooked noodles, and warm through. Remove from the heat, stir in the lime juice, and season the soup with salt and white pepper. Ladle into warm serving bowls and garnish with the parsley.

SERVES 4 TO 6

BUFFALO CHICKEN WINGS
WITH BLUE CHEESE DRESSING AND CELERY STICKS

Some Europeans we know are convinced this is a recipe for preparing buffalo; they are the same ones who think Chicken-Fried Steak (see page 36) is a chicken recipe! The name for this straightforward deep-fried chicken dish comes from the city in upstate New York; it originated at the Anchor Bar in Buffalo in the mid-1960s. Another fact you should know when making these wings is that July 29 is Chicken Wing Day, as decreed by the city of Buffalo. Mark the date on your calendar—what better way to celebrate than to fix these "more-ish" morsels?

The idea here is that the celery and cooling dip counterbalance the fiery wings; your guests should alternate between the two. This make-ahead dish makes great party and buffet food or informal hors d'oeuvres. If you prefer, serve the wings with a spicy tomato sauce (see page 143) instead of the Tabasco mixture, and save any extra blue cheese dressing for a fresh green salad another time.

To prepare the dressing, place the blue cheese, sour cream, and mayonnaise in a mixing bowl and thoroughly combine. Stir in the onion, lemon juice, and garlic, and season with salt and cayenne.

To prepare the chicken, cut off the wing tips and use for stock (freeze if not using immediately). Cut the wings at the joint. Heat the oil in a saucepan to 375°F. and deep-fry the chicken in batches for about 10 minutes, until cooked through and golden brown. Remove with a slotted spoon and drain on paper towels. Meanwhile, melt the butter over medium-low heat in a saucepan. Add the Tabasco and vinegar, whisk together, and warm through. Brush over the chicken pieces and serve with the dressing and celery sticks.

SERVES 4

FOR THE BLUE CHEESE DRESSING:
8 ounces blue cheese, crumbled
$1/2$ cup sour cream
$1/2$ cup mayonnaise
2 tablespoons finely diced onion
1 tablespoon freshly squeezed lemon juice
1 teaspoon minced garlic
Salt and cayenne to taste

FOR THE CHICKEN WINGS:
20 chicken wings (about 4 pounds), rinsed and patted dry
3 to 4 cups peanut or vegetable oil
4 tablespoons butter ($1/2$ stick)
$1/4$ cup Tabasco sauce
1 tablespoon white wine vinegar
4 celery sticks, cut in half crosswise, for garnish

BROWN DERBY COBB SALAD
WITH CHICKEN, BACON, AND EGGS

This famous salad is one of the most visually arresting of all, with the ingredients arranged in strips across the top of the greens. It makes a terrific summer lunch entrée. The Cobb salad is named after its creator, Bob Cobb, the Executive Chef of the Brown Derby restaurant on Wilshire Boulevard in Los Angeles. Some time in the 1930s, the story goes, he decided to chop up some ingredients that were lying around in the kitchen to put on top of the salad he was making for himself. He realized its potential, and a classic was born. There are many options when it comes to preparing this recipe, although the more changes you make, the less authentic the Cobb will become. It's a great way of using leftover chicken, and you can poach or sauté the chicken, rather than grill it. For a nouveau version, you might try shrimp instead of chicken, a mesclun mix instead of the greens called for here, or the addition of diced cooked beets.

Prepare the grill. (Alternatively, the chicken can be sautéed.) Brush the chicken breasts with the oil, season with salt and pepper, and grill over direct medium heat for 5 to 6 minutes per side, or until cooked through. (If sautéing, heat the oil in a sauté pan and season the chicken with salt and pepper. Sauté the chicken over medium heat for 6 or 7 minutes per side, or until well cooked through.) Set aside, let cool, and julienne. Bring a saucepan of salted water to a boil. Place an egg in a large spoon and gently lower onto the bottom of the pan. Repeat with the other egg, and reduce the heat to low or medium-low. Simmer for 10 minutes, until hard-cooked. Remove with a slotted spoon and transfer to a bowl of ice water. Let cool, peel, and dice. While the eggs are cooking, place the bacon in a dry skillet and sauté over medium heat until crispy, about 5 or 6 minutes, turning once or twice. Let cool and roughly crumble.

Place the romaine, Boston lettuce, frisée, and watercress in a large salad bowl and toss together. Arrange the chicken in a strip down the center of the salad. Arrange the tomato and avocado in separate strips on either side of the chicken. Arrange the eggs in a separate strip next to the tomato, and the bacon next to the avocado. Arrange the cheese evenly around the edge of the salad and sprinkle the chives over the top.

To prepare the vinaigrette, combine the vinegar, lemon juice, mustard, and garlic in a bowl. Season with salt and pepper. Gradually whisk in the oil until incorporated. Pour the vinaigrette over the salad at the table, toss together, and serve.

SERVES 4

FOR THE SALAD:
2 boneless, skinless chicken breast halves (about 4 ounces each)

1 tablespoon olive oil

Salt and freshly ground black pepper to taste

2 eggs

5 slices bacon

3 ounces romaine lettuce, roughly torn

3 ounces Boston, Bibb, or green leaf lettuce, roughly torn

2 ounces frisée leaves

2 ounces watercress leaves

3/4 cup seeded and diced plum tomato

1 large avocado, peeled, pitted, and diced

3/4 cup crumbled Roquefort cheese

2 tablespoons finely sliced fresh chives

FOR THE VINAIGRETTE:
2 tablespoons white wine vinegar

1 tablespoon freshly squeezed lemon juice

2 teaspoons Dijon mustard

1 clove garlic, minced

Salt and freshly ground black pepper

1/2 cup safflower or peanut oil

POULTRY AND FOWL

MARINATED GRILLED
ASIAN CHICKEN
WITH CABBAGE SLAW AND BLACK SESAME SEED RICE

There's no doubting which continent provides the main influence for this dish! Some time ago, we enjoyed an Asian-style cabbage slaw at Alan Wong's restaurant in Honolulu, and this slaw recipe evolved from that defining moment. It is delightfully crisp and refreshing, without the cloying creaminess of some cabbage slaws. Mirin, a flavor element in the slaw, is a Japanese sweet rice cooking wine that is sometimes labeled "rice wine." The short-grain rice that we use here is also known as "sticky rice" or "Japanese rice" because it is favored in that country. As the name suggests, sticky rice is starchier and more glutinous than long-grain rice. Calrose short-grain rice is a commonly available brand.

FOR THE MARINADE AND CHICKEN:

¼ cup soy sauce

¼ cup freshly squeezed lemon juice

2 tablespoons honey

2 tablespoons peanut oil or light sesame oil

1 tablespoon roasted sesame oil

1 teaspoon Chinese five-spice powder

1 teaspoon Asian chile sauce with garlic, such as sambal oelek

1 teaspoon peeled and minced fresh ginger

3 cloves garlic, minced

8 boneless, skinless chicken breast halves (about 4 ounces each)

FOR THE CABBAGE SLAW:

3 cups julienned Chinese or Napa cabbage

1 cup julienned purple cabbage

½ cup sliced snow peas

1 red bell pepper, seeded and julienned

1 yellow bell pepper, seeded and julienned

2 tablespoons scallions finely sliced on the bias

2 tablespoons mirin

1 tablespoon freshly squeezed lemon juice

2 tablespoons minced fresh cilantro leaves

1 teaspoon Asian chile sauce with garlic, such as sambal oelek (optional)

FOR THE RICE:

2 cups short-grain rice

2 cups cold water

1 tablespoon black sesame seeds

To prepare the marinade, place the soy sauce, lemon juice, honey, peanut oil, roasted sesame oil, five-spice powder, chile sauce, ginger, and garlic in a mixing bowl, and whisk together. Transfer to a baking dish and add the chicken. Marinate in the refrigerator for 3 to 4 hours, turning occasionally.

Meanwhile, prepare the slaw. Place the cabbages, snow peas, red and yellow bell peppers, scallions, mirin, lemon juice, cilantro, and chile sauce in a mixing bowl and gently toss together. Keep refrigerated.

Prepare the grill.

Wash the rice several times in cold water. Rinse and drain until the water runs fairly clear. Place the rice in a heavy saucepan and cover with the 2 cups of cold water. Bring to a boil over medium-high heat, reduce the heat to low, and cover the pan. Steam the rice for 15 minutes; do not remove the lid while the rice is cooking. Turn off the heat and let the rice sit for another 10 minutes before removing the lid. Fluff with a fork and garnish with the sesame seeds just before serving.

While the rice is cooking, remove the chicken from the marinade and drain well. Grill over medium-high direct heat for 5 to 6 minutes on each side, or until well cooked through. Transfer to warm serving plates, sliced, and serve with the rice and slaw.

SERVES 4

GREEN CHILE ENCHILADAS
WITH RED CHILE SAUCE AND BLACK BEANS

In the Southwest, and especially down New Mexico way, chile sauce is a way of life. When ordering in restaurants, you may well be asked, "Green, red, or Christmas?" This refers to the preferred color of chile sauce, with "Christmas" referring to both green and red served side by side on top of the food. Red chile sauce is usually made with dried chiles, and the green with fresh, roasted, or frozen chiles, making the flavors and textures entirely different. In this recipe, we offer a variation on the dual-sauce theme to go with these enchiladas, a staple of the region.

Place the chicken in a large saucepan and cover with water. Press the cloves into the onion and add to the pan. Add the celery, carrot, peppercorns, thyme, and bay leaf and bring to a boil. Reduce the heat, partially cover the pan, and simmer for 30 minutes, or until the chicken is poached through and tender. Remove and let cool; reserve 1¹/₂ cups of the poaching broth for this recipe, and the rest for soup or stock. Remove the skin and shred the chicken. Reserve 2¹/₂ cups of meat for the enchiladas; use the rest for other recipes.

While the chicken is cooking, prepare the sauce. Heat the oil in a large sauté pan and add the onion and garlic. Sauté over medium-high heat for 5 minutes, or until lightly golden. Add the cumin, oregano, salt, and cinnamon, stir well, and remove from the heat. Transfer the mixture to a food processor and add the chile powder, the reserved 1¹/₂ cups of chicken broth, and the tomatoes. Purée until smooth, adding a little more broth if necessary. Heat the peanut oil in a large, heavy skillet, and when almost smoking, add the sauce. Refry for 3 or 4 minutes, stirring constantly. Set aside.

Preheat the oven to 375°F. To prepare the enchiladas, heat the vegetable oil in a large sauté pan and add the onion and garlic. Sauté over medium-high heat for 3 minutes. Add the chiles, tomatoes, marjoram, cumin, salt, and Worcestershire sauce, and cook for 2 minutes longer. Add the 2¹/₂ cups of shredded chicken meat and combine. Remove from the heat. Heat the peanut oil in a small sauté pan and using tongs, briefly fry the tortillas, one at a time, over medium-high heat for 10 seconds to soften. Drain on paper towels and place the chicken mixture in a line down the center of each tortilla. Roll up and place seam-side down in a baking dish just large enough to hold them all snugly. Pour the reserved red chile sauce over and sprinkle with the cheese. Transfer to the oven and bake for 15 to 20 minutes, or until the cheese is bubbling. Place 3 enchiladas and sauce on each warm serving plate and serve with the beans. Pass the sour cream at the table.

SERVES 4

FOR THE CHICKEN:
1 chicken (about 2¹/₂ pounds)
3 whole cloves
1 onion
1 stalk celery, sliced
1 carrot, sliced
1 teaspoon black peppercorns
2 sprigs fresh thyme
1 bay leaf

FOR THE RED CHILE SAUCE:
2 tablespoons vegetable oil
¹/₂ cup finely diced onion
2 cloves garlic, minced
1 teaspoon ground cumin
1 teaspoon dried oregano
³/₄ teaspoon salt
¹/₄ teaspoon ground cinnamon
¹/₂ cup pure red chile powder
4 plum tomatoes, roasted and chopped (page 228)
2 tablespoons peanut oil

FOR THE ENCHILADAS:
2 tablespoons vegetable oil
¹/₂ cup finely diced onion
3 cloves garlic, minced
3 Anaheim or New Mexico green chiles, or 2 poblano chiles, roasted, peeled, seeded, and finely diced (page 228)
2 plum tomatoes, seeded and finely diced
1 teaspoon dried marjoram
1 teaspoon ground cumin
³/₄ teaspoon salt
¹/₄ teaspoon Worcestershire sauce
1 cup peanut or vegetable oil
12 yellow or blue corn tortillas
1¹/₂ cups grated Monterey Jack cheese

Mark Miller's Black Beans (page 226)
¹/₄ cup sour cream, for garnish

POULTRY AND FOWL

BISTEEYA:
MOROCCAN CHICKEN PIE
WITH PHYLLO DOUGH AND CINNAMON-SUGAR TOPPING

Bisteeya (also spelled Bstila, Bastilla, and B'steeya, depending on the source) is a Moroccan dish served for celebrations; it is usually one of many offerings at the table. However, we think this unusual and time-consuming (but fun-to-make) dish deserves to be the main event. Because it is very rich, we suggest serving it with a crisp green salad and a bottle of dry white wine. In Morocco, it is usually prepared with pigeon and handmade pastry sheets, called ouarka, but chicken and phyllo dough are fine substitutes. Phyllo usually comes in sheets measuring 12 x 17 inches, and you will need about half a standard-size box to make this recipe. In Morocco, the pie is usually eaten with the fingers, but you may offer forks, if desired.

2 sticks butter (16 tablespoons)

3 tablespoons olive oil

1 chicken (about 2$^1/_2$ pounds), cut into 8 pieces

Salt and freshly ground black pepper to taste

1 large onion, minced

$^1/_2$ cup minced fresh flat-leaf parsley

$^1/_2$ cup minced fresh cilantro leaves

2$^1/_2$ teaspoons ground cinnamon

$^1/_2$ teaspoon saffron

$^1/_2$ teaspoon ground cumin

5 eggs, beaten

$^1/_4$ cup confectioners' sugar

4 ounces sliced almonds, blanched (about 1$^1/_4$ cups)

16 sheets phyllo dough

Heat 3 tablespoons of the butter and 2 tablespoons of the oil in a flameproof casserole, Dutch oven, or large sauté pan over medium-high heat. Season the chicken with salt and pepper and sauté for about 10 minutes, until golden brown on all sides. Remove the chicken and set aside. Add the onion to the pan and sauté for about 5 minutes, until softened. Add the parsley, cilantro, 1$^1/_2$ teaspoons of the cinnamon, the saffron, and cumin, and cook for 2 minutes longer. Return the chicken to the pan and add $^1/_2$ cup of water. Cover and simmer for about 45 minutes, until the chicken is tender. Remove the chicken and let cool slightly. Reduce the heat to low, gradually add the eggs to the sauce, and scramble for 2 or 3 minutes, stirring constantly, until the eggs are just cooked. Remove the chicken meat from the bones and discard the bones and skin. Shred or cut the chicken into 1 or 2 inch pieces and return to the sauce. Season with salt and pepper and set aside.

While the chicken is cooking, combine the remaining 1 teaspoon of cinnamon with the confectioners' sugar. Heat the remaining tablespoon of olive oil in a nonstick skillet and sauté the almonds over medium heat for about 1 minute, or until golden. Transfer to a food processor, add 1 tablespoon of the cinnamon-sugar mixture, and coarsely chop. Melt the remaining butter and set aside.

Preheat the oven to 350°F. To assemble the pie, lay the phyllo sheets on a clean dry surface and cover with plastic wrap and a lightly dampened cloth. (Since phyllo dries out very quickly, keep it covered as much as possible while preparing the pie.) Using a pastry brush, lightly butter a sheet of parchment paper placed on a large pizza pan or baking sheet (at least 14 inches across). Lay out one sheet of phyllo and brush with butter. Add another sheet of phyllo overlapping the first and begin to form a pinwheel, brushing each

(CONTINUED ON PAGE 190)

sheet with butter. Working with 1 sheet at a time, continue to add phyllo until you have placed 5 sheets in a circular fashion, with about a third of each sheet overhanging from the center. Brush the entire surface of each sheet with butter (including the overhang) as you lay it. After laying the first 5 sheets, begin again and form another pinwheel of 5 sheets over the first. Lay a folded piece of phyllo in the center and brush with butter. Sprinkle about $1/4$ cup of the almond mixture in a 10-inch circle in the center of the phyllo. Pile the chicken and sauce over the almonds. Lay a folded piece of phyllo over the chicken and brush with butter. Sprinkle the remaining almonds over the phyllo. Fold the overhanging phyllo over the almonds, brushing with butter, until the entire pinwheel is folded and the pie is closed. Take 4 more sheets of phyllo and arrange in a decorative ruffled or crimped style on top and around the pie. Brush with a little more butter and sprinkle the remaining cinnamon sugar over the top. Bake for about 50 minutes, until golden brown. Cut the pie into portions and serve warm.

SERVES 6

HAZELNUT-STUFFED CHICKEN
WITH ROASTED VEGETABLES AND WORCESTERSHIRE GRAVY

Stuffing poultry makes roasting one of the most flavorful means of cooking it. The range and combinations of flavors and textures that can be incorporated into the meal by means of stuffings are endless. Many stuffings are based on bread crumbs, and here, we have added more elements than usual, including herbs, nuts, eggs, chicken livers, and cheese. The results will delight you. Manchego, used in the stuffing, is a Spanish sheep cheese with a characteristic hard, black (and inedible) crosshatched rind. Look for the words "La Mancha" on the label, indicating its origin; if absent, it may not be the genuine article. Italian Pecorino or Cheddar makes a fine substitute. You can use pine nuts instead of the hazelnuts if you prefer.

Preheat the oven to 425°F.

To prepare the stuffing, heat the oil in a sauté pan and add the onion and garlic. Sauté over medium-high heat for 5 minutes, and then transfer to a mixing bowl. Add the chicken livers, eggs, bread crumbs, cheese, hazelnuts, wine, and basil, and season with salt and pepper. Thoroughly combine, and then stuff the chicken with the mixture. (Place any excess stuffing in a small, ovenproof casserole, cover with foil, and refrigerate. About 30 minutes before you are ready to serve, transfer the stuffing to the oven and roast.) Truss the chicken with butcher's twine. Place the stuffed chicken in a large, lightly buttered roasting pan.

Place the potatoes, sweet potatoes, parsnips, and artichokes in a mixing bowl, and drizzle with the oil. Season with salt and pepper, and toss to coat the vegetables completely. Arrange the vegetables in the roasting pan around the chicken and transfer the roasting pan to the oven. Roast for 50 minutes to 1 hour, or until the internal temperature reaches 170°F. Remove from the oven and let rest for 5 to 10 minutes before carving. (The internal temperature will rise to about 175°F.) Transfer the roasted vegetables to a serving bowl.

While the chicken is resting, prepare the gravy. Pour 2 tablespoons of the drippings from the roasting pan into a small saucepan set over medium heat. Whisk in the flour, add the stock and Worcestershire sauce, and bring just to a boil, stirring continuously. Reduce the heat and simmer for 2 minutes. Season with salt and pepper and transfer to a gravy boat.

Arrange the carved chicken and stuffing on a warm serving platter. Serve family-style at the table with the vegetables and gravy.

SERVES 4

FOR THE STUFFING AND CHICKEN:
2 tablespoons olive oil
1/2 onion, diced
2 cloves garlic, minced
3 ounces chicken livers, chopped
1 hard-boiled egg, chopped
1/2 cup fresh bread crumbs
1/2 cup crumbled manchego cheese
1/2 cup chopped hazelnuts
2 tablespoons dry white wine
1 tablespoon chopped fresh basil or tarragon leaves
Salt and freshly ground white pepper to taste
1 chicken (about 3 1/2 pounds)

FOR THE VEGETABLES:
8 ounces Yukon Gold potatoes, chopped
8 ounces sweet potato, peeled and chopped
8 ounces parsnips, peeled and chopped
5 artichokes bottoms, quartered (optional)
2 tablespoons olive oil
Salt and freshly ground white pepper to taste

FOR THE GRAVY:
1 tablespoon all-purpose flour
1 cup hot Chicken Stock (page 225)
1 teaspoon Worcestershire sauce
Salt and freshly ground white pepper to taste

POULTRY AND FOWL

DORO WAT: ETHIOPIAN STEW
WITH BERBERE SAUCE AND INJERA BREAD

Doro Wat is an Ethiopian stew, usually made with chicken. It contains a hot chile spice blend, called berbere, and although this recipe makes about twice as much as you will need, save the rest to season meat, stews, and vegetables. Injera is a traditional Ethiopian flatbread, typically made of teff flour over the course of two or three days. (Teff is a tiny grain indigenous to North Africa with a nutty flavor.) Our version adapts the recipe for convenience's sake; the texture will be like a spongy crepe. To serve this dish in its traditional style, pass the bread and place the stew in the center of the table, so that all guests can reach it. The bread is used in place of utensils to scoop up the stew and put it in your mouth. Alternatively, your guests can place their bread on a plate, scoop some of the stew onto the bread, and then use their fingers to eat. In any case, the combination of the fiery juices from the stew and the spongy bread is not to be missed. If desired, add sliced carrots, okra, or green beans to the onions during the cooking process.

FOR THE BERBERE:

1 teaspoon cumin seeds

$1/2$ teaspoon fenugreek seeds

$1/2$ teaspoon black peppercorns

$1/4$ teaspoon coriander seeds

3 cardamom pods

2 whole cloves

1 cup tightly packed, small, dried red chiles, such as tepín, pequín, or de arbol, (about 1 ounce), stemmed and seeded, or 3 tablespoons cayenne

1 teaspoon salt

$1/2$ teaspoon ground dried ginger

$1/2$ teaspoon turmeric

$1/4$ teaspoon ground allspice

FOR THE DORO WAT:

1 stick butter (8 tablespoons)

3 onions (about $1 1/2$ pounds), diced

2 cloves garlic, minced

$1/4$ cup tomato paste

1 chicken (about 3 pounds), skin removed and meat cut into bone-in, bite-size pieces (about 20 pieces total: 4 pieces from each breast and 2 from each drumstick, thigh, and wing)

2 tablespoons chopped fresh mint leaves (optional)

2 tablespoons chopped fresh basil leaves (optional)

4 hard-boiled eggs (page 87), peeled

Salt and freshly ground black pepper to taste

To prepare the sauce, heat a small sauté pan over medium heat and toast the cumin, fenugreek, peppercorns, coriander, cardamom, and cloves for about 1 minute, just until fragrant. Do not allow them to scorch, or they will become bitter. Transfer to a spice grinder or a mortar and pestle, and grind until smooth. Set aside. Remove the stems and seeds from the chiles and grind until smooth. Combine the toasted spices and chile peppers in a bowl, and mix with the salt, ginger, turmeric, and allspice. Set aside.

To prepare the doro wat, melt the butter in a large flameproof casserole or Dutch oven, add the onions and garlic, and cook over medium-high heat for about 7 minutes, or until soft. Reduce the heat to medium, add 2 tablespoons of the reserved berbere mixture and the tomato paste and cook for about 10 minutes, stirring occasionally. With a knife, score each piece of chicken several times, and add a few pieces at a time to the stew, stirring constantly to make sure that the chicken is coated with the sauce. Stir in $1/2$ cup of water, the mint, and basil, if desired. Cover and simmer the stew for about 20 minutes. (Add more water if necessary, but the stew should be thick.) Lightly score the eggs 2 or 3 times lengthwise, and add them to the stew. Season with salt and pepper. Continue to simmer, covered, for 20 to 30 minutes longer, or until the chicken is completely cooked.

While the stew is cooking, prepare the injera. Combine the flours and baking powder in a large mixing bowl. Stir in the club soda and water. Mix thoroughly. Heat a large nonstick skillet over medium heat and pour about $1/2$ cup of the batter over the bottom of the pan, swirling the pan to spread the batter as thinly and evenly as possible. When bubbles have formed on the surface and the bread is dry, remove it and keep warm. (The bread should be cooked on one side only.) Ideally, the bread should be moist and spongy on both sides and should not be browned on the bottom or be pasty. If necessary, thin the batter with more water to achieve this result. Keep the stack of injera covered with a cloth while cooking the remaining breads.

To serve, place the stew in a large serving dish in the center of the table and pass the injera. Alternatively, arrange the injera in a overlapping circular pattern on a large deep platter and spoon the stew into the center of the platter.

SERVES 4

FOR THE INJERA:
2 cups self-rising flour
$1/2$ cup whole-wheat flour
1 teaspoon baking powder
1 cup club soda
2 cups water

POULTRY AND FOWL

ORANGE-BASIL CHICKEN BREAST
WITH WILD RICE SALAD AND MANGO-AVOCADO SALSA

In this recipe, the chicken is subtly—and delightfully—infused with the light and fruity flavors of the basil and orange. The lush, tropical salsa matches its flavor, while the rice offers a contrasting nutty, slightly earthy quality. This versatile wild rice salad makes a great side for most red meats, as well as fish. The colorful salsa can be made ahead of time, but it's best eaten the same day, as it will not keep well.

To prepare the marinade, heat 2 tablespoons of the oil in a saucepan and add the shallot and garlic. Sauté over medium heat for 4 or 5 minutes, until translucent. Pour into a baking dish, and add the remaining oil, the orange juice, basil, salt, and peppercorns. Stir to combine and add the chicken. Marinate in the refrigerator for 2 hours, turning occasionally.

Meanwhile, prepare the salsa. Gently mix the mango, avocado, onion, bell pepper, cilantro, scallions, lime juice, tomato, and chile in a mixing bowl. Season with salt and pepper and refrigerate.

To prepare the rice salad, heat 1 tablespoon of the oil in a saucepan and add 1/4 cup of the shallots. Sauté over medium heat for 3 or 4 minutes, until translucent. Add the wild rice and stir for 1 minute, or until well coated. Add 1 cup of the stock and enough water to cover the rice by 2 inches. Bring to a boil, cover, and reduce the heat. Simmer for 40 to 45 minutes, or until al dente and the rice has absorbed the liquid. Transfer to a mixing bowl and let cool. Heat the remaining tablespoon of oil in a separate saucepan and add the remaining 1/4 cup of shallots. Sauté over medium heat for 3 or 4 minutes, until translucent. Add the white rice and stir for 1 minute, or until well coated. Add the remaining cup of stock and enough water to cover the rice by 2 inches. Bring to a boil, cover, and reduce the heat. Simmer for about 15 minutes, or until tender and the rice has absorbed the liquid. Add to the mixing bowl. Blanch the corn in a saucepan of boiling water for 1 minute; drain and add to the bowl with the bell pepper and pine nuts. Place the basil, vinegar, lemon juice, garlic, salt, and pepper in a bowl and whisk together. Gradually add the olive oil until incorporated, and then pour the dressing over the salad.

While the rice is cooking, prepare the grill. Remove the chicken from the marinade, draining off any excess liquid. Grill over direct medium-high heat for 5 or 6 minutes per side, or until well cooked through. Transfer to serving plates and serve with the rice and salsa.

SERVES 4

FOR THE ORANGE-BASIL MARINADE AND CHICKEN:
1/2 cup olive oil
1 shallot, minced
2 cloves garlic, minced
Juice of 2 oranges
1/2 tablespoon chopped fresh basil leaves
1/4 teaspoon salt
1/2 tablespoon crushed black peppercorns
8 boneless, skinless chicken breast halves (about 4 ounces each)

FOR THE MANGO-AVOCADO SALSA:
1 mango, peeled, pitted, and finely diced
1 avocado, peeled, pitted, and finely diced
2 tablespoons sliced red onion
2 tablespoons finely diced red bell pepper
2 tablespoons chopped fresh cilantro leaves
1 tablespoon finely sliced scallions
1 tablespoon freshly squeezed lime juice
1 plum tomato, finely diced
1 serrano chile, seeded and minced
Salt and freshly ground black pepper to taste

FOR THE WILD RICE SALAD:
2 tablespoons olive oil
1/2 cup minced shallot
1/2 cup wild rice, rinsed and drained
2 cups Chicken Stock (page 225)
1/2 cup long-grain white rice, rinsed and drained
1 cup fresh corn kernels
1/2 cup finely diced red bell pepper
1/4 cup pine nuts, toasted (page 229)
2 tablespoons julienned fresh basil leaves
1 tablespoon sherry vinegar
1 tablespoon freshly squeezed lemon juice
1/2 teaspoon minced garlic
1/2 teaspoon salt
1/4 teaspoon freshly ground black pepper
1/4 cup extra-virgin olive oil

POULTRY AND FOWL

CILANTRO-GARLIC
CHICKEN BREAST
WITH BLACK BEAN CHILE RELLENOS
AND TOMATILLO SAUCE

196

The intense tomatillo sauce echoes the aromatic flavor combination of cilantro, garlic, and lime juice in the marinade. Yet in their final form, these two elements complement, rather than duplicate, each other. Tomatillos have a tart, fruity flavor and are particularly favored in Mexico for sauces. They must be husked and rinsed before use because of the sticky resin on the skin. Rellenos are most commonly stuffed with cheese, but all sorts of fillings can be used for the chiles, the only limit being your imagination. By all means, sauté the chicken, rather than grill it.

FOR THE CILANTRO-GARLIC MARINADE AND CHICKEN:

1 cup chopped fresh cilantro leaves

1 cup freshly squeezed lime juice

⅓ cup white wine vinegar

¼ cup finely diced white onion

2 tablespoons minced garlic

1 tablespoon dried oregano

½ tablespoon salt

½ tablespoon freshly ground black pepper

½ tablespoon ground cumin

1 cup olive oil

8 boneless, skinless chicken breast halves (about 4 ounces each)

FOR THE TOMATILLO SAUCE:

2 tablespoons olive oil

1 onion, chopped

2 cloves garlic, chopped

1 pound tomatillos, husked, rinsed, and blackened (page 228)

¼ cup chopped fresh cilantro leaves

1 teaspoon light brown sugar

1 teaspoon salt

2 teaspoons freshly squeezed lime juice

FOR THE BLACK BEAN RELLENOS:

2 cups cooked black beans (page 226)

2 canned chipotle chiles in adobo, minced

2 teaspoons adobo sauce

½ teaspoon ground cumin, toasted (page 229)

¼ teaspoon salt

4 Anaheim or green New Mexico chiles, roasted and peeled (page 228)

2 eggs, beaten

2 tablespoons milk

½ cup all-purpose flour

2 cups cornmeal

¼ teaspoon cayenne

Peanut oil, for deep-frying

To prepare the marinade, place the cilantro, lime juice, vinegar, onion, garlic, oregano, salt, pepper, and cumin in a food processor and purée. Gradually pour in the oil, mixing until incorporated. Transfer the marinade to a mixing bowl and add the chicken. Marinate in the refrigerator for 2 hours, turning occasionally.

Prepare the grill.

To prepare the sauce, heat the olive oil in a sauté pan and add the onion and garlic. Sauté over medium heat for 5 minutes, until soft and translucent. Transfer to a food processor, add the tomatillos, cilantro, sugar, and salt, and purée. Transfer to a saucepan, stir in the lime juice, and warm through just before serving.

Preheat the oven to 250°F. To prepare the rellenos, place the beans, chipotles, adobo sauce (from the canned chipotles), cumin, and salt in a food processor and purée until smooth. Set aside. Leaving the stems intact, carefully make a lengthwise incision in the chiles and remove the seeds and ribs. Spoon the purée mixture into the chiles, being careful not to overstuff or rip the chiles. Mix the eggs and milk together in a shallow bowl. Place the flour on a plate. On a separate plate, mix together the cornmeal and cayenne. Dredge the stuffed chiles first in the flour and then into the egg wash, letting any excess drip off. Finally, dredge the chiles on the cornmeal and coat well. Heat the peanut oil in a deep-fryer or large saucepan to 350°F. Carefully place the rellenos in the hot oil and fry for about 1 minute, until golden brown. Remove from the oil with tongs and drain on paper towels. Keep warm in the oven.

Remove the chicken from the marinade and pat dry with paper towels. Grill over direct medium-high heat for about 5 or 6 minutes on each side, or until well cooked through.

Spoon the sauce on warm serving plates and arrange the chicken breasts on top. Serve with the chile rellenos.

SERVES 4

OMAHA STEAKS MEAT

Honey-Mustard
BBQ Chicken
with Cilantro-Potato Salad and
Mixed Greens with Artichokes

The perfect recipe for a summer cookout consists of grilled chicken, potato salad, and a green salad. No sweating in a hot kitchen here! And it is also a great do-ahead meal. The barbecue sauce in this recipe is a simpler version of the mustardy North Carolina–style sauce we use with the pork ribs on page 88, and like it, it contains tomatoes. Some purists might frown at this "adulteration," but we think it combines the best of all possible barbecue worlds! Traditionalists might also prefer regular American mustard to the Dijon variety; you can make this substitution, but the French mustard has a sharpness and pungency to it that brings out the best in other ingredients.

To prepare the chicken, place the honey and mustard in a mixing bowl and stir together. Add the tomatoes, vinegar, Worcestershire sauce, salt, and cayenne, and mix well. Place the chicken pieces in a baking dish and add the honey-mustard mixture. Transfer the dish to the refrigerator and marinate for 1 hour, turning once or twice.

Prepare the grill.

To prepare the salad, rub the trimmed artichokes with the lemon halves to prevent discoloration. Place the artichokes in a steamer set over a saucepan of boiling water. Cover tightly and steam for 7 or 8 minutes, or until tender. Meanwhile, in a bowl, whisk together the oil and vinegar. Add the basil and season with salt and pepper. Transfer the steamed artichokes to a mixing bowl, and toss with half of the vinaigrette while still warm. Just before serving, place the salad greens in a separate bowl, add the artichokes and 2 tablespoons of the remaining vinaigrette. Toss together and sprinkle with the Parmesan cheese. Serve the remaining vinaigrette at the table.

Remove the chicken from the marinade. Pour the marinade into a saucepan and bring to a boil. Reduce the heat and simmer for 5 minutes; keep warm. Reserve $1/2$ cup of the marinade for plating the dish. Use the remaining marinade to baste the chicken while grilling. Grill the chicken over direct medium-high heat for about 5 or 6 minutes on each side, or until well cooked through. Brush the chicken with the honey-mustard glaze once or twice while it is grilling.

Transfer the chicken to serving plates and pour over some of the remaining glaze. Serve with the potato salad and the mixed greens.

Serves 4

For the BBQ Chicken:
$1/3$ cup honey
$1/4$ cup Dijon mustard
1 cup canned crushed tomatoes
$1/4$ cup apple cider vinegar
3 tablespoons Worcestershire sauce
1 teaspoon salt
$1/2$ teaspoon cayenne
4 boneless, skinless chicken breast halves (about 4 ounces each)
4 skinless chicken thighs (about 4 ounces each)

For the Mixed Greens and Artichokes:
8 baby artichokes, outer leaves trimmed off
1 lemon, cut in half
5 tablespoons extra-virgin olive oil
2 tablespoons red wine vinegar
$1/2$ tablespoon minced fresh basil leaves
Salt and freshly ground black pepper to taste
3 cups mixed greens, such as mesclun mix
$1/4$ cup freshly shaved Parmesan cheese

Cilantro-Potato Salad (page 59)

POULTRY AND FOWL

PUEBLA CHICKEN
WITH CHOCOLATE MEXICAN MOLE SAUCE AND CORN-SCALLION PANCAKES

Chicken or turkey served with the chocolatey mole poblano stands as one of the best-known Mexican dishes of all. "Poblano" means "from Puebla," the city in which the sauce originated in the 17th century. "Mole" is a word borrowed from the Nahuatl (Aztec) language meaning "mixture," and there is certainly an extended mixture of ingredients in most mole sauces. Although the recipe may appear lengthy, this is actually a simplified version of the classic dark mole. Don't be put off by its length; it's definitely worth the effort. It's both sweet and hot, so reduce the chiles to match your heat tolerance! For a shortcut, serve with plain long-grain white rice instead of the pancakes.

Preheat the oven to 250°F. Place the dried ancho, mulato, pasilla, and chipotle chiles in a single layer on 1 or 2 baking sheets and toast them in the oven for 4 or 5 minutes, until fragrant but not burned. (Toast in batches if necessary.) Transfer to a large mixing bowl, cover with warm water, and let sit for 30 minutes, or until softened. (Use a saucepan lid or plate to weight the chiles down to keep them submerged.) Drain the chiles, reserving 1 cup of the liquid. Transfer to a food processor or blender and add just enough of the reserved liquid to make puréeing possible (about 3/4 cup); use the remaining liquid if necessary. Purée and set aside. Heat a dry skillet and add the tortillas, cooking until they are dried and brittle but not burned. Tear into pieces and set aside. Heat the olive oil in a large saucepan and add the onion and garlic. Sauté over medium heat for 5 minutes, until softened. Add the reserved puréed chiles and tortillas. Add the raisins, pumpkin seeds, almonds, sesame seeds, tomatoes, tomatillos, stock, cinnamon, salt, thyme, allspice, and cloves. Stir well and bring to a boil. Reduce the heat to low, partly cover to avoid spattering, and simmer for 30 minutes. Add the chocolate, stir until melted, and remove the pan from the heat. Transfer to a food processor and purée in batches until smooth. Strain into a clean saucepan, add the lime juice, and warm through, but do not boil.

While the mole is cooking, prepare the chicken. Heat the oil in a large heavy skillet and season the chicken breasts with salt and pepper. Sauté the chicken over medium-high for 3 minutes per side. Reduce the heat to medium-low, add the warm mole sauce, and cook the chicken and sauce for 15 to 20 minutes, or until the chicken is cooked through. Transfer the chicken and sauce to warm serving plates, and serve with the corn-scallion pancakes.

SERVES 4

FOR THE MOLE SAUCE:

6 dried ancho chiles, stemmed and seeded

6 dried mulato chiles, stemmed and seeded

3 dried pasilla chiles, stemmed and seeded

2 dried chipotle chiles, stemmed and seeded

3 corn tortillas

2 tablespoons olive oil

1 cup diced onion

1/2 tablespoon minced garlic

1/3 cup raisins

1/4 cup pumpkin seeds, toasted (page 229)

1/4 cup chopped almonds

1/4 cup white sesame seeds

3 plum tomatoes, roasted, peeled, and chopped (page 228)

4 tomatillos, husked, rinsed, roasted, peeled, and chopped (page 228)

6 cups Chicken Stock (page 225)

1 teaspoon ground cinnamon

1 teaspoon salt

1/2 teaspoon dried thyme

1/4 teaspoon ground allspice

1/8 teaspoon ground whole cloves

12 ounces Mexican chocolate, preferably Ibarra, chopped, or 6 tablespoons cocoa powder

2 tablespoons freshly squeezed lime juice

FOR THE CHICKEN:

2 tablespoons peanut oil

8 boneless, skinless chicken breast halves (about 4 ounces each)

Salt and freshly ground black pepper to taste

Corn-Scallion Pancakes (page 162)

POULTRY AND FOWL

CHICKEN LEG ROULADES
WITH SWEET CORN COULIS AND SUN-DRIED TOMATO HASH

The slices of aromatic chicken filled with vegetables make a very attractive presentation and provide an abundance of wonderful flavors in this dish. You can just as easily use chicken breast halves instead of boneless legs; just lightly pound the breasts flat between sheets of waxed paper, spread the stuffing on top, and then roll up, securing with toothpicks. Both the coulis—defined as a thick, puréed sauce—and the sun-dried tomato and potato hash are versatile sides.

FOR THE CORN COULIS:

2 tablespoons butter (¼ stick)

½ cup diced onion

2 cloves garlic, minced

¼ cup dry white wine

1½ cups fresh corn kernels (about 2 ears)

1 teaspoon chopped fresh marjoram leaves

½ teaspoon salt

¾ cup heavy cream

FOR THE CHICKEN LEG ROULADES:

½ cup fresh bread crumbs

¼ cup Chicken Stock (page 225)

2 tablespoons olive oil

¾ cup thinly sliced leek, white and light green parts

¾ cup finely diced mushrooms

½ tablespoon minced fresh flat-leaf parsley

½ teaspoon dried sage

Salt and freshly ground black pepper to taste

8 boneless chicken thighs (skin on)

4 thin slices ham

2 tablespoons clarified butter or olive oil

FOR THE SUN-DRIED TOMATO HASH:

1 pound Yukon Gold potatoes, diced

2 tablespoons olive oil

2 tablespoons minced shallot

1 clove garlic, minced

¼ cup chopped sun-dried tomatoes (packed in oil)

1 teaspoon white wine vinegar

Salt and freshly ground black pepper to taste

To prepare the coulis, heat the butter in a saucepan and add the onion and garlic. Sauté over medium-high heat for 2 minutes. Add the wine and bring to a simmer. Add the corn, marjoram, and salt, and return to a simmer. Add the cream, warm through, and reduce the heat to medium-low. Keep the mixture hot, while not simmering or boiling it, for 7 or 8 minutes. Transfer to a blender and purée. Strain into a clean saucepan and warm through just before serving.

Preheat the oven to 375°F. To prepare the roulade, place the bread crumbs in a bowl, add the stock, stir together, and let soak. Heat the oil in a sauté pan, add the leek, mushrooms, parsley, and sage, and sauté over medium heat for 5 or 6 minutes, until tender. Season with salt and pepper. Add the soaked bread crumbs, mix together thoroughly, and remove from the heat. Lay out the chicken thighs, cut-side up and skin-side down. Place a slice of ham over the "inside" of the chicken thighs and spread the leek and mushroom mixture over the ham. Close up the thigh meat and secure with toothpicks. Heat the clarified butter in a sauté pan or skillet, and when hot, sear the chicken over medium heat for 2 or 3 minutes per side, or until golden. Transfer to a baking dish and roast in the oven for 12 to 15 minutes, or until well cooked though.

While the chicken is cooking, prepare the hash. Bring a saucepan of salted water to a boil, add the potatoes, and blanch for 5 minutes. Drain and set aside. Heat the oil in a sauté pan, add the shallot and garlic, and sauté over medium-high heat for 2 minutes. Add the blanched potatoes and sun-dried tomatoes, and sauté for 3 or 4 minutes, or until the potatoes are tender. Sprinkle the vinegar over the potatoes and season with salt and pepper.

Spoon the coulis onto warm serving plates and arrange the chicken roulades on top. Serve with the sun-dried tomato hash.

SERVES 4

COCONUT CURRIED CHICKEN
WITH LENTILS AND RICE

Traditionally, coconut milk comes from simmering fresh or dried coconut flesh with water and then straining, but in the United States we have the convenience of using the canned product. It is an important ingredient in the cuisines of India, southeast Asia, and many parts of South America and Africa. This recipe is in the style of southern India, where curries commonly include coconut, with our addition of the subtle flavoring of lemongrass, an herb featured in the cooking of many southeast Asian countries, most notably Thailand. All the exotic ingredients called for can be found in Asian markets.

Place the lentils in a bowl, cover with plenty of water, and let soak for 2 hours. Drain and transfer to a saucepan. Add 3 cups of water, the turmeric, coriander, and cumin. Bring to a boil, reduce the heat, and simmer for 20 to 25 minutes, or until just tender. (Add a little more water if necessary to keep moist.) Let cool slightly, and then transfer half of the mixture to a blender and purée. Lightly mash the remaining lentils in the pan, and return the puréed lentils to the pan. Stir in the chile, tomatoes, and curry leaves, and season with salt. Cover the pan and cook over low heat for 30 minutes. Just before serving, if desired, heat the clarified butter in a small skillet and add the onion. Sauté over medium heat until golden brown and pour over the lentils. Garnish with the cilantro.

To prepare the curry, combine the coconut milk, lime leaves, and lemongrass in a saucepan and bring to a boil. Reduce the heat and simmer for 5 minutes. Remove from the heat and let sit to infuse. Season the chicken with the chile powder. Heat 2 tablespoons of the oil in a large saucepan and when hot, add the chicken. Cook over medium-high heat for 5 or 6 minutes, turning often, or until browned on all sides. Remove the chicken and set aside. Add the remaining tablespoon of oil to the pan, and when hot, add the ginger and garlic. Sauté for 1 minute, and then add the onion, bell pepper, and scallions. Sauté for 3 minutes longer, stir in the curry powder, and cook for 2 minutes. Add the stock and tomatoes and bring to a boil. Strain the coconut milk mixture into the pan, add the chicken, stir, and cover. Reduce the heat to low and simmer the curry for about 20 minutes. Uncover the pan, raise the heat to medium, and add the cilantro. Simmer for about 10 minutes longer, or until the chicken is tender and the sauce is thickened slightly.

Spoon the rice onto warm serving plates and arrange the curried chicken and sauce on top. Serve with the lentils.

SERVES 4

FOR THE LENTILS:
1 cup yellow or red lentils, rinsed
1/2 teaspoon ground turmeric
1/2 tablespoon ground coriander
1/2 tablespoon ground cumin
1 jalapeño chile, seeded and minced
1 cup canned crushed tomatoes
5 curry leaves (optional)
Salt to taste
1/2 tablespoon clarified butter (optional)
1 tablespoon minced onion (optional)
1 tablespoon minced fresh cilantro leaves, for garnish

FOR THE CHICKEN CURRY:
2 cups canned coconut milk
3 kaffir lime leaves or 1 teaspoon lime zest
1 tablespoon minced fresh lemongrass
1 chicken (about 3 1/2 pounds), cut into 8 pieces
2 teaspoons pure red chile powder
3 tablespoons peanut oil
1 tablespoon peeled and minced fresh ginger
1 teaspoon minced garlic
1/2 cup sliced sweet onion
1 red bell pepper, seeded and finely diced
2 scallions, finely sliced
2 tablespoons curry powder
1 cup Chicken Stock (page 225)
1 cup canned crushed tomatoes
1/4 cup minced fresh cilantro leaves

Basmati or Long-Grain White Rice (page 227)

POULTRY AND FOWL

BRUNSWICK STEW
WITH POACHED CHICKEN, FRESH CORN, AND LIMA BEANS

This chicken dish is named after Brunswick County in Virginia, although counties with the same name in other Southern states, such as North Carolina and Georgia, have also laid claim to it. The stew originated in the early 19th century, almost certainly with origins in Native American cooking. In its earliest form, the principal ingredients were squirrel and corn. Since there is not much call for squirrel these days, you will find this updated combination of flavors most satisfying. Lima beans, onions, tomatoes, and corn are essential ingredients; okra is favored but optional; and you can add other vegetables of your choice to personalize the stew. Use frozen vegetables, if need be, and serve with rice, if desired.

FOR THE CHICKEN:
1 chicken (about 3 1/2 pounds), washed
1 onion, chopped
1 carrot, sliced
1 stalk celery, sliced
2 bay leaves
1 teaspoon black peppercorns
1 teaspoon salt

FOR THE STEW:
2 tablespoons olive oil
1 onion, sliced
1 green bell pepper, seeded and diced
1 stick celery, sliced
1 carrot, sliced
2 cloves garlic, chopped
1 pound potatoes, chopped
1 (14-ounce) can crushed tomatoes
2 cups fresh corn kernels (3 or 4 ears)
2 cups fresh or frozen small lima beans
1 cup sliced okra or fresh peas (optional)
1/2 cup freshly squeezed lemon juice
1/4 cup ketchup
2 tablespoons Worcestershire sauce
1 tablespoon Tabasco sauce
1/4 teaspoon ground allspice
Salt and freshly ground black pepper to taste
2 tablespoons chopped fresh flat-leaf parsley, for garnish

Place the chicken in a stockpot and add the onion, carrot, celery, bay leaves, peppercorns, salt, and 2 quarts of water. (Add more water if necessary to cover the chicken.) Bring to a boil, cover, and reduce the heat to low. Poach gently for about 1 hour, or until tender and cooked through. Remove the chicken, and let cool; strain the stock and reserve. When the chicken is cool, remove and discard the skin, shred the meat, and set aside.

While the chicken is poaching, prepare the stew. Heat the oil in a large, flameproof casserole, and add the onion, bell pepper, celery, carrot, and garlic. Sauté over medium-high heat, stirring often for 7 or 8 minutes, or until soft. Add the reserved stock and the potatoes, cover the pan, and bring to a boil. Reduce the heat to low and simmer for 30 minutes. Add the tomatoes, corn, beans, okra, lemon juice, ketchup, Worcestershire sauce, Tabasco, and allspice; season with salt and pepper. Return to a simmer and cook for 30 minutes more, stirring often. Add the cooked shredded chicken and adjust the seasonings. Ladle into warm serving bowls and garnish with the parsley.

SERVES 6 TO 8

GRILLED CHICKEN
BARBECUE PIZZA
WITH THREE CHEESES

So many barbecue sauces, so little time . . . This is a great barbecue sauce for chicken, but if you have your own favorite—or if you want to save time by using a store-bought variety—by all means, go ahead and use them. Adding one or two minced canned chipotle chiles (or a little of their adobo sauce) will add a nice smoky tone, in which case, you might want to cut down on—or eliminate—the jalapeños. Using more than one type of cheese on the pizzas adds to the flavor dimensions, especially with the addition of smoked cheese, which plays off the barbecue sauce. It goes without saying that if you are not fond of smoked cheese, use another kind. Serve with a side salad, if you like.

Prepare the pizza dough according to the recipe on page 120.

To prepare the chicken, heat the olive oil in a sauté pan and add the onion, chiles, garlic, and ginger. Sauté over medium-high heat for 5 minutes, or until tender. Stir in the ketchup, vinegar, ale, sugar, mustard, Worcestershire sauce, and honey, and bring to a boil. Reduce the heat to medium-low and simmer, uncovered, for 20 minutes, or until thickened slightly. Strain into a large bowl and let cool. Place the chicken breasts in a large plastic zipper-lock bag, add 1 cup of the barbecue sauce, and let marinate in the refrigerator for 1 hour. Reserve the remaining sauce.

Prepare the grill. Remove the chicken from the marinade and transfer the chicken marinade to a saucepan. Bring to a boil, reduce the heat, and simmer for 3 or 4 minutes. Divide the marinade in half. Grill the chicken over direct medium-high heat for 5 or 6 minutes on each side, or until well cooked through, brushing with half of the boiled marinade glaze. Remove from the grill and let cool. Cut the cooled chicken into strips and set aside.

Preheat the oven to 450ºF. To assemble the pizzas, heat 2 tablespoons of the olive oil in a large sauté pan, and add the bell peppers. Sauté over medium-high heat for 5 or 6 minutes, or until softened. Brush each of the 4 prepared servings of pizza dough with 1/2 tablespoon of the remaining olive oil, and then spoon with the other half of the reserved marinade, spreading it out evenly to within 1/2 inch of the edges. Sprinkle the chicken strips and bell peppers over the sauce, and top with a mixture of the cheeses. Transfer to a pizza brick or pizza pans, and bake in the oven for 12 to 15 minutes, or until the crusts are golden brown.

SERVES 4

Pizza Dough (page 120)

FOR THE BARBECUED CHICKEN:
2 tablespoons olive oil
1 onion, diced
2 jalapeño chiles, seeded and minced
2 cloves garlic, minced
1 teaspoon peeled and minced fresh ginger
1 1/4 cups ketchup
1/2 cup white wine vinegar
1/2 cup ale or dark beer
1/4 cup packed light brown sugar
1/4 cup Dijon mustard
3 tablespoons Worcestershire sauce
2 tablespoons honey
8 boneless, skinless chicken breast halves (about 4 ounces each)

FOR THE PIZZAS:
4 tablespoons olive oil
1 small red bell pepper, seeded and julienned
1 small yellow bell pepper, seeded and julienned
1/4 cup grated smoked mozzarella, smoked Cheddar, or gouda cheese
2 tablespoons grated Monterey Jack cheese
2 tablespoons grated Parmesan cheese

PYRÉNÉES CHICKEN
WITH BRAISED VEGETABLES AND SUN-DRIED TOMATO MASHED POTATOES

The Basque region sits in far southwest France and northeast Spain, and includes much of the Pyrénées. The people are proudly independent and the native language they speak is, surprisingly, derived from neither French nor Spanish. Some say the Basques are the descendants of the lost continent of Atlantis, and there is little doubt their culture is ancient. The cuisine of the region is also distinctive, sharing more in common with that of the rest of northern Spain than France. Most dishes contain bell peppers, which are grown in profusion everywhere. Bayonne ham is another specialty of the region, and although we use bacon in this recipe, this comforting dish reflects flavors typical of Basque country. If you wish, after braising, place the chicken pieces in a roasting pan under the broiler for 5 minutes to nicely brown the skin. Serve with rice instead of potatoes, if preferred.

FOR THE CHICKEN:

1 cup diced bacon

4 pounds bone-in chicken pieces (skin on), chopped into bite-size pieces

2 tablespoons olive oil

1 cup diced onion

1 cup diced leek, white and green parts

½ tablespoon minced garlic

1 small red bell pepper, seeded and sliced

1 small yellow bell pepper, seeded and sliced

1 small green bell pepper, seeded and sliced

5 plum tomatoes, diced

1 cup Chicken Stock (page 225)

1 teaspoon chopped fresh oregano leaves

Salt and freshly ground black pepper to taste

FOR THE MASHED POTATOES:

Mashed Potatoes (page 36)

¼ cup diced sun-dried tomatoes (packed in oil)

2 tablespoons minced shallot

4 sprigs fresh thyme, for garnish

Preheat the oven to 375°F. To prepare the chicken, place the bacon in a flameproof casserole or baking dish, and sauté over medium heat for 2 or 3 minutes per side, or until cooked through but not crisp. Remove with a slotted spoon and drain on paper towels. Add the chicken and sauté until browned on all sides, about 5 minutes. Remove with a slotted spoon and drain on paper towels. Add the oil to the casserole and when heated through, add the onion, leek, and garlic. Sauté for 5 minutes, and then add the bell peppers. Sauté for 8 minutes longer, stirring occasionally, until softened. Add the tomatoes, stock, and oregano, and season with salt and pepper. Add the bacon and chicken to the casserole and bring just to a boil. Transfer to the oven and braise for about 40 minutes, or until the chicken is tender.

While the chicken is cooking, prepare the mashed potatoes. Reserving the tomatoes, drain the oil from the sun-dried tomatoes into a nonstick sauté pan. Add the shallots, and sauté over medium-high heat for 3 or 4 minutes, until soft. (Add a little more olive oil if necessary.) Stir the shallots and sun-dried tomatoes into the mashed potatoes, and adjust the seasonings.

Spoon the braised chicken onto warm serving plates and spoon the mashed potatoes next to the chicken. Garnish with the thyme.

SERVES 4

SAUTÉED CHICKEN
WITH MUSHROOMS AND
LEMON-MUSTARD SAUCE ON LINGUINE

Lemon is a flavoring with chicken that transcends national cuisines. From Italy and France to the eastern Mediterranean and China, the two ingredients suit each other very well. Cilantro and basil are other "bright" herbal flavors that complement chicken to great effect. In this recipe we offer the option of marinating the chicken in a zipper-lock bag. It's a useful technique as it keeps the liquid in contact with more of the chicken during the marinating process, and it avoids any messiness. As with other chicken recipes in this chapter, by all means use whole breasts rather than half breasts if you like. Fettuccine or spaghetti can be substituted for the linguine.

FOR THE MARINADE AND CHICKEN:
½ cup freshly squeezed lemon juice

½ cup olive oil

2 tablespoons minced fresh cilantro leaves

2 cloves garlic, minced

¼ teaspoon salt

¼ teaspoon freshly ground black pepper

4 boneless, skinless chicken breasts (about 7 ounces each)

2 tablespoons olive oil

FOR THE LEMON-MUSTARD SAUCE:
2 tablespoons butter (¼ stick)

2 tablespoons olive oil

1 small onion, finely diced

8 ounces sliced mushrooms

¼ cup freshly squeezed lemon juice

1 tablespoon Dijon mustard

¾ cup heavy cream

Salt and freshly ground white pepper to taste

14 ounces fresh linguine or 12 ounces dried

4 teaspoons minced fresh basil leaves, for garnish

To prepare the marinade, place the lemon juice, oil, cilantro, garlic, salt, and pepper in a mixing bowl and whisk together. Transfer to a large baking dish or large plastic zipper-lock bag, add the chicken breasts, and marinate in the refrigerator for 1 hour, turning once or twice.

Remove the chicken from the marinade. Heat the oil in a large nonstick sauté pan and cook over medium-high heat for 6 to 7 minutes on each side, or until well cooked through. Let the chicken cool a little and cut it into thin strips.

To prepare the sauce, heat the butter and oil in a large sauté pan, and when the butter is melted, add the onion. Sauté over medium heat for 5 minutes, until translucent. Add the mushrooms and sauté for 5 more minutes, stirring often, or until tender. Reduce the heat to low and add the chicken strips. Combine the lemon juice and mustard in a cup, and then add to the pan. Add the cream and warm through; do not boil. Season with salt and pepper.

While the sauce is cooking, bring a saucepan of salted water to a rapid boil and add the linguine. Cook until al dente and drain. Arrange the linguine in warm serving bowls or plates and spoon the chicken and mushroom mixture on top. Garnish with the basil.

SERVES 4

CLASSIC
BEAUJOLAIS COQ AU VIN
WITH TOASTED CROUTONS

This classic stew—one of the most famous poultry dishes of France—is a specialty of Burgundy, and the city of Dijon in particular. Here, we use a fruity, young wine from the Beaujolais region in southern Burgundy to marinate and cook the chicken. While traditional recipes do not call for marinating, we recommend it here, as it gives the chicken an even more intense flavor. Use a good-quality bottle of wine—the results will depend on it—and enjoy the same wine to accompany the meal. Fried croutons are an authentic accompaniment to coq au vin, and you may fry the croutons—slices of French bread—in olive oil or butter instead of toasting them, if you prefer. Alternatively, serve the stew with rice, noodles, or potatoes.

Place the chicken in a large baking dish and add the wine, garlic, and bouquet garni. Marinate in the refrigerator for at least 3 hours, and preferably overnight.

Remove the chicken from the marinade and pat dry with paper towels. Reserve the marinade. Place the flour on a plate, season with salt and pepper, and dredge the chicken pieces in the mixture. Set aside. Blanch the pearl onions in a saucepan of boiling water for 1 minute, and then drain. Heat 3 tablespoons of the oil in a heavy flameproof casserole and add the bacon and pearl onions. Sauté over medium-high heat for 5 minutes, stirring often, until the onions are translucent. Remove the bacon and pearl onions with a slotted spoon and reserve. Add the chicken pieces to the casserole in 2 batches, and sauté each batch, turning once or twice, for 6 or 7 minutes, or until browned. Remove the chicken and reserve. Add the mushrooms and brandy to the casserole and sauté for 3 minutes, stirring often. Add the reserved marinade and stir to deglaze the pan. Return the chicken pieces, bacon, and onions to the pan, add the stock, and bring to a boil. Reduce the heat to medium-low, cover, and simmer for 35 to 40 minutes, until the chicken is tender and cooked through; stir after 15 minutes. Remove the chicken and keep warm. Uncover the casserole, raise the heat to medium-high, and reduce the cooking liquid for 8 or 10 minutes, or until thickened, stirring occasionally. Adjust the seasonings and return the chicken to the casserole.

Preheat the broiler. Brush the bread with the remaining 3 tablespoons of olive oil and place on a baking sheet, in 2 batches if necessary. Toast under the broiler for 2 or 3 minutes, until golden brown. Serve 2 pieces of chicken on each warm serving plate and spoon the vegetables and sauce over and around the chicken. Serve with the toasted croutons.

SERVES 4

1 chicken (about 4 pounds), cut into 8 pieces

1 bottle (750 ml) Beaujolais red wine (about 3 1/2 cups)

2 cloves garlic, chopped

1 Bouquet Garni (page 226) or 1/2 tablespoon Herbes de Provence

1 cup all-purpose flour

Salt and freshly ground black pepper to taste

4 ounces pearl onions

6 tablespoons olive oil

2/3 cup diced bacon

10 ounces button mushrooms

3 tablespoons brandy

2 cups Chicken Stock (page 225)

20 slices baguette loaf, cut on the bias

POULTRY AND FOWL

VERACRUZ BRAISED CHICKEN
IN PEANUT SAUCE WITH JÍCAMA-MANGO SALAD

You might expect to find this colorful dish in the Mexican Gulf state of Veracruz. The sauce—actually a mole (see also page 199)—is typical of the region, as well as of the southern states of Oaxaca and the Yucatán. When preparing the chicken, either cut a whole bird into 8 pieces or use only your favorite parts—drumsticks or thighs or bone-in breast, for instance. The salad tastes both lushly tropical and crisply refreshing. Jícama is widely available, especially in Hispanic markets, but you can substitute water chestnuts for a similar crunchy texture. Serve with rice, if desired.

To prepare the salad, place the jícama in a mixing bowl and add the citrus juices. Toss well and let sit in the refrigerator for 1 hour, tossing occasionally. Add the mango, cilantro, onion, chile powder, and salt, and gently combine. When you are ready to serve, place a radicchio leaf on each serving plate and spoon the salad onto and next to the leaves.

To prepare the sauce, place the cinnamon and allspice in a hot, dry, small skillet. Toast over medium heat for about 1 minute, or until fragrant. Transfer to a bowl and add the pepper. Heat 1 tablespoon of the peanut oil in a sauté pan, and add the onion and garlic. Sauté over medium heat for 5 minutes, or until translucent. Transfer to a blender, and add the toasted spice mixture, the peanut butter, tomatoes, chiles, stock, and vinegar. Purée until smooth. Heat another 2 tablespoons of the oil in a large, cast-iron skillet, and when hot, add the chicken. (Cook in 2 batches if necessary.) Sauté over medium-high heat for about 5 or 6 minutes per side, or until cooked through and light golden. Set aside. Add the remaining tablespoon of oil to the skillet if necessary, and add the puréed sauce. Cook over medium heat for 3 or 4 minutes, stirring constantly. Stir in 1 1/2 cups of water and return to a boil. Add the cooked chicken, reduce the heat to low, and simmer for 20 minutes. Add the coconut milk, bring to a simmer, and reduce the heat to low. Cook for 10 more minutes, or until the sauce is thickened. (If not adding coconut milk, simmer the chicken for a total of 30 minutes.)

Serve 2 chicken pieces per plate and spoon with some of the sauce. Garnish with the cilantro and serve with the salad.

SERVES 4

FOR THE JÍCAMA-MANGO SALAD:

1 pound jícama, peeled and finely julienned into matchsticks

1/4 cup freshly squeezed lime juice

1/4 cup freshly squeezed orange juice

1 cup finely diced mango (2 small mangoes)

1/4 cup chopped fresh cilantro leaves

1/4 cup minced red onion

1/2 tablespoon pure red chile powder, preferably New Mexican

Salt to taste

4 large radicchio leaves

FOR THE BRAISED CHICKEN AND PEANUT SAUCE:

1/2 teaspoon ground cinnamon

1/4 teaspoon ground allspice

1/2 teaspoon freshly ground black pepper

4 tablespoons peanut oil

1/2 cup diced onion

2 cloves garlic, minced

1 cup peanut butter

3 plum tomatoes, roasted, peeled, seeded, and chopped (page 228)

3 canned chipotle chiles in adobo, seeded and chopped

2 cups Chicken Stock (page 225)

2 tablespoons red wine vinegar

4 pounds bone-in chicken pieces, chopped

1/2 cup canned unsweetened coconut milk (optional)

2 tablespoons chopped fresh cilantro leaves, for garnish

HONEY-ROASTED TURKEY
WITH ROASTED PARSNIPS AND POTATOES AND BACON BRUSSELS SPROUTS

This simple and rewarding dish makes an ideal centerpiece for the Thanksgiving or Christmas table. Remove the turkey from the refrigerator about 1 hour before you plan on cooking it, and pour the honey mixture over it. Let rest, basting a few times while the turkey is coming to room temperature. Serve with the Cranberry-Orange Spread (page 211), left chunky as the recipe headnote suggests, and the gravy recipe on page 36.

FOR THE HONEY-ROASTED TURKEY AND POTATOES:

1 young turkey (about 10 pounds)

$2/3$ cup honey

$5\,1/3$ tablespoons butter ($1/3$ cup)

$1/2$ tablespoon pure red chile powder (optional)

FOR THE POTATOES AND PARSNIPS:

1 pound parsnips, peeled and cut in half lengthwise, and then crosswise

1 pound russet potatoes, peeled and halved

FOR THE BACON BRUSSELS SPROUTS:

1 pound Brussels sprouts, trimmed and cut in half lengthwise

$1/2$ cup diced bacon

2 tablespoons butter ($1/4$ stick)

Salt and freshly ground black pepper to taste

Preheat the oven to 425°F. Place the turkey in a large roasting pan. Place the honey, butter, and chile powder in a saucepan, and cook over low heat until the butter is melted, stirring well. Pour the mixture over the turkey and baste again with the mixture in the pan. Arrange the parsnips and potatoes in the pan around the turkey, cut-sides down. Transfer to the oven and roast for 20 minutes. (The honey mixture will have darkened.)

Reduce the oven temperature to 350°F., and baste the turkey again. Loosely cover with foil. Continue roasting for $2\,3/4$ to 3 hours, or until the internal temperature reaches 170°F. and the juices run clear, basting every 30 minutes or so. Remove the vegetables after about 1 hour, or when cooked through. Reserve and warm through in the oven before serving. Remove the foil over the turkey for the last 20 minutes of cooking to allow the skin to become crispy. Take out of the oven and let rest for 10 minutes before carving. (The internal temperature will rise to about 175°F.)

To prepare the sprouts, bring a saucepan of salted water to a boil. Add the sprouts and blanch for 7 or 8 minutes, or until just tender. Drain. Meanwhile, sauté the bacon in a nonstick sauté pan over medium-high heat for about 5 or 6 minutes, or until just crispy. Drain the bacon on paper towels and set aside. Heat the butter in a clean sauté pan and add the blanched sprouts. Toss to coat with the butter, add the bacon, and season with salt and pepper. Transfer to warm serving plates and serve with the turkey, potatoes, and parsnips.

SERVES 4

ROASTED TURKEY SANDWICHES
WITH CRANBERRY-ORANGE SPREAD
AND RED CHILE CHIPS

This recipe offers another great way to use up leftover turkey meat. The spread is versatile, as it can be left a little chunkier and served as cranberry sauce with roast turkey. You can make it with fresh cranberries, in which case use about 1½ cups. As there will be no need to rehydrate them, just purée them with the orange juice in the food processor. The brioche gives these sandwiches a soft richness, but you can use a French baguette or whole-grain bread, if you prefer.

To prepare the spread, place the cranberries and orange juice in a bowl and let sit for 30 minutes. Transfer to a food processor, and add the pecans, sugar, and lime zest. Purée until smooth. Stir in the cilantro and season with salt. Keep refrigerated.

To prepare the chips, fill a metal bowl with cold water. Slice the potatoes as thinly as possible with a mandoline or a very sharp knife, and add to the bowl. Rinse well, drain on paper towels, and pat dry. Heat the oil in a deep-fryer or large saucepan to 375°F. Fry the potatoes in batches in the oil for 1 or 2 minutes, until golden brown and crisp. Remove with a slotted spoon and drain on paper towels. Transfer to a large bowl, and sprinkle with the chile powder and salt. Toss together, sprinkle in some of the juice from the lemon, and toss again.

To assemble the sandwiches, spread each slice of bread with about 1 tablespoon of the orange-cranberry spread. Place a red bell pepper half on top of 4 of the slices, and then top with the turkey. Arrange the arugula on top of the turkey and close the sandwiches with the 4 remaining slices of bread. Cut each sandwich in half on the diagonal and serve with the potato chips.

SERVES 4

FOR THE CRANBERRY-ORANGE SPREAD:
1 cup dried cranberries (about 4 ounces)
¾ cup freshly squeezed orange juice
¼ cup chopped pecans, toasted (page 229)
2 tablespoons sugar
Zest of ½ lime
3 tablespoons minced fresh cilantro leaves
Salt to taste

FOR THE RED CHILE CHIPS:
1 pound Yellow Finn or Yukon Gold potatoes, peeled
4 cups peanut oil
1 teaspoon pure red chile powder, or to taste
¼ teaspoon salt
½ lemon, seeded

FOR THE SANDWICHES:
8 slices brioche or challah bread
2 red bell peppers, roasted, peeled, seeded, and cut in half lengthwise (page 228)
4 (5-ounce) slices Honey-Roasted Turkey breast meat (page 210), smoked turkey, or other cooked turkey breast meat
1 cup firmly packed arugula leaves or green lettuce

PACIFIC RIM TURKEY SAUSAGE
WITH JEAN-MARIE'S MACADAMIA NUT AND PINEAPPLE RICE PILAF

In July of every year, a spectacular culinary event occurs on the Big Island of Hawaii called Foods of the Sun. Californian food writer Janice Wald Henderson and Honolulu-based chef Alan Wong devise the program hosted by The Mauna Lani Bay Hotel on the Kona coast. Chefs specifically from sunny climates are invited to lead seminars, offer food demonstrations, and most important, to cook for the event participants. There is something in the spirit and flavors of foods from the Mediterranean, Florida and the Caribbean, Hawaii, and southeast Asia, for example, that really is a shared phenomenon. This dish is typical of the bright flavors and colors, and the lightness of texture and "mouth-feel" that these cuisines feature. The pilaf is the creation of the French-born and trained chef, Jean-Marie Josselin, owner of A Pacific Cafe, a fine-dining restaurant on three of the Hawaiian islands. He is also author of A Taste of Hawaii, *a best-selling book on contemporary Hawaiian cuisine.*

FOR THE TURKEY SAUSAGE:
3 tablespoons butter

2 tablespoons minced onion

1 tablespoon peeled and minced fresh ginger

1 tablespoon minced fresh lemongrass

1/2 tablespoon minced garlic

2 serrano chiles, seeded and minced

2 fresh kaffir lime leaves, minced, or
  1 teaspoon minced lime zest

1 1/4 pounds high-quality ground turkey meat

1 egg, beaten

2 teaspoons white sesame seeds

1 teaspoon black sesame seeds

Salt and freshly ground black pepper

1 tablespoon peanut oil

FOR THE RICE PILAF:
1 tablespoon butter

1 1/2 cups long-grain white rice

2 teaspoons minced garlic

1/4 cup diced red bell pepper

1/4 cup diced yellow bell pepper

3 cups Chicken Stock (page 225)

1/2 cup golden raisins

1/2 cup chopped macadamia nuts, toasted

1 fresh sage leaf

1 teaspoon salt

1/3 cup chopped fresh cilantro leaves

1 cup diced fresh pineapple

2 tablespoons fresh cilantro leaves, for garnish

To prepare the sausage, heat the butter in a large skillet, and add the onion, ginger, lemongrass, garlic, chiles, and lime leaves. Stir well and sauté over medium-high heat for 2 minutes. Transfer to a mixing bowl, let cool, and add the turkey meat. Add the egg, the white and black sesame seeds, salt, and pepper, and thoroughly combine. Divide the mixture into 8 patties and let sit in the refrigerator while making the rice pilaf.

Preheat the oven to 375°F. In a flameproof casserole, melt the butter and add the rice. Stir over medium heat for 10 seconds, until the rice is well coated. Add the garlic and stir for 10 seconds longer. Add the bell peppers and stir for 30 seconds. Add the stock and bring the mixture to a boil. Add the raisins, nuts, sage, and salt. Cover the casserole, transfer to the oven, and bake for about 18 minutes. Remove from the oven and let rest for 10 minutes. Stir in the cilantro and pineapple, and adjust the seasonings if necessary.

Meanwhile, heat the peanut oil in a nonstick sauté pan, and when hot, add the turkey sausage patties. Sauté over medium heat for 5 or 6 minutes per side, or until lightly browned and well cooked through. Transfer to serving plates, serve with the pilaf, and garnish with the cilantro.

SERVES 4

HILL COUNTRY TURKEY CHILI
WITH BUTTERMILK CORN BREAD

This dish has a similar format to the Venison Chili with Pueblo Blue Corn Bread (page 163), but the flavors are quite different. By all means use the blue corn bread recipe here, if you prefer. For notes on chili, see the venison recipe. If you have more leftover Thanksgiving turkey than you know what to do with, this recipe might just be one solution. Finely chop the turkey meat and sauté with the onions for 1 or 2 minutes only. We call for serving the corn bread on the side, but you might consider placing a square in the center of each serving bowl and ladling the chili around it.

Preheat the oven to 375°F. To prepare the corn bread, place the cornmeal, flour, sugar, baking powder, and salt in a mixing bowl. In a separate bowl, whisk together the butter, buttermilk, milk, and egg yolks. Whisk the liquid ingredients into the dry just until they are combined; do not over-mix. Fold in the corn and cilantro with a spatula. Whisk the egg whites in a bowl until they form stiff peaks. Gently fold into the batter. Pour the batter into an oiled, 11 x 7-inch or 10-inch square baking pan, and bake in the oven for 20 to 25 minutes, or until springy and lightly browned. Remove from the oven and let cool in the pan on a rack.

To prepare the chili, heat the olive oil in a saucepan and add the onions, bell pepper, and garlic. Sauté over medium-high heat for 7 or 8 minutes, or until soft. Add the turkey and sauté for 7 or 8 minutes longer, or until browned, stirring to break up any lumps of meat. Stir in the chile powder, cumin, and oregano, and sauté for 2 minutes. Add the wine, stock, beans, tomatoes, tomato paste, and corn, and bring to a boil. Reduce the heat to medium-low and simmer, uncovered, for 30 to 40 minutes, or until thickened. Add the salt and adjust the seasonings as necessary.

Ladle the chile into warm serving bowls and garnish with the cilantro. Cut the corn bread into squares and serve on the side.

SERVES 4

FOR THE CORN BREAD:

1 cup yellow or blue cornmeal

1 cup all-purpose flour

2 tablespoons sugar

1 teaspoon baking powder

1 teaspoon salt

1/4 cup melted butter

3/4 cup buttermilk

1/2 cup milk

3 eggs, separated

1/2 cup fresh corn kernels (about 1 ear)

2 tablespoons minced fresh cilantro leaves

FOR THE TURKEY CHILI:

2 tablespoons olive oil

2 onions, chopped

1 red bell pepper, diced

3 cloves garlic, minced

1 1/2 pounds high-quality ground turkey

3 tablespoons pure red chile powder

1 teaspoon ground cumin

1 teaspoon dried oregano

1 cup red wine, such as Merlot or Cabernet Sauvignon

1 1/2 cups Chicken Stock (page 225)

3 cups cooked black beans (page 226), or canned black beans or pinto beans, drained

3 cups canned crushed tomatoes

1/4 cup tomato paste

1 cup fresh corn kernels

Salt to taste

4 teaspoons chopped fresh cilantro leaves, for garnish

POULTRY AND FOWL

BRAISED DUCK À L'ORANGE
WITH WATERCRESS SALAD

This recipe adapts the style of dish called "à la bigarade" in French cuisine, referring to a brown sauce flavored with bitter oranges. Seville (marmalade) oranges are the preferred variety here, or at least some type that is not too sweet. Roasting the bird before braising it helps to give the skin a darker color and draws off some of the fat. The combination of duck with orange is a traditional favorite, and it pairs wonderfully with the refreshing, spicy watercress salad garnished with pecans and cranberries.

FOR THE BRAISED DUCK:
1 duck (about 5 pounds)
Salt and freshly ground black pepper to taste
2 oranges, peeled, seeded, and chopped
2 green apples, peeled, cored, and chopped
1 bay leaf, crumbled
1 cup dry white wine
1 onion, sliced
1 carrot, sliced
1 stalk celery, sliced
1 cup Chicken Stock (page 225)
3/4 cup freshly squeezed orange juice
1 tablespoon arrowroot or cornstarch
1 tablespoon freshly squeezed lemon juice
1/4 cup julienned orange zest
1 tablespoon grated lemon zest

FOR THE WATERCRESS SALAD:
1/2 cup dried cranberries
1/4 cup olive oil
2 tablespoons red wine vinegar
1 tablespoon chopped fresh tarragon or mint leaves
6 cups fresh watercress leaves or 2 large bunches watercress (about 1 pound)
1/2 cup chopped pecans, toasted (page 229)
Salt and freshly ground black pepper to taste

Preheat the oven to 425°F. Season the cavity of the duck with salt and pepper. In a mixing bowl, combine the oranges, apples, and bay leaf, and stuff into the cavity. Truss the bird with butcher's twine, and lightly pierce the skin all over with a skewer to better allow the release of fat. Place the duck in a roasting pan and roast in the oven for about 1 hour, basting once or twice with the fat from the pan. Remove the duck from the oven, take out of the roasting pan, and transfer to an ovenproof casserole. Pour off the fat from the roasting pan and reserve. On the stove top, add the wine to the roasting pan and stir to deglaze the pan. Reduce the liquid by half over medium heat. Add to the casserole.

Pour 3 tablespoons of the duck fat in a large sauté pan, and sauté the onion, carrot, and celery over medium heat for 5 or 6 minutes, or until softened. Add the stock and bring to a boil. Transfer to the casserole, cover, and braise the duck in the oven for 30 minutes. Uncover the casserole and braise for 25 to 30 minutes longer. Transfer the duck to a serving platter and cover loosely with foil to keep warm. Strain the liquid from the casserole into a clean saucepan, and degrease by removing the duck fat from the surface with a large spoon. Add all but 2 tablespoons of the orange juice. Mix the remaining orange juice with the arrowroot, and add to the pan. Stir in the lemon juice, orange zest, and lemon zest. Bring to a boil, stirring constantly, and simmer over medium-low heat for 2 minutes, or until thickened. Adjust the seasonings. Carve the duck and serve a little of the fruit from the cavity, if you wish. Drizzle with the sauce, and pass the remaining sauce at the table.

While the duck is braising, prepare the salad. Rehydrate the cranberries in warm water for 20 minutes. Place the oil, vinegar, and tarragon in a bowl and whisk together. Place the watercress in a serving bowl. Drain the cranberries and add to the watercress. Add the pecans to the salad, and season with salt and pepper. Toss the salad with the dressing, and serve with the duck.

SERVES 4

MAGRET DE CANARD: DUCK BREAST
WITH APRICOT SAUCE AND PINWHEEL POTATOES

Magret refers to the meaty breast of the moulard duck, a specially bred hybrid of the lean, meaty Muscovy and the flavorful Long Island duck (better known as Peking ducks in France). Trimmed of fat and sliced, the finely grained magret can almost be mistaken for beef. In France, magret—and duck dishes in general—is one of the specialties of the Gascony region, where it is said that there are almost as many recipes for duck as there are Gascons. This dish is inspired by multiple versions of duck breast and fruit sauces enjoyed on a recent trip through Gascony and the Périgord—and especially by a magnificent dish enjoyed at the acclaimed three-star Troisgros restaurant in Roanne, in central France.

To prepare the sauce, place the preserves and $1/2$ cup of water in a saucepan. Bring to a boil, while stirring continuously. In a cup, combine 1 tablespoon of water with the arrowroot and add to the pan. Return to a boil and stir until thickened. Remove from the heat and stir in the lemon juice, cayenne, and sugar. Warm through just before serving.

To prepare the potatoes, lightly butter a sheet of parchment paper set on a baking sheet. Cut the potatoes crosswise into very thin slices with a mandoline or sharp knife, pat dry, and arrange in a single layer on the parchment paper in 8 small circular pinwheel patterns with the slices overlapping. Brush the pinwheels with the butter and sprinkle with salt and pepper. Bake in the oven for 20 to 25 minutes, or until golden and crisp. Garnish with the parsley just before serving.

To prepare the duck, heat the oil in a large nonstick sauté pan. Season the duck with salt and pepper, and when the oil is hot, place in the pan, skin-side down. Cook for 8 to 10 minutes, or until the skin is golden and crisp; pour off any excess fat. Turn the breasts over and cook for 2 or 3 more minutes for medium-rare, about 4 minutes for medium, or to the desired doneness. Remove the duck from the pan, let rest for 5 minutes, and then cut each breast into 4 or 5 slices.

Spoon 2 or 3 tablespoons of the apricot sauce onto warm serving plates. Arrange the sliced duck breasts in a fan on top of the sauce and serve with 2 potato pinwheels on each plate.

SERVES 4

FOR THE APRICOT SAUCE:
$1/2$ cup good-quality apricot preserves, preferably Bonne Maman

1 teaspoon arrowroot or cornstarch

2 tablespoons freshly squeezed lemon juice

$1/2$ teaspoon cayenne (optional)

Sugar to taste (optional)

FOR THE PINWHEEL POTATOES:
$1 1/2$ pounds russet potatoes, peeled

2 tablespoons melted butter

Salt and freshly ground black pepper to taste

2 teaspoons minced fresh flat-leaf parsley, for garnish

FOR THE MAGRET DE CANARD:
$1/2$ tablespoon olive oil

4 single duck breasts (skin on) (about 5 ounces each)

Salt and freshly ground black pepper to taste

POULTRY AND FOWL

SPICE-RUBBED
CORNISH GAME HENS
WITH RICE FLORENTINE AND RED BELL PEPPER COULIS

Cornish game hens are not, as some might assume from the name, game birds—that is, wild fowl. Instead, these miniature birds are young Cornish chickens or Cornish-White Rock chicken hybrids. By definition, Cornish game hens are a few weeks old; as the birds mature, they become (by definition) frying chickens, and then, a few weeks later still, roasters. The flavor of the game hens' white meat is delicate (there is no dark meat), and the spice rub in this recipe provides some assertiveness and character. For this reason, too, marinades are also favored for game hens. With the red bell pepper coulis, this dish contains plenty of color contrast. Sprinkle the rice with 2 tablespoons of freshly grated Parmesan cheese, if you like.

FOR THE SPICE RUB AND CORNISH GAME HENS:

1 1/2 tablespoons dried tarragon

1 tablespoon paprika

1 tablespoon freshly ground black pepper

2 teaspoons garlic powder

2 teaspoons dried marjoram

1 teaspoon dried sage

1 teaspoon dried thyme

1 teaspoon ground cumin

1 teaspoon pure red chile powder

1 teaspoon salt

4 Cornish game hens (about 1 1/4 pounds each), cut in half

1 tablespoon olive oil

FOR THE RED BELL PEPPER COULIS:

2 tablespoons olive oil

1 onion, minced

2 cloves garlic, minced

3 large red bell peppers, roasted, peeled, seeded, and chopped (page 228)

1/2 cup tomato paste

2 tablespoons dry white wine

2 tablespoons chopped fresh basil leaves

1/2 teaspoon chopped fresh thyme leaves

1 teaspoon honey

Salt and freshly ground black pepper to taste

FOR THE RICE FLORENTINE:

1 tablespoon butter

1 cup long-grain white rice

2 cups Chicken Stock (page 225)

4 cups chopped spinach leaves

2 tablespoons Dijon mustard

To prepare the rub, place the tarragon, paprika, black pepper, garlic powder, marjoram, sage, thyme, cumin, chile powder, and salt in a bowl, and thoroughly combine. Rub the game hens with the oil and then rub with the spice mixture. Let sit in the refrigerator for 2 or 3 hours.

To prepare the coulis, heat the olive oil in a saucepan, and add the onion and garlic. Sauté over medium heat for 3 or 4 minutes, until soft. Add the bell peppers, tomato paste, wine, basil, thyme, and honey, and season with salt and pepper. Cover, reduce the heat to low, and simmer for 20 minutes, until thickened. (Add a little more wine if necessary). Transfer to a blender and purée until smooth. Transfer to a clean saucepan and reheat just before serving.

Prepare the grill. Lightly oil the cooking grate and place the game hens skin-side down on the grill over medium heat. Grill for 25 to 30 minutes, turning occasionally and moving over indirect heat if the birds appear to be cooking too fast. They should be crisp and golden brown and the juices should run clear when the meat is pierced near the leg bone.

To prepare the rice, heat the butter in a saucepan, add the rice, and stir over medium heat for 1 minute, until the rice is coated. Add the stock and bring to a boil. Cover, reduce the heat to low, and simmer for 10 minutes. Stir in the spinach and mustard, cover, and simmer for 5 to 10 minutes longer, until the rice has absorbed the liquid and is tender.

Spoon some of the sauce onto warm serving plates. Place the game hens on top of the sauce and serve with the rice.

SERVES 4

GARLIC AND THYME–
STUFFED QUAIL
WITH ROASTED YAMS AND FENNEL SAUCE

Quail enjoyed in the United States is not really quail at all. Or at least, that's what Europeans will tell you! The earliest European explorers named the native American species after the distantly related flight-averse bird that it most resembled from the Old World; for the same reason, quail are known as partridges in parts of the South. The most common type of American quail, the bobwhite—named after its distinctive call—is almost exclusively farm-raised. This recipe demonstrates how well fennel is suited to the flavors of fowl, just as it is to game meat, such as venison. Use Red Chile–Mashed Potatoes (page 151) instead of the yams if you prefer, or substitute sweet potatoes for the yams. Although the two tubers are unrelated, they are usually interchangeable on the plate.

FOR THE FENNEL SAUCE:

1 cup red wine, preferably
  Cabernet Sauvignon

1/2 cup Chicken Stock (page 225)

1 tablespoon tomato paste or ketchup

1/2 tablespoon fennel seeds

Salt and freshly ground black pepper to taste

FOR THE SPICY YAMS:

1 pound yams, peeled and cubed

8 ounces white or russet potatoes, peeled
  and cubed

1 tablespoon olive oil

Salt to taste

1 teaspoon cayenne

FOR THE STUFFED QUAIL:

8 quail (about 5 ounces each)

Salt and freshly ground black pepper

1 tablespoon minced garlic

24 sprigs fresh thyme

1/4 cup olive oil

Preheat the oven to 450°F.

To prepare the sauce, heat the wine in a saucepan, bring to a boil, and reduce by half. Add the stock, tomato paste, and fennel. Return to a boil, and reduce the liquid by half until about 1/2 cup is left. Season with salt and pepper and keep warm, or reheat just before serving.

While the sauce is reducing, place the yams and potatoes in a roasting pan and toss with the olive oil, salt, and cayenne. Roast in the oven for 35 to 40 minutes, or until tender.

Meanwhile, season the quail with salt and pepper, and stuff with the garlic and thyme. Heat the olive oil in a roasting pan over medium-high heat, and sear in the hot oil for about 5 minutes, or until browned on all sides. Transfer the roasting pan to the oven and roast at 450°F. for about 15 minutes, or until cooked through and the juices run clear.

Spoon the sauce onto warm serving plates. Serve 2 quail per person, and arrange the yams next to the quail.

SERVES 4

CILANTRO-MARINATED
GRILLED QUAIL
WITH SAUTÉED LEEKS AND BUTTON MUSHROOMS

Farm-raised bobwhite quail (also called blue quail in some parts of the United States) has delicate meat, and some connoisseurs prefer the darker, gamier meat of wild quail, available at specialty butchers. The thick, pesto-like marinade we use here is inspired by a recipe of Philadelphia chef Jim Coleman (see page 134), and it can also be used with chicken. An alternative method for marinating (which works equally well in other recipes) is to pour the marinating liquid into a couple of plastic zipper-lock bags (rather than a baking dish), and then let the quail marinate in the refrigerator. If you prefer, sauté or broil the quail instead of grilling it. If button mushrooms are unavailable, use larger mushrooms cut into halves or quarters.

To prepare the quail, place the cilantro, stock, oil, garlic, lime juice, sugar, and pepper in a food processor or blender, and purée until smooth. Transfer to a large baking dish (or 2 smaller dishes), and add the quail. Cover the dish and marinate in the refrigerator for 3 or 4 hours.

Prepare the grill. Remove the quail from the marinade, wiping off any excess marinade, and bring to room temperature.

Meanwhile, prepare the leeks and mushrooms. Heat 2 tablespoons of the oil in a large sauté pan and sauté the leeks over medium-high heat for 4 to 5 minutes, or until soft. Remove from the pan and set aside. Add the remaining 2 tablespoons of oil and when heated through, add the mushrooms. Toss the mushrooms for about 5 minutes, until cooked through. Return the leeks to the pan, and add the sun-dried tomatoes, wine, corn bread crumbs, marjoram, salt, and pepper. Toss together and cook for 3 or 4 minutes longer, or until the liquid has almost evaporated.

While the leeks and mushrooms are cooking, grill the quail over direct medium-high heat for 4 or 5 minutes on each side, or until cooked through and the juices run clear. Transfer to warm serving plates and serve with the leek and mushroom mixture.

SERVES 4

FOR THE CILANTRO MARINADE AND QUAIL:

1 1/2 cups fresh cilantro leaves

3/4 cup Chicken Stock (page 225)

1/4 cup olive oil

6 cloves garlic, chopped

3 tablespoons freshly squeezed lime juice

1/2 tablespoon sugar

1/2 tablespoon freshly ground black pepper

8 boneless quail (about 4 ounces each), pressed flat

FOR THE LEEKS AND MUSHROOMS:

4 tablespoons extra-virgin olive oil

2 leeks, white and light green parts only, thinly sliced

12 ounces button mushrooms, cleaned

2 tablespoons chopped sun-dried tomatoes (packed in oil)

3 tablespoons dry white wine or Chicken Stock (page 225)

1/4 cup Campfire Skillet Corn Bread crumbs (page 144) or store bought

1 teaspoon minced fresh marjoram leaves

Salt and freshly ground black pepper to taste

POULTRY AND FOWL

DUCK BREAST
WITH CUMBERLAND SAUCE AND WARM GOAT CHEESE SALAD

About two-thirds of the duck meat sold commercially in the United States comes from the white-feathered Long Island breed, a type of mallard also known as Peking duck. Virtually all of the farm-raised birds in this country are descended from three Peking ducks brought to Long Island from China in 1873, making that part of New York State the center of the duck industry for decades. The salad is a simple, classic French presentation; use a dressing of your choice for the salad, if you prefer. Cumberland sauce is the traditional English accompaniment for game meat and ham, named in honor of the Duke of Cumberland (1845–1923). It is a classic accompaniment for venison, pork, and ham, as well as duck and chicken.

To prepare the sauce, place the red currant jelly and port in a saucepan. Bring to a boil, reduce the heat to low, and simmer for 10 minutes, uncovered, until reduced by one-quarter. Remove from the heat and add the citrus juices, lemon zest, mustard, and nutmeg. Combine thoroughly and return to medium heat. Bring to a boil, cook for 2 minutes, and set aside. Just before serving, warm through.

Prepare the broiler. To prepare the salad, place the frisée, watercress, and tomatoes in a mixing bowl. In a separate bowl, mix together the thyme, pepper, and lemon zest. Cut the goat cheese into 4 equal rounds and place on a baking sheet. While the duck is cooking, place the cheese under the broiler for about 1 minute, until the tops are bubbly and light golden. (Do not let the cheese become too runny.) Remove with a spatula. Toss the salad with the vinaigrette and arrange in a neat stack on one side of each serving plate. Place the goat cheese on top and sprinkle with the thyme mixture.

Season the duck breasts with salt and pepper. Heat the butter in a sauté pan, and when hot, add the duck, skin-side down. Sauté over medium heat for about 4 minutes on each side. Remove from the pan and let cool slightly. Cut each breast on the bias into 6 to 8 slices, and transfer to warm serving plates, arranging them in a fan next to the salad. Spoon some of the sauce over the duck and pass the rest at the table.

SERVES 4

FOR THE CUMBERLAND SAUCE:
1 cup red currant jelly
1/2 cup port
2 tablespoons freshly squeezed orange juice
2 tablespoons freshly squeezed lemon juice
1 tablespoon minced lemon zest
1 teaspoon Dijon mustard
1/4 teaspoon ground nutmeg

FOR THE SALAD:
3 cups frisée leaves, torn
1 cup watercress leaves
10 cherry or teardrop tomatoes, cut in half
1/2 teaspoon minced fresh thyme leaves
1/4 teaspoon freshly ground black pepper
1/4 teaspoon minced lemon zest
8 ounces fresh goat cheese (in log form)
2 tablespoons Papa's Real French Vinaigrette (page 32)

FOR THE DUCK BREAST:
4 boneless, skinless single duck breasts (about 5 ounces each)
Salt and freshly ground black pepper, to taste
2 tablespoons clarified butter

POULTRY AND FOWL

ROASTED STUFFED PHEASANT
WITH CRANBERRY-CHIPOTLE SAUCE AND ROASTED CORN MASHED POTATOES

Pheasant is a popular wild game bird in both the United States and Europe, although much of the commercial supply these days comes farm-raised and frozen. The bird is originally native to the Caucasus region of western Asia. It yields a mild but flavorful and slightly sweet meat that is lean and, therefore, prone to dryness. Pheasant should not be overcooked or it will become stringy and tough, and basting frequently with butter will help to keep the meat moist. For a shortcut, buy ready-made corn bread, or in a pinch, leave the pheasant unstuffed. This sauce, with its complex fruity-smoky flavors, makes a great accompaniment for other fowl and game, including venison. If necessary, substitute frozen cranberries for fresh; the method will remain the same.

FOR THE CRANBERRY-CHIPOTLE SAUCE:

1 tablespoon butter

2 cloves garlic, minced

2 tablespoons minced shallot

1 cup fresh cranberries

1/4 cup packed dark brown sugar

1/2 cup dry red wine

1 cup Chicken Stock (page 225)

1 tablespoon grated orange zest

1 canned chipotle chile in adobo, minced

1 teaspoon adobo sauce (from the canned chipotles)

Salt to taste

FOR THE PHEASANT:

2 pheasants (about 2 1/2 pounds each)

Salt and freshly ground black pepper to taste

4 cups roughly crumbled Campfire Skillet Corn Bread (page 144) or store-bought

1/2 tablespoon chopped fresh thyme leaves

1/2 tablespoon chopped fresh sage leaves

1/4 cup melted butter

FOR THE ROASTED CORN MASHED POTATOES:

Mashed Potatoes (page 36)

1 1/2 cups fresh corn kernels (about 2 large ears), roasted (page 229)

1/2 tablespoon minced fresh cilantro leaves or flat-leaf parsley (optional)

2 tablespoons chopped pecans, toasted (page 229)

To prepare the sauce, heat the butter in a small sauté pan. Add the garlic and shallot, and sauté over medium-high heat for 2 minutes, until softened. Remove from the heat and set aside. Place the cranberries, sugar, and wine in a saucepan and bring to a boil. Reduce the heat to a simmer and cook until the cranberries "burst," about 5 minutes. Add the reserved shallot mixture, the stock, orange zest, chipotle, and adobo sauce. Raise the heat to medium-high and reduce the liquid by half, 8 to 10 minutes. Season with salt and rewarm just before serving.

Preheat the oven to 425°F. To prepare the pheasant, season the birds with salt and pepper. Mix together the corn bread, thyme, and sage in a bowl, and stuff the pheasants. Truss with butcher's twine and place in a roasting pan, breast-side up. Brush with the melted butter and roast in the oven for 10 minutes. Reduce the heat to 350°F. and baste again. Roast for 45 to 50 more minutes, or until the juices run clear, basting with the butter every 10 minutes or so. Remove from the oven and let rest for 5 to 10 minutes before carving at the table.

With the mashed potatoes in a mixing bowl, add the corn and cilantro. Fold in to thoroughly combine.

Place the pheasant on each warm serving plate with a spoonful of the stuffing. Pour the sauce over the pheasant and garnish the sauce with the pecans. Serve with the potatoes.

SERVES 4

BACON-WRAPPED SQUAB
WITH MRS. SIMON'S POTATO PUDDING AND MUSHROOM-WINE SAUCE

Squab is the cooking term for young pigeons, usually farm-raised, with a tender, dark, and lean meat. Like pheasant (page 222), squab is prone to dryness, and laying bacon or pork butt over game birds to baste them while they cook is a classic technique known as "barding." This is another family recipe, this time from Fred's grandmother, Mrs. B. A. Simon. The potato pudding is a version of potato kugel, a traditional Jewish dish. Beatrice Sommer, a friend of the family who knew Fred's grandparents and provided us with the recipe, comments, "You'll enjoy the recipe as long as you are not too concerned about calories, fat, or cholesterol. It just goes to show how eating patterns have changed over the last 50 years." By all means, add some sautéed leeks and shallots to the potato mixture, if you like.

Preheat the oven to 400°F.

To prepare the potato pudding, place the potatoes in a large mixing bowl. Add the eggs, fat, and salt, and mix thoroughly. Place in a large gratin dish or in individual cup molds, and bake in the oven for 45 to 50 minutes, or until golden. (Less time is necessary if using cup molds.)

To prepare the mushroom sauce, heat the duck fat in a large sauté pan. Sauté the shallots over medium-high heat for about 3 minutes, until softened. Add the mushrooms and peppercorns, and cook for 3 or 4 minutes, until softened. Add the red wine and cook for 7 or 8 minutes longer, until reduced by half. Add the stock and cook for 5 minutes more. Just before serving, stir in the butter, thyme, mustard, and salt until well incorporated.

About 25 minutes before you are ready to serve, prepare the squab. Season the birds with salt and pepper. Place the butter in a roasting pan and briefly melt in the oven; do not let the butter brown. Place the squab breast-side down in the pan, brush with the melted butter, and cover each bird with 2 half-strips of bacon. Roast in the oven for 10 minutes. Remove the bacon slices and finish roasting for 3 to 5 minutes longer, or until the juices run clear. Remove from the oven and let rest for 5 minutes.

Place the squab on warm serving plates—with the bacon, if desired. Spoon the sauce over the birds and serve with the potato pudding.

SERVES 4

FOR THE POTATO PUDDING:
3 russet potatoes (about 8 ounces each), peeled and finely grated
2 eggs, beaten
3 tablespoons rendered duck or chicken fat
Pinch of salt

FOR THE MUSHROOM-WINE SAUCE:
1 tablespoon rendered duck fat or butter
2 tablespoons minced shallots
8 ounces mushrooms, sliced
1 teaspoon coarsely cracked black peppercorns
1/2 cup dry red wine
1/2 cup Chicken Stock (page 225)
1 1/2 tablespoons butter, diced
1 teaspoon minced fresh thyme leaves
1/2 teaspoon Dijon mustard
Salt to taste

FOR THE SQUAB:
4 squab (about 14 ounces each)
Salt and pepper to taste
3 tablespoons butter
4 slices bacon, cut in half

BASIC RECIPES, TECHNIQUES, AND DEFINITIONS

Beef, Veal, or Lamb Stock

This flavorful stock can be adapted to make veal or lamb stock by simply substituting the beef bones and meat with veal or lamb. Keep the stock refrigerated and freeze any that you will not be using within 2 or 3 days. For ease of use later on, freeze the stock in ice-cube trays, then transfer to zipper-lock bags. Remove individual cubes of stock as needed.

Preheat the oven to 450°F.

Place the beef bones, meat, and trimmings in a roasting pan with the carrots and onions. Roast in the oven for 30 to 40 minutes, stirring occasionally, until the mixture is browned. Transfer to a stockpot. Pour off the fat from the roasting pan, add the hot water, and stir to deglaze the pan. Add this mixture to the stockpot, along with the leek, celery, tomatoes, garlic, parsley, bay leaves, thyme, and vinegar. Add enough water to cover the mixture by 2 inches, and bring to a boil. Reduce the heat and simmer the stock for at least 4 hours, uncovered. Occasionally skim off any impurities that rise to the surface as it cooks. Add more water as necessary to keep the mixture covered. Strain, discard the solids, and let the stock cool. Cover and refrigerate until needed.

2 pounds beef bones, meat, and trimmings
3 carrots, chopped
2 small onions, chopped
2 cups hot water
1 leek, chopped
1 celery stalk, coarsely chopped
2 tomatoes, quartered, or 1 cup canned plum tomatoes
3 cloves garlic, crushed
8 sprigs fresh flat-leaf parsley
2 bay leaves
4 sprigs fresh thyme or $1/2$ teaspoon dried
2 tablespoons champagne vinegar or white wine vinegar

Yields about 2 quarts (8 cups)

Chicken Stock

This recipe is low in sodium, with less than 10 mg per cup, much lower than most ready-to-use canned stocks. Keep the stock refrigerated and freeze any that you will not be using within 2 or 3 days.

Place the water, chicken bones, onion, carrots, celery, garlic, and peppercorns in a stockpot or large saucepan and bring to a boil. Add the bouquet garni to the pan and reduce the heat to low. Partially cover the pan and simmer for at least 4 hours, and up to 6 hours, occasionally skimming any fat or impurities that rise to the surface. Add water as needed to keep all the ingredients covered.

Strain the stock into a large bowl and let sit for 15 minutes. Carefully skim the fat and then strain again into another bowl. Refrigerate the stock until the fat congeals on the surface, and then skim off the fat once again. Cover and keep stored in the refrigerator for up to 3 or 4 days, or freeze for up to 3 months.

3 quarts cold water
3 pounds uncooked chicken bones and/or raw wings and backs from 2 to 3 chickens
1 onion, chopped
2 carrots, sliced
1 stalk celery, sliced
2 cloves garlic
$1/2$ teaspoon black peppercorns
Bouquet Garni (page 226)

Yields about 2 quarts (8 cups)

BASIC RECIPES, TECHNIQUES, AND DEFINITIONS

MARK MILLER'S BLACK BEANS

Add the barbecue sauce for spicy Southwestern-style beans, but leave it out if you prefer beans without a smoky flavor.

1 teaspoon ground cumin
1 teaspoon ground coriander
1 teaspoon dried ground oregano
1 teaspoon dried ground marjoram
2 cups dried black beans, picked through and rinsed
1 onion, finely diced
3 cloves garlic, minced
2 serrano chiles, seeded and minced
2 bay leaves
1 cup tomato purée
1 tablespoon salt
1 cup barbecue sauce, preferably a smoky-flavored sauce (optional)

Place the cumin, coriander, oregano, and marjoram in a dry, heavy skillet, and toast over low heat for about 1 minute, stirring frequently, until fragrant. (Do not scorch or the mixture will become bitter.) Transfer to a large saucepan, and add the beans, onion, garlic, serranos, bay leaves, and tomato purée. Add enough water to cover the beans by 2 to 3 inches. Bring the beans to a simmer over medium heat. Cook at a low simmer for about 2 hours, or until the beans are just tender. (Add more water if necessary to keep the beans covered as they cook.) Season with salt, stir in the barbecue sauce, and continue cooking the beans for about 10 minutes, or until almost all of the liquid has been absorbed.

YIELDS ABOUT 4 CUPS

BOUQUET GARNI

If fresh herbs are unavailable, use dried herbs: substitute ¼ teaspoon each of dried parsley and dried thyme, and ⅛ teaspoon each of dried oregano and tarragon. Add the bay leaves, place in a double layer of cheesecloth, and tie securely.

2 sprigs fresh flat-leaf parsley
2 sprigs fresh thyme
1 sprig fresh oregano or marjoram
1 sprig fresh tarragon
2 bay leaves

Tie all the herbs together securely with kitchen twine.

MUSTARD GREENS

This vegetable side, paired with the T-bone steaks on page 20, can be relied upon to provide both flavor and zip to many meat dishes.

2 tablespoons olive oil
1 tablespoon minced garlic
1 cup Chicken Stock (page 225)
2 pounds mustard greens, washed and stemmed
Salt and freshly ground black pepper to taste

To prepare the mustard greens, heat the olive oil in a large sauté pan and sauté the garlic over medium heat for 2 minutes. Add the stock and bring to a simmer. Pile the greens into the pan, cover, and simmer for 6 to 8 minutes, or until the greens are just wilted. Raise the heat to high, uncover, and simmer, tossing the greens in the broth to reduce some of the cooking liquid. Season with salt and pepper.

SERVES 4

Glazed Gingered Carrots

The sweet-and-tart glaze coupled with the ginger give these carrots character and a robust flavor. We pair them with the pork roast on page 122.

To prepare the carrots, melt the butter in a saucepan, and then add the carrots. Sauté over medium heat for 2 minutes, stirring gently once or twice. Season with salt and pepper, and add the wine, orange juice, honey, and ginger. Cover and cook for 3 minutes. Uncover and simmer for 8 to 10 minutes longer, or until the carrots are glazed and the liquid has evaporated. Garnish with the parsley.

SERVES 4

2 tablespoons butter (¼ stick)
5 medium carrots (about 1 pound), peeled and sliced
Salt and freshly ground black pepper to taste
¼ cup white wine
Juice of 1 orange
2 tablespoons honey
½ tablespoon peeled and grated fresh ginger
1 tablespoon minced fresh flat-leaf parsley, for garnish

Long-Grain White Rice

This is a multi-purpose rice recipe. For Indian cuisine, substitute fragrant long-grain basmati (or the domestic Texmati) rice. For Southeast Asian recipes, we recommend Jasmine Rice provided below.

Place the rice, 2 cups of water, and salt in a saucepan with a tight-fitting lid. Bring to a boil, and reduce the heat to a simmer. Stir once and cook, covered, for 15 to 20 minutes, or until the rice has absorbed all the liquid. Remove from the heat and let sit for 5 minutes. Fluff with a fork before serving.

YIELDS ABOUT 3 CUPS

1 cup long-grain white rice
Pinch of salt

Jasmine Rice

Jasmine rice is an aromatic, delicately scented long-grain rice native to Thailand but now grown in California. (Lundberg Family Farms brand, available at many natural foods markets and supermarkets, tastes superb.)

Place the rice, 1½ cups of water, the butter, and salt in a saucepan with a tight-fitting lid. Bring to a boil, and reduce the heat to a simmer. Cover and cook for 20 minutes, or until the rice has absorbed all the liquid. (Add a little more water if the rice is not yet tender.) Remove from the heat and let sit for 5 minutes. Fluff with a fork before serving.

YIELDS ABOUT 2 CUPS

1 cup jasmine rice
1 tablespoon butter
Salt to taste

BASIC RECIPES, TECHNIQUES, AND DEFINITIONS

BLANCHING TOMATOES

Blanching makes tomatoes very easy to peel, and in certain dishes, it is advantageous to remove the relatively tough outer skin. Blanching also keeps the texture intact.

Bring a saucepan of water to a boil. Score the base of the tomatoes with an "X" and immerse in the water for 30 seconds. Remove with a slotted spoon and transfer to an ice bath to stop the cooking process. Peel with the tip of a knife, starting at the base end of the tomatoes.

ROASTING AND BLACKENING TOMATOES AND TOMATILLOS

This technique is common in Southwestern and Mexican cooking to give more robust and complex flavors to a dish. The ingredients are then used, blackened parts and all.

For tomatillos, remove the husks and rinse. For both tomatoes and tomatillos, remove the stems and place on a rack over a gas flame (or under a broiler) until the exterior parts blister, crack, and blacken (but do not overly blacken). Chop or process as directed, with the blackened parts. Alternatively, they can be blackened in a dry, cast-iron skillet.

ROASTING BELL PEPPERS AND FRESH CHILES

Roasting bell peppers and chiles gives them an attractive smoky and complex flavor. It also makes peeling the tough (and sometimes bitter-tasting) outer skin possible.

You can roast the bell peppers or chiles on the grill, under the broiler, or on a wire rack placed over a gas flame on top of the stove. Blister and blacken the skins evenly, taking care not to burn the flesh. Transfer to a bowl and cover with plastic wrap; let the chiles "steam" for about 15 minutes. Uncover, and remove the charred skins with your fingers or the tip of a sharp knife. Cut open and remove the seeds and internal ribs to help moderate the heat of the chiles.

Take care to wash your hands thoroughly after handling chiles, and never touch your face or eyes with your hands until you have done so. If you have sensitive skin, wear rubber gloves when handling chiles.

ROASTING GARLIC

Roasting garlic gives it a sweet, mellow flavor.

Place unpeeled garlic cloves in a heavy skillet and dry-roast over low heat for about 30 minutes, shaking or stirring the skillet occasionally, until the garlic becomes soft. Alternatively, place the garlic cloves in a roasting pan and roast in a preheated oven at 350°F. for 25 to 30 minutes. (Cook at 300°F. for 45 minutes to 1 hour to make the garlic sweeter yet.) When the garlic has roasted, peel the cloves, or squeeze it out of the skin. For roasted garlic purée, smash the roasted garlic with the side of a knife or chop very finely.

If you have a toaster oven, roast garlic cloves in that—it's more energy efficient.

ROASTING AND BLANCHING CORN

Roasting gives corn a smoky quality that enhances its natural flavor.

Cut the kernels from the cob with a sharp knife, taking care not to cut too deeply into the cob. Heat a large, dry skillet or nonstick sauté pan for 3 to 4 minutes over high heat, and when hot, add the corn in a single layer. Roast for 3 to 4 minutes, tossing after 2 minutes, until dark.

To blanch corn, add the fresh kernels to a saucepan of lightly salted boiling water for 1 minute. Transfer to a bowl of ice water to stop the cooking process, and then drain.

TOASTING SPICES

Toasting spices, such as cumin and coriander seeds, is a technique used especially in Southwestern and Indian cuisines to bring out more complex flavor tones.

Place the spices in a dry skillet over low heat and toast for about 1 minute, until fragrant, stirring frequently. Take care not to scorch spices, as they will taste bitter.

TOASTING SEEDS AND NUTS

This technique brings the roasty, rich flavor of the seeds or nuts.

For toasted pumpkin seeds, place the seeds in a single layer in a hot, dry skillet over medium-high heat for 2 to 3 minutes, stirring with a wooden spoon. The seeds will pop and brown slightly. Take care not to burn them. Toast sesame seeds for 45 seconds to 1 minute, and stir constantly, until golden and shiny.

Nuts take longer to toast. Place in a hot, dry skillet over medium-high heat. Toast pine nuts, chopped walnuts, pecans, or almonds for 3 to 5 minutes; walnut or pecan halves or whole almonds will take 5 to 7 minutes. The nuts are toasted when they look slightly browned and smell aromatic.

TOASTING, REHYDRATING, AND PURÉEING DRIED CHILES

This standard technique for preparing dried chiles in Southwestern and Mexican cooking can be done ahead of time.

Stem and seed the chiles, place in a single layer in a dry heavy skillet, and toast over medium heat for 2 to 3 minutes. Shake the skillet occasionally and do not let the chiles blacken or burn, as they will taste bitter. Transfer the chiles to a large bowl and cover with hot water. Weigh the chiles down with a lid or plate to keep them submerged. Let stand for 30 minutes until rehydrated and soft. Transfer the chiles to a blender. Taste the water in which the chiles were soaking; if not bitter tasting, add enough to the blender to make puréeing possible. If the water tastes bitter, use plain water. Purée the chiles and strain.

DEFINITIONS AND GLOSSARY

DEFINITIONS OF INGREDIENTS AND EQUIPMENT

— All ingredients are medium size, unless stated otherwise.

— Onions, garlic, and carrots are all peeled, unless stated otherwise.

— Chiles and bell peppers are seeded, unless stated otherwise.

— Herbs are fresh, unless stated otherwise; bay leaves are dried.

— Butter is unsalted, unless stated otherwise.

— Eggs are extra-large, unless stated otherwise.

— Tomatoes taste best in summer months at the height of ripeness. When tasty, ripe tomatoes are not available, feel free to substitute canned tomatoes. Unlike many canned goods, tomatoes work well canned and will not hurt the flavor of your dish.

— All stocks can be substituted by good-quality, low-sodium canned varieties.

— Salt and pepper "to taste": start by seasoning in small increments, tasting as you go, until you reach the desired flavor. Remember, you can always add more at the table, so err on the side of caution.

— Chipotles are smoked jalapeños, and they have a hot, smoky flavor. Chipotle chiles en adobo are canned. "En adobo" refers to the spicy pickling liquid in which the chiles are packed. Chipotles are also available dried, in which case they need rehydrating.

— Roasted sesame oil is the dark brown, fragrant, and strongly flavored oil favored in Asian cooking. It is a different product than regular sesame oil, which is much lighter in color.

— Zest of citrus fruit is the aromatic, outermost layer of the skin; that is, it excludes the bitter white pith. Citrus zest can be removed with a zester, fine grater, vegetable peeler, or a sharp knife.

— All bowls and pans are nonreactive (ceramic, glass, or stainless steel). Avoid aluminum cookware.

GLOSSARY

— Deglaze: adding a liquid, such as water, wine, or stock, to a hot cooking pan and scraping the bottom with a spatula or wooden spoon to dislodge the browned bits of food that are stuck to the pan.

— Dice: cutting ingredients into neat $1/2$-inch cube shapes (the shape of dice). "Finely diced" or "cut into small dice" refers to $1/4$-inch cubes, while "coarsely diced" or "cut into large dice" refers to $3/4$-inch cubes. Larger cuts are considered "chopped"; smaller ones are referred to as "minced."

— Julienne: cutting ingredients (usually vegetables) into sticks about $1/8$ inch wide and 1 or 2 inches long.

— Mince: cutting food very finely and neatly. Minced ingredients are less coarsely cut than diced or chopped ones.

— Reduce: cooking a liquid rapidly to decrease its volume by evaporation, thereby thickening it and concentrating the flavor.

— Sear: browning meat or other food quickly over high heat, usually as a prelude to further cooking.

INDEX

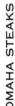

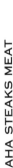
OMAHA STEAKS MEAT